A sense of place

Manchester University Press

A sense of place

Regional British television drama, 1956–82

Lez Cooke

Manchester University Press

Manchester and New York

distributed in the United States exclusively by Palgrave Macmillan

Published by Manchester University Press
Oxford Road, Manchester M13 9NR, UK
and Room 400, 175 Fifth Avenue, New York, NY 10010, USA
www.manchesteruniversitypress.co.uk

Distributed in the United States exclusively by
Palgrave Macmillan, 175 Fifth Avenue, New York,
NY 10010, USA

Distributed in Canada exclusively by
UBC Press, University of British Columbia, 2029 West Mall,
Vancouver, BC, Canada V6T 1Z2

British Library Cataloguing-in-Publication Data
A catalogue record for this book is available from the British Library

Library of Congress Cataloging-in-Publication Data applied for

ISBN 978 0 7190 8678 6 hardback

First published 2012

Typeset in 10/12 Photina
by Servis Filmsetting Ltd, Stockport, Cheshire
Printed in Great Britain
by CPI Anthony Rowe Ltd, Chippenham, Wiltshire

In memory of my mother, father and brother

Contents

Acknowledgements

Most of the research for this book was carried out as part of the AHRC-funded project *Cultures of British Television Drama: 1960-82* and I would like to extend thanks to the project directors, Jonathan Bignell, John Ellis and Stephen Lacey, and the postdoctoral researcher Helen Wheatley, who collaborated on a very productive project. My research for the project was written up as a PhD thesis, *Television Drama in the English Regions, 1956-82* (Manchester Metropolitan University, 2007) and I am grateful to my supervisors, Stephen Lacey and Robin Nelson, for their guidance and comments (and for tolerating the amount of time I spent writing a book on Troy Kennedy Martin while working on the PhD!). I am especially grateful to Robin, who took over as my PhD Director of Studies at MMU following Stephen's departure to Glamorgan, not just for guiding me through the final stages of the PhD but for his continued support during the three years when I was a research fellow at MMU. I am also grateful to my PhD examiners, Julia Hallam and John Hill, for their constructive criticisms and comments.

Many thanks are due also to Kathleen Dickson at the British Film Institute for enabling me to track down and view material produced by BBC English Regions Drama and Granada, to the staff of the BFI National Library, especially David Sharp who sorted through boxes of dusty Granada press cuttings and publicity material in the BFI store at Berkhamsted, to Liz Silvester and Pauline Hutchinson for the painstaking work involved in transcribing some very long interviews, to Kathleen Luckey at the BFI National Archive, Marion Hewitt at the North West Film Archive, the staff of the BBC Written Archives Centre at Caversham, especially Trish Hayes, and the staff at Birmingham Central Library, Manchester Central Library and the National Media Museum in Bradford. I am grateful to the BBC

Written Archives Centre for allowing me to quote extensively from BBC documents.

I am extremely grateful to all my interviewees who helped to make the process of research so enjoyable, often giving up more time to talk to me than I might have hoped for. Special thanks go to David Rose, who was always generous with his time, and John Finch, an inveterate emailer who provided me with much information about his work at Granada and put me in touch with a number of ex-Granada personnel. Other interviewees and correspondents to whom I owe thanks include Peter Ansorge, Derek Bennett, Peter Cheeseman, Michael Cox, Peter Duguid, Denis Forman, Barry Hanson, June Howson, Julia Jones, Mike Leigh, Elizabeth MacLennan, Christopher Martin, Bob Millington, Alan Plater, Philip Purser, Willy Russell, Philip Saville, Roger Smith, Tara Prem, Michael Wearing and Herbie Wise, several of whom are sadly no longer with us.

Finally, many thanks are due to Matthew Frost and Kim Walker at Manchester University Press for commissioning the book when other publishers thought it too parochial, and to the (anonymous) readers for their comments on the proposal and for a very positive report on the manuscript.

Introduction

At a time of cultural flux, and in the light of recent debates about globalisation and global culture, the question of regional identity and regional culture has re-emerged on to the field of academic and social inquiry. In the field of broadcasting, concerns have been expressed – by academics, practitioners and viewers – about the potential impact of global media culture on indigenous regional and local broadcasting in Britain (see Kidd and Taylor, 2002). These concerns were exacerbated by the series of mergers and takeovers among the network of regional Independent Television (ITV) companies in the UK between 1994 and 2000, resulting in the eventual establishment in 2004 of a single company – ITV plc – which, it was argued by City financiers and shareholders, would be better equipped to compete in a global marketplace with commercial companies such as British-Sky-Broadcasting (BSkyB), which had grown from its establishment in 1990 to become a major player in the UK market by the early 2000s, purchasing and producing programmes designed to have a global, rather than local, appeal. In this competitive international market-place the onus has fallen on the BBC, as a public service broadcaster, to cater for regional audiences and retain elements of regional production, while at the same time striving to compete with ITV, BSkyB and other companies in the new global environment.

In the light of these developments it is perhaps timely to review the origins and development of regional television in Britain, paying particular attention to a dominant form of television production – drama – and the output of two important regional producers – Granada Television and BBC English Regions Drama – in the period often referred to as the 'golden age' of television drama, from the late 1950s to the early 1980s (see Bignell, Lacey and Macmurraugh-Kavanagh, 2000; Caughie, 2000; Cooke, 2003).

As the first chapter of this book explains, 'regionalism' has been a topical issue since long before the word first appeared in public discourse in the late nineteenth century, when its adoption reflected 'a feeling of reaction against the gradually increasing centralisation of government' (Read, 1964: 282).[1] In fact, as Helen Jewell has shown in her scholarly historical study *The North–South Divide: The Origins of Northern Consciousness in England*, regional concerns about the centralising of power can be traced back to the eighth century and the writings of Bede and Eddius whose 'perception was very much in terms of political power: Bede thought of Northumbrian and Southumbrian power blocks, and Eddius wrote of southern nations united against Wilfred's Northumbria' (Jewell, 1994: 207–8).

Regional identity has traditionally been expressed through regional accents and dialect, through a shared social and industrial history, and through regional cultural practices. Occasionally indigenous regional culture and identity have come to national, and sometimes international, attention. One twentieth-century example is the 'New Wave' of provincial art, literature, theatre, cinema and television of the 1950s–60s, which brought English regional culture, especially Northern working-class culture, to national consciousness. While regional television drama featured as an important part of the New Wave, and was accordingly given some attention in certain studies (see Laing, 1986, and Lacey, 1995), there has been no systematic analysis of the history and development of regional television drama in Britain, from the 1950s, when television first became available in the English regions, to the present day, when television is ubiquitous and there are many regionally based production companies making programmes for both local and national audiences.

Regional television drama takes two main forms: (1) drama that is *set* in the regions but produced by a national broadcaster for a national audience, e.g. *Z Cars* (BBC, 1962–78), set in Liverpool, *When the Boat Comes In* (BBC, 1976–81), set in the North East, and *Cutting It* (BBC, 2002–5), set in Manchester, and (2) drama that is *produced* in the regions by a regionally based company for both local and national audiences. In the latter case such regionally produced drama need not necessarily reflect the region in which it is produced – for example the internationally set *The Jewel in the Crown* (ITV, 1984) was produced by Granada Television, based in Manchester – but, more often than not, regional companies do produce drama which reflects the region in which the company is based, such as Granada's *Coronation Street* (ITV, 1960 to present), Yorkshire Television's *Emmerdale* (formerly *Emmerdale Farm*, ITV, 1972 to present) and *Heartbeat* (ITV, 1992–2010), and the Mancunian dramas *Queer as Folk* (C4, 1999–2000) and *Clocking Off* (BBC, 2000–3), produced by the Manchester-based independent production company Red Production for Channel Four and the BBC respectively.

The economics of television drama production dictate that programmes are rarely produced solely for a regional audience by a regional broadcaster. Regional television drama has nearly always – except for a few pre-1980s examples cited in Chapters 3 and 4 – been produced for a national audience. This is not to suggest, however, that regional segments of that national audience will interpret the different idioms and accents in regional television drama in exactly the same way. The consumption of television drama produced in one region and consumed by audiences in another adds a layer of complexity to the analysis of regional television drama that is largely beyond the scope of this particular study.

In their report for the Independent Television Commission (ITC) on *Television in the Nations and Regions: Television Broadcasting and Production outside London* (ITC, 2002) Mike Kidd and Bill Taylor focus on 'three separate, although related issues, which are often lumped together under the umbrella description of "regional broadcasting"':

- The *production* of regional and network programmes in locations outside London.
- The *broadcasting in specific Nations and Regions* of regional programmes which reflect the diversity of life in the UK outside London (such as the highly successful *Lesser Spotted Ulster*, which is broadcast only by UTV).
- The *broadcasting on the national networks* of television programmes which reflect the diversity of life in the UK outside London (an obvious and long-standing example being *Coronation Street*, which is produced in Manchester and broadcast across the ITV networks). (Kidd and Taylor, 2002: 2)

In the same publication Sylvia Harvey makes a related, but politically nuanced, distinction between the opportunity given to regional broadcasters not only to 'opt out' of the national network and show regionally-produced programmes for regionally specific audiences but also to 'opt in' to the national network in order to bring regional culture to a national audience:

> The history of regionalism in the BBC and ITV was very much about allowing the regions to have a little bit of airtime to opt out of the network, which is something I very much support and should continue. But what is tremendously important culturally and economically is that producers from the regions can opt in to the ITV Network, so they have a presence culturally for what they want to say and also so they have access to network budgets. (Kidd and Taylor, 2002: 27–8)

One of the aims of this book is to explore the different definitions and interpretations of regional broadcasting, with particular reference to television drama produced in the period from 1956 to 1982, in other words from the year in which the first regional ITV companies began broadcasting to the arrival on to the British broadcasting landscape of a fourth television channel in November 1982, a moment which signalled the end of the BBC/ITV duopoly and the beginning of a new era in the history of British television, a 'third age' if you like, following the 'first age' of the BBC monopoly from 1936 to 55 and the 'second age' of the BBC/ITV duopoly from 1955 to 1982.

I have taken 1956 as the starting point not only because it was the year in which the first regional ITV companies, ABC, ATV and Granada, began broadcasting in the Midlands and the North of England but also because 1956 has a particular resonance in British culture, being the year of John Osborne's *Look Back in Anger* and the beginning of a period of artistic production in the theatre, and subsequently the cinema, which had a significant impact on the development of regional television drama in Britain. It should be noted, however, that in Chapters 1 and 2 I have ventured much further back in order to provide a historical context for the discussion of regionalism, regional culture and identity, and regional broadcasting, and that, in the Conclusion, I discuss recent developments, and future possibilities, in the production and transmission of regional British television drama.

Chapter 1 provides a brief historical context, considering some of the ways in which regionalism, regional culture and regional identity have been defined and discussed by historians, geographers, economists, sociologists, playwrights and cultural historians, from the Middle Ages to the present day. Chapter 2 examines the history and development of regional broadcasting in the United Kingdom, from the beginnings of the BBC in the 1920s to the arrival of Channel Four in 1982, paying particular attention to the regional organisation of the ITV network and the structure and organisation of regional broadcasting in the Midlands, using a Midlands-based theatre company as a case study in order to examine the relationship between regional theatre and regional television in the 1960s–70s. Chapter 3 provides a detailed examination of Granada Television's drama output from 1956 to 1982, considering the company's development from the mid-1950s to its position as the biggest and most important regional ITV company at the beginning of the 1980s. Chapter 4 provides a detailed examination of BBC English Regions Drama, from its establishment in 1971 to the beginnings of its decline in the early 1980s, when a number of key personnel departed to work at the new Channel Four. The Conclusion reflects on whether this 'second age' of British television, from the mid-1950s to the early 1980s, might be considered, in retrospect, a 'golden age' for regional British television drama, before proceeding to consider the present situation and future possibilities for regional television drama in an era of global, multi-channel television and new media platforms such as the internet.

It should be stressed that the main focus of this book is the English regions, rather than what the BBC used to refer to as the 'National Regions' of Scotland, Wales and Northern Ireland. It will become apparent, however, that one of the most significant issues concerning regional television producers, then and now, is not the relationship between the nations and the regions, but the relationship between the regions and London, where most of the power, economically and politically, has resided. As Geraint Talfan Davies, the former controller of BBC Wales, wrote in his contribution to the ITC report on *Television in the Nations and Regions*: 'Centralised organisation has been accompanied by a centralised cultural mindset. The notion of regional production centres, for anything other than programmes for the local audience, is often regarded as a tiresome parochialism, out of tune with markets and the economies of the industry' (Davies, 2002: 77).

In contrast, the cultural historian Dorothy Hobson, in her contribution to the ITC report, felt that 'Cultural centralisation is a contradiction in terms'. She suggests that national identity, and national culture, is formed out of an accumulation of regional identities and cultures: 'The English define their identity from their village, town or city. It is the sum of those cultural experiences which amalgamate and coalesce into a national culture' (Hobson, 2002: 35). Hobson did, however, agree with Davies and Sylvia Harvey that: 'Broadcasters must recognise their special relationship to our sense of community and national identity. One of the most effective ways in which they can do this is by enabling more programmes to be made both by the regions for the regions and – equally important – by companies within the regions for network transmission' (Hobson, 2002: 35).

Returning to the beginnings of regional television in England provides an opportunity to take a historical perspective on questions of regional identity and regional culture, in relation to national identity and national culture, through re-examining the practices, products and representations of an earlier period. The methodology adopted here is largely empirical. In Chapter 1 I have drawn on interdisciplinary research in order to provide a conceptual and historical framework for the general analysis of regional broadcasting that forms Chapter 2 and the specific analyses of Granada Television and BBC English Regions Drama in Chapters 3 and 4. In the latter chapters textual analysis, of the aesthetic and representational strategies adopted by television drama practitioners on a range of productions, is combined with contextual analysis of the social, cultural, institutional, technological and political conditions within which regional television drama was produced in the period from 1956 to 1982.

The problems of historical research in the field of television are well known and this research has encountered the usual problems of the unavailability of primary material, in terms of programmes which no longer exist because they were transmitted live and not recorded, or because they have since been wiped or junked. While written documentation can compensate to some extent for the absence of recorded programmes there is an additional problem with obtaining such material from the archives of regional broadcasters. Either the archives have not been maintained and only selective material has found its way to national archives such as the BBC Written Archives Centre or the BFI National Library or, in the case of no longer extant commercial broadcasters (such as Granada) which may have merged with, or been taken over by, other companies or corporations, there is the problem of locating, and then gaining access to, whatever material may have been preserved.[2]

While a substantial amount of recorded material from Granada and BBC English Regions Drama is available to view in the BFI National Archive, and a certain amount of useful written documentation about

BBC English Regions Drama productions is collected in the BBC Written Archives Centre at Caversham, there is a shortage of documentation about the regional policies of both Granada and BBC English Regions Drama, although publications such as West Midlands Arts' *Films and Plays from Pebble Mill: Ten Years of Regional Television Drama* (1980), the BFI Dossier *Granada: The First 25 Years* (Buscombe, 1981) and *Granada Television: The First Generation* (Finch, 2003) are invaluable.

In the absence of both visual and written material I have drawn on original interviews with practitioners – executives, writers, producers, directors and actors – who worked for Granada and BBC English Regions Drama or were involved in regional productions during this period. There are some dangers with using interview material – memories can be fallible and sometimes misleading (and many of the first generation of television practitioners still alive are now in their eighties or nineties) – but interviews are sometimes the only source of information about certain productions and they can help to illuminate the intention behind a production, or the operation of a particular practice or policy, in a way that viewing a recording or reading an official document cannot.

This study, I hope, contributes to the project of uncovering and re-evaluating some of the 'lost' history of British television drama. In Chapter 3 I discuss a number of relatively unknown Granada dramas, such as the 'Manchester Plays' of Harold Brighouse, Stanley Houghton and Allan Monkhouse, the anthology play series *The Younger Generation*, *The Villains*, *City '68* and *The System*, and the 'telenovels' of Northern writers such as Stan Barstow and John Finch. In Chapter 4 I discuss BBC English Regions Drama plays such as *The Fishing Party*, *Land of Green Ginger* and *The Roses of Eyam*, the anthology series *Second City Firsts*, and serials such as *Trinity Tales*, *Gangsters* and *Empire Road*. These and other dramas from Granada and BBC English Regions Drama tend not to form part of the 'canon' of British television drama and have been unduly neglected.[3] For this reason alone, as well as for what they reveal about regional British television, regional culture and regional identity between the mid-1950s and the early 1980s, they are ripe for reassessment.

Notes

1 In his book *The English Provinces c. 1760–1960: A Study in Influence*, the historian Donald Read notes that 'The word "regionalism" seems to have first

appeared in 1874, and it has certainly been in common use since about 1890' (Read, 1964: 282).

2 These problems are discussed in a special issue of *Critical Studies in Television*, 'TV Archives: Accessing TV History', 5:2, Autumn 2010.

3 For more on the 'canon' in British television see Bignell (2006), Creeber (2004) and Ellis (2005 and 2007). Appendix 1 lists all the television dramas produced by Granada Television in the period from 1956 to 1982 and Appendix 2 lists all the television dramas produced by BBC English Regions Drama from 1972 to 1982.

1

Regionalism, regional culture and regional identity

What is a region? The question has preoccupied geographers for more than a century. While early twentieth-century geographers, such as A.J. Herbertson, developed a theory of the region based on 'natural' characteristics, suggesting a region was defined by 'a certain unity of configuration, climate and vegetation' (Herbertson, 1905: 309), subsequent definitions have taken social as well as environmental factors into consideration. Accordingly, a region came to be defined not only on the basis of its physical geography but also by the ways in which humankind has interacted with the environment. To define a region as 'an area of common living' (Gilbert, 1960: 158) moves traditional geography towards sociology and cultural studies, suggesting that a region might be defined not simply as 'a unit area of the Earth's surface' (Professor E.G.R. Taylor, quoted in Gilbert, 1951: 346) but as 'an area where people [share] a common sense of belonging shaped by physical features and historical tradition' (Sergeant, 2003: 17). The latter definition makes it possible to begin exploring regionalism in relation to concepts such as 'regional culture' and 'regional identity' and the myriad ways in which these are represented and reproduced in British television drama.

Regionalism: 'The Idea of the Region'

Considering some contrasting definitions of the region in his 1960 Herbertson Memorial Lecture, entitled 'The Idea of the Region', the geographer E.W. Gilbert compared regions to the changing personality of individuals:

> [I]t appears that the unifying factor which makes a mere *area* into a *region* may be a natural one, or it may have been impressed on the area

by some form of human use. In either case the region is often so clearly distinguishable as a separate entity that it receives recognition in the shape of a distinct name. Take for example the Lake District, the Black Country, the Vale of the White Horse . . .

Now geography is, in my view, the art of recognizing, describing and interpreting the personalities of regions. Regions, like individuals, have very different characters; moreover, the character of regions, like those of individuals, are constantly changing or developing. (Gilbert, 1960: 158)

Gilbert insists that defining a region is an 'art' rather than an 'exact science' and he proceeds to consider 'the geographer's idea of the region', as both 'natural' and 'human', 'the political idea of the region', where the country is divided into regions for the purpose of political administration, and 'artistic' descriptions of a region, by novelists such as Arnold Bennett, Charlotte Brontë, George Eliot, Elizabeth Gaskell and Thomas Hardy who 'have been able to produce a synthesis, "a living picture of the unity of place and people", which so often eludes geographical writing. The geographer often speaks of the "personality" of a region and this is exactly what the novelist has brought out so strongly' (Gilbert, 1960: 168).

Gilbert's tripartite analysis is a useful starting point for exploring concepts of regionalism, regional culture and regional identity. From the geographer's point of view, Gilbert says, 'it is now fully realized that there are very few "natural" regions. Human occupation has transformed almost every region wholly or at least in part' (Gilbert, 1960: 160). Among these human interventions, possibly the most significant and sustained period of transformation occurred with the Industrial Revolution of the late eighteenth and nineteenth centuries. Before the Industrial Revolution notions of regional difference in England were largely based on an opposition between town and country, with London the metropolitan centre of political and cultural activity while the rest of the country was a largely rural, agricultural landscape, pocketed with small villages and market towns. With the advent of the Industrial Revolution, however, the rapid growth of provincial towns and cities in the Midlands and the North of England challenged not only the economic supremacy of London but also its cultural and political superiority (Read, 1964: 1–2).

The Industrial Revolution saw a new definition of regional difference replace the earlier distinction between town and country. The growth of the industrial towns of the North led to a polarisation between North and South, an industrial and social divide which Elizabeth Gaskell turned into a 'living picture' in her mid-nineteenth-century novel *North and South* (1855), in which she 'contrasts the peaceful life of a rural county in the south with the "almost brutal strenuousness of the manufacturing north" as the author had seen it in "Milton", that is Manchester' (Gilbert, 1960: 163). This North/South regional divide may have been exacerbated by the Industrial Revolution but the idea of a more refined and civilised South, in contrast to the rough barbarity of the industrial North, has a longer history. The historian Donald Read traces it back to the reign of King John in the thirteenth century when 'The barons from north of the Trent who forced Magna Carta upon the king in 1215 were nick-named "the Northerners" by John's friends because this seemed to emphasise their barbarity' (Read, 1964: 276). Such descriptions have fuelled stereotypes of the 'rough, ignorant Northerner' in contrast to the 'refined, educated Southerner' which still persist in popular culture.

While the nature of the North/South divide changed as a result of the Industrial Revolution, as northern cities grew in economic importance to rival London, the concept returned to the political agenda with the gradual industrial and economic decline of the North during the course of the twentieth century, a process accelerated by Conservative government policy in the 1980s which re-established London as the political and economic powerhouse of the United Kingdom. Since the 1980s the balance of economic and political power has been firmly located in London and the Home Counties, although attempts have been made to regenerate the old industrial cities in the Midlands and the North in order to counter the new North/South divide (see Lewis and Townsend, 1989; Smith, 1989; Baker and Billinge, 2004).

In his book *North and South: Britain's Economic, Social and Political Divide*, David Smith considers the problem of dividing the country into regions, prior to deciding where (and how) the line should be drawn between North and South. Noting how regions have been defined 'according to the sphere of influence of major cities, or the transmission areas of the independent television companies', Smith announces his intention to use 'the government's standard regions' whereby the United Kingdom is divided into eight English and three national regions. Adopting this political and administrative regional breakdown Smith then separates the North – comprising the three nations of Scotland, Northern Ireland and Wales and the three north-ernmost English regions of the North, North West, and Yorkshire and Humberside – from the South – the five remaining English regions of the South East, South West, East Anglia, East Midlands and West Midlands. As Smith admits, 'It would be surprising if the economic, political and other differences between North and South followed a neat line according to the boundaries of the government's standard regions. But it is probably the best we can do' (Smith, 1989: 5).

Smith does accept that the designation of the two Midlands regions is problematic, but provides a rationale for their inclusion on the basis that 'in the case of the east midlands, the region has been a clear beneficiary of spillover activity and prosperity from the south east', while 'The west midlands has been, since the 1930s, part of a zone of prosperity, originally based on manufacturing industry, which stretched from London to Birmingham. This was interrupted in the early 1980s, but it appeared to be well on the way to becom-ing re-established as this book was being written' (Smith, 1989: 5). Smith's division highlights the fluctuating nature of the North/South divide when based on an economic rationale, positing the Midlands as a transient region residing between North and South, with no real allegiance to either, 'an area which in economic terms first swung into the North during the early 1980s but has since rejoined the South' (Smith, 1989: 3). Smith's difficulty in deciding where to draw the line between North and South highlights the problem of a largely economic approach which takes little cognisance of socio-cultural factors, leaving such aspects to be explored by others, such as Beryl Bainbridge in her book *Forever England: North and South* (1987) and Helen Jewell in her exemplary historical study *The North–South Divide: The Origins of Northern Consciousness in England* (1994).

In contrast to economic or geographic analyses of the North/South divide, it is worth considering an alternative conception of region-alism that emerged with the growth of provincial cities during the Industrial Revolution. The opposition here is between 'metropolitan' and 'provincial', with the latter carrying derogatory connotations that betray the word's metropolitan origins. Dr Johnson, in his 1755 *Dictionary*, defined 'provincial' as 'rude' and 'unpolished' and the term continued to have negative connotations in much of its subsequent usage (Read, 1964: 2).

The derogatory use of the term 'provincial' was evident in the nineteenth-century writings of the cultural theorist Matthew Arnold who, in arguing for the establishment of an Academy of English Literature, warned against 'provinciality', which he equated with cultural philistinism. In literature and culture throughout the nineteenth century the connotations of 'provincial' were largely negative, the implication being that anyone who 'came from or lived in the provinces was likely by this fact to have a talent in some way in need of improvement' (Read, 1964: 262).

Such an attitude is evident in the 'New Wave' of literature, theatre and cinema that appeared in the mid to late 1950s, where the central character is often desperate to escape the 'dour restrictions of the provinces and go to London, where new opportunities beckon' (Lacey, 1995: 80). In much of the New Wave, London is seen as the centre of artistic and cultural activity, associated with 'modernity', whereas the industrial North is described far more negatively: 'The term "provincial" had, in this context, pejorative overtones that largely displaced the connotations of authenticity that were important elsewhere, and drew on a different set of stereotypes. Provincial – and northern – signified a grey, constricting drabness, that was the embodiment of limited ambitions and a philistine cultural outlook' (Lacey: 1995: 80).

Regional culture

In his book *The English Provinces c.1760–1960: A Study in Influence*, Donald Read puts a more positive gloss on the emergence of provincial writers and artists, following Rayner Heppenstall in suggesting that the provinces have been a 'seed-bed of talent, away from the stultifying conformism of the capital' (Read, 1964: 261). As an example, Read notes the establishment of repertory theatre companies in provincial towns and cities in the early years of the twentieth century, one of which – Annie Horniman's Manchester-based company – became associated with the 'Manchester School' of Northern dramatists, which included Harold Brighouse, Stanley Houghton and Allan Monkhouse. Discussing this regional development in *The Repertory Movement: A History of Regional Theatre in Britain*, George Rowell writes:

> It is customary to describe this as 'Lancashire drama', and its authors as 'the Manchester school', a custom manifestly apt in the case of its two most famous titles, *Hindle Wakes* and *Hobson's Choice*, since these plays

are quickened to life by Lancashire folk and the Lancashire idiom, and
were written by two Mancunians born and bred: Stanley Houghton and
Harold Brighouse respectively. (Rowell and Jackson, 1984: 42–3)

When the regional ITV company Granada Television began producing 'Lancashire drama' in the late 1950s it turned, first of all,
to the work of the Manchester School playwrights as one source of
regional material, prior to nurturing a new generation of Northern
writers in the late 1950s and 1960s in order to offer contemporary
regional drama from the North for both a local and a national television audience. Granada's regional counterpart in the North, ABC
Television, which shared the franchise for the North of England with
Granada until 1968, also contributed to the New Wave of Northern
drama during this period, most notably by commissioning Northern
writers to contribute original plays to its prestigious *Armchair Theatre*
series, a weekly networked anthology series which, along with
Granada's *Coronation Street*, helped to popularise Northern culture
and idioms for a national audience, through the network of regional
ITV companies.

Despite the negative connotations of 'provincialism' previously
noted, the renaissance in provincial writing in the mid-twentieth
century was profoundly significant, challenging the idea that cultural
and artistic production in the provinces was qualitatively inferior to
that of London. Many of the novels and plays by Northern writers
such as John Braine, Alan Sillitoe, David Storey, Stan Barstow, John
Arden and Shelagh Delaney were adapted for film and television in
the late 1950s and early 1960s, extending and consolidating the cultural importance of the New Wave. Meanwhile, writers such as David
Mercer, Alun Owen, Alan Plater and Dennis Potter began writing
original plays for television about provincial life, largely drawn from
their own experience. Anthology play series such as *Armchair Theatre*
and the BBC's *The Wednesday Play* provided an outlet for some of this
'provincial' drama while the popular success of new drama series,
such as Granada's *Coronation Street* and the BBC's Z *Cars*, provided
confirmation that the New Wave of Northern drama had entered the
mainstream of British culture.

From the mid-1950s to the mid-1960s provincial, working-class
drama was current and contemporary, a sign that the landscape
of British culture was changing as a new generation sought to
shake off the middle-class cultural conservatism of the 1940s–50s

as Britain emerged from the torpor of postwar austerity. The New Wave, however, was short-lived, and the election of a new Labour government in 1964, after thirteen years of Conservatism, coincided with a cultural shift towards new forms of popular culture which saw the New Wave of Northern realism returned to its provincial roots, superseded by a revived metropolitan culture that was largely associated with London. In the new era of 1960s modernity the cultural phenomenon of the 'swinging sixties' was, to all intents and purposes, synonymous with that of 'swinging London'.

In a reaction against the 'limited ambitions' and 'philistine cultural outlook' of the provinces, many films and television dramas produced after 1963, the end point of the New Wave, showed young people 'escaping' the constricting influence of the industrial North and Midlands and fleeing down South to London, the new cultural Mecca. The journey from North to South is the starting point in a number of post-New Wave film and television narratives. Examples include Alun Owen's *A Hard Day's Night* (1964), at the beginning of which The Beatles travel by train to London where their new-found fame has preceded them and they are mobbed on the streets. At the beginning of *Diary of a Young Man* (BBC1, 1964), a six-part television drama written by Troy Kennedy Martin and John McGrath, Joe and his friend Ginger are seen arriving in London by train in search of 'a bird, a pad and some money', while in Jeremy Sandford's *Cathy Come Home* (BBC1, 1966) the eponymous heroine hitches a ride down South on a lorry at the beginning of the drama as her narrational voiceover explains: 'Well, I *was* a bit fed up . . . didn't seem to be much there for me . . . you know how these little towns are . . . *one* coffee bar . . . it was closed on a Sunday' (Sandford, 1976: 23). For Cathy, as for Joe and Ginger, the reality does not match the myth of London as 'the promised land', yet these and other 1960s representations trade on and perpetuate deep-rooted notions of a North/South divide, offering the possibility of escape from a dour and debilitating provincial culture to the bright lights and glamorous modernity of the metropolis.

In theatre, the late 1960s and 1970s saw a renaissance in provincial culture with the establishment of regional repertory theatre companies in Liverpool, Manchester, Nottingham and Stoke-on-Trent. This development proved important for regional television drama in the same period, especially following the establishment by the BBC of a regional drama department at the new Pebble Mill studios in Birmingham in 1971. While the experienced television producer and director David Rose was appointed head of the department, Barry Hanson was a significant appointment as script editor for he had previously worked at the Royal Court Theatre in London and been Artistic Director at Hull Arts Centre, where he worked with Alan Plater, among other regional writers. Plater subsequently became one of a number of regional playwrights to contribute to BBC English Regions Drama's portfolio of plays, along with other writers from regional theatre such as Alan Bleasdale, Mike Bradwell, David Halliwell, Henry Livings, Mary O'Malley, Willy Russell and Peter Terson. The symbiosis between regional theatre and regional television drama proved very productive throughout the 1970s. Not only did BBC English Regions Drama enable a number of regional playwrights to break into television, the department also drew upon a range of personnel from regional theatre companies, including actors, producers and directors.

In the 1980s, however, the cultural backlash that accompanied Margaret Thatcher's stringent monetarist policies decimated regional theatre, as it did so many aspects of regional culture. It is perhaps no coincidence that regional television drama appeared to go into decline during this period as economic power and cultural production became increasingly centralised in London and the South. With the demise of Thatcherism, however, and the election of a New Labour government in 1997, there was something of a regional renaissance, with the old industrial cities of the Midlands and the North undergoing a gradual process of regeneration and renewal on a number of levels: economic, social, industrial, architectural and cultural. On the cultural level this revival is evident in what might be described as a 'postmodern new wave' of British television drama which emerged in the late 1990s (see Cooke, 2005a). Drama series such as *Cold Feet* (Granada, 1996–2003), *Queer as Folk* (C4, 1999–2000), *Clocking Off* (BBC, 2000–3) *At Home with the Braithwaites* (Yorkshire, 2000–3), and *Cutting It* (BBC, 2002–5) provide clear evidence in their narratives, characters, visual style and iconography of the 'postmodern makeover' which many Northern cities were experiencing at the turn of the century.

Regional identity

An important aspect of the popularisation of Northern culture and identity in the late 1950s and early 1960s was the presentation on the national airwaves and cinema screens of Northern accents and dialect. Previously, British television had been notable for its lack of regional accents. Indeed, apart from imported American programmes and the occasional regional accent heard in a televised British feature film, Southern, middle-class voices (and values) predominated.

The hierarchies of the British class and education systems have had a determining influence on attitudes towards regional accents. The adoption by the BBC of Received Pronunciation, 'a prestigious form of nonlocal British English pronunciation used by many educated British people, especially in the south' (*Longman Dictionary of the English Language*, 1991: 1342) merely perpetuated the notion that recipients of a public-school education spoke 'correctly', whereas regional accents were a sign of a lack of education. Exploring the historical disparity in educational opportunities between North and South, Donald Read observes how the elevation of a courtly 'Southern English' over Northern speech patterns and dialect dates back to the Elizabethan era:

> As early as 1589 the author of *The Arte of English Poesie* advised poets never to use 'any speech used beyond the river of Trent', which was 'not so Courtly nor so current as our Southern English is, no more is the far Western man's speech'; he recommended them to follow the 'usual speech of the Court, and that of London and the shires lying about London within LX miles'. The idea of 'Establishment' English as the only correct way of speaking was thus adopted early, although it is well to remember that Elizabethan 'Establishment' English sounded very different from twentieth-century 'Establishment' English. (Read, 1964: 275)

Regional accents and dialect are one of the most obvious and immediate signifiers of regional identity and regional difference. As we have seen with attitudes towards 'Northerners' as 'ignorant' and 'barbaric' in earlier centuries, strong regional accents have historically been used to signify an 'uncouth' or 'uneducated' person. Assessing 'The literary and linguistic evidence' in the final chapter of her book, *The North–South Divide: The Origins of Northern Consciousness in England*, Helen Jewell refers to Nevill Coghill's observation, in *Chaucer: The Canterbury Tales*, that Geoffrey Chaucer makes two characters in 'The Reeve's Tale' speak in a Northern dialect and idiom, 'the first time known to him that dialect was used in English fictional writing for comic effect' (Jewell, 1994: 191). This may be one of the earliest examples of regional stereotyping in English literature, where regional dialect is used for comic effect, a practice still evident in British films, television and radio programmes.

Jewell's consideration of Chaucer's fourteenth-century literary style reveals that he 'repeatedly characterised the north by distance' (Jewell, 1994: 191) and she provides another example from 'The Reeve's Tale' where the same two characters, John and Alan, 'are described as both born in the same village, Strother, "Fer in the north, I kan nat telle where"' (Jewell, 1994: 191) as an illustration of Chaucer's Southern perspective on the North in *The Canterbury Tales*. Another example comes from 'The Friar's Tale' where the yeoman 'describes himself as living "fer in the north contree"' (Jewell, 1994: 191), a description not only evoking distance but positioning the North as 'another country'.

Six centuries later Alan Plater, in his third production for BBC English Regions Drama, would pay tribute to Chaucer with his 1975 reworking of *The Canterbury Tales* as a six-part television drama called *Trinity Tales*, in which a group of Wakefield Trinity supporters travel from Yorkshire to London for the Rugby League Cup Final, exchanging bawdy stories on their circuitous journey. Plater's story retains much of the flavour of Chaucer's original but is firmly grounded in the regional identity of his characters as Northerners, without any of the derogatory connotations or aspersions often cast on Northern characters by Southern writers. Two years before, in his second production for English Regions Drama, Plater gave a more positive account of a character living 'fer in the north contree' in his 1973 *Play for Today*, *Land of Green Ginger*, in which 'a North country maid down to London has strayed' but who returns, for the duration of the play, to her 'North country home', as the folk group The Watersons sing on the soundtrack to the play.

In a 1977 article, Alan Plater wrote about the importance of using regional voices and dialect to convey human emotion in drama in an authentic manner: 'in everyday speech there is a richness and music that makes the voice the most powerful and sensitive instrument for human emotion . . . this exists as a tool for the dramatist at its most useful when the voice speaks with a local accent or dialect' (Plater, 1977: 38). As Plater and other Northern writers have shown on many occasions, not only are regional accents and dialect important as a 'powerful and sensitive instrument for human emotion', they are central to communicating regional identity and regional culture in television drama.

2

Regional broadcasting

Since the 1920s the development of regional broadcasting in the UK has been subject to a number of interrelated factors: technological, geographical, cultural, financial and political. Among these the technological and geographical have arguably been the most significant. The designation of geographical regions has been determined mainly by the availability of broadcasting frequencies and the range of transmitters, rather than by any idea of shared community interests or indigenous regional identities. Writing about regional and local radio in his *History of Broadcasting in the United Kingdom*, Asa Briggs notes how 'the BBC's Regional boundaries in England had been originally fixed purely in terms of engineering practicalities. Geographical, demographical, and cultural considerations had been left out of the reckoning' (Briggs, 1995: 623). He goes on to describe the extent of the geographical areas which formed the three English regions (Scotland, Wales and Northern Ireland were designated as separate 'national regions'):

> The huge North Region, with its headquarters in Manchester, stretched deeply into the North Midlands and Lincolnshire; the Midland Region, with its headquarters in Birmingham, spanned a group of counties from the Welsh borders to East Anglia; and the West Region, with its headquarters in Bristol, extended as far east as Brighton. (Briggs, 1995: 623)

Each of these English regions embraced not only a large number of counties but also, one might surmise, a diversity of regional cultures and identities. It is evident, therefore, that these regions were not formed on the basis of collective regional identity but were geographical constructs determined by technology.

That London and the South East was not designated as a separate region was clearly an important political decision. While the area was served by its own transmitter, it was not allocated a separate frequency, as were the other regions. London was the administrative centre of the BBC where decisions were made which determined the structure and composition of the national broadcasting service and where the vast majority of the programmes that were broadcast to the nation were produced. Since its establishment as a public corporation, the BBC had seen itself primarily as a national broadcaster, with its headquarters in London, and its regional broadcasting activities, especially in television, have always been determined by institutional policy devised in the metropolis.

When ITV was introduced in 1955 its federal constitution and regional structure were fundamentally different from these of the BBC. The fourteen regional ITV companies operated out of regional production centres from all over the UK with a degree of autonomy which the BBC regional production centres rarely achieved. While the ITV companies formed a national network, with the four largest companies producing the majority of the programmes, the regional structure of ITV meant that its network operations, at least during its first four decades, allowed for regional differentiation and diversity in its programming to a far greater extent than was possible within the BBC.

The remainder of this chapter will explore the regional nature of this broadcasting duopoly, from the beginnings of the BBC in 1922 to the end of that duopoly in 1982, when the launch of Channel Four marked the beginning of a new era in British broadcasting.

The BBC and regional broadcasting, 1922–60

As Paddy Scannell has indicated, before nationalisation and the establishment of the British Broadcasting Corporation on 1 January 1927, the British Broadcasting Company, established in 1922, was organised on a local rather than a national basis, with nineteen locally based radio stations operating throughout the UK (Scannell, 1993: 27–9). The General Manager of the company, and future Director-General of the Corporation, John Reith, initially envisaged a broadcasting system which was genuinely 'regional' in its structure and programming, 'with radio stations eventually grouped according to the regional characteristics of the populations in the areas they covered' (Scannell, 1993: 29). From 1924, however, Reith's vision of broadcasting changed: 'More and more he thought of the BBC as a national institution providing a national broadcasting service (Scannell, 1993: 30). In 1926 Reith's vision of the BBC as a national institution was realised when the BBC was transformed from a private company serving the interests of radio manufacturers to become a public corporation with a remit to provide a national service. Subsequently the loose network of nineteen local radio stations was developed into a national broadcasting system with (initially) five regional centres, forming the basis of the regional structure that the BBC was to operate for the next four decades.

In radio a National Programme was established in 1930, based in London, to be joined over the next decade by a Regional Programme, with material being produced for the latter by the different regional stations (although the Regional Programme also took material from the National Programme). During this period, the region with the strongest sense of regional identity, Scannell suggests, was the North:

> Of the three English regional production centres the one with the clearest sense of a particular character rooted in place and people was North Region, based in Manchester . . . What was most clearly reflected in the differences between the output of Manchester and London were most generally those between North and South, a theme with a long history in English life and culture. Those differences were as much based on class as on differences of place. Manchester held together, not without difficulty, a sense of place and people in which perhaps working-class identity was the common factor among audiences drawn from many different localities (for example, the major towns and cities of Lancashire, Yorkshire and Tyneside), each with their own sense of local identity and pride. In the National Programme the ordinary life and experience of working people was marginal. It was central to North Region's programme service for its largely working-class audiences. (Scannell, 1993: 35–6)

On the outbreak of the Second World War the Regional Programme was closed down and the National Programme became responsible for broadcasting to the nation for the duration of the war. After the war the Regional Programme was not reintroduced. Instead the BBC's radio service was reorganised into three national channels: the Home, Light and Third Programmes, channels which 'reclassified the audience not in terms of differences of place and identity (local, regional, national) but in terms of broad differences of social and cultural tastes' (Scannell, 1993: 36).

The fledgling television service that was introduced in 1936 was

London-based, with a small, mainly middle-class audience in and around the metropolis, with programming tailored for that audience. Questions of regional identity and the regional composition of the audience were not an issue in television until the service began to expand after the war, gradually becoming available in other parts of the country. Even then, there was no real attempt to cater for regional audiences and regional tastes, in the way there had been in the North Region with radio, until after the arrival of ITV in 1955.

Although television was established as a national service, the range of the Alexandra Palace transmitter meant that it could initially be received only in the London area. When a new transmitter was built at Sutton Coldfield in 1949 the television service became available for the first time in the Midlands and in 1952 new transmitters at Holme Moss and Kirk o'Shotts extended the service to the North of England and to Scotland. Thereafter television gradually became available throughout the United Kingdom. In December 1958, in a document on 'Regional Broadcasting' presented to the General Advisory Council, the BBC was able to claim of its television service: 'Today it is available to 98.4 per cent. of the entire population with the result that the BBC has the most nearly complete coverage of any Television Service in the world.'[1]

The development of television as a national service by the BBC meant that it was never able to develop 'from below' in the way that radio had. As Briggs notes, with the gradual extension of the television service to the whole of the UK, 'what regional activity was permitted was grafted on to a national system' (Briggs, 1995: 623). The BBC was slow to build regional television studios, initially making use of Outside Broadcast (OB) units to produce regional programmes. Looking back on the development of regional television in 1960, Cecil McGivern, Deputy Director of Television, wrote in an internal BBC document:

> There was no Regional television until October 1951, when the first Regional O.B. unit began to be shared between Midland and North. In 1952, a unit was shared between North and Scotland and in 1953 one between Wales and West. This was a most uncomfortable period for the Regions, the system being not only extremely difficult to work, but uneconomic and time-wasting in long travel and periods at base for maintenance.
>
> The policy of the then D.G., as seen by the Television Service, was that the expenditure of money on television should be gradual and should

go hand in hand with the growth of licences. There would be no sudden increases. The D.G. foresaw that there should be an O.B. unit in each Region, but he did not envisage studios in the regions, at least for years to come. Also, the output from the Regions should be primarily, if not totally, for the network . . .

With the coming of a new D.G. in 1952, the policy about Regional studios changed. Perhaps it would have changed had the former D.G. remained. It was agreed that there should be in each Region (except Northern Ireland) a general purpose studio, modestly equipped. The first Regional studio run-in began in West Region in October 1953 (2 years before the operation of equipping each Region with its own O.B. unit had been completed). From then the growth in the number of Regional studios was steady, as was the growth in the complexity of their studio equipment though they are still behind London standards.

The philosophy behind the building of Regional studios is important. It was that they should help importantly to service a second programme or a significant increase in hours. D.G. instructed the Television Service to proceed with television studios in the Regions on the firm assumption that we would obtain a second programme. Meantime, their primary use should be for the network and that there should be no significant increase in opting-out. Actually, there *could* be no significant increase as in each Region there was only one crew to service both Studio and O.B. unit.[2]

Although the possibility of the BBC acquiring a second channel seemed to be the initial motivation for the building of regional studios (nearly a decade before the BBC was actually given a second channel), the situation changed with the arrival of ITV. By the late 1950s, according to McGivern, 'there was little or no thought that regional plans and development should be based on a second programme. The main reasons for development seemed to be because of I.T.A. competition and because of the "natural" needs of a Region as regards television.'[3] Once the regional ITV companies were operational, regional BBC controllers 'began to state that they must have more opt-outs in order to protect themselves and the BBC in general'.[4]

While the initial impetus for the development of regional television was to support the network, the introduction of ITV, it seems, brought calls for the BBC Regions to be able to opt-out of the network at certain times in order to compete with the regional ITV companies with locally produced programmes made specifically for their own regional audiences. McGivern's reference to 'the "natural" needs of a Region as regards television' suggests that many people at the BBC, especially perhaps the regional controllers, saw the provision of regional pro-grammes for regional audiences as an important part of the BBC's public service commitment.

By the mid-1950s the three English regional production centres at Birmingham, Bristol and Manchester were suitably equipped to enable them to produce drama. There was, however, some initial concern about the quality of the plays being produced in the regions. Referring to a half-hour play called *Fresh as Paint* (3 July 1956), pro-duced by the Midland Region for the network, Cecil McGivern wrote in an internal memorandum:

> This play was too thin and feeble for a transmission at peak time trans-mission in the BBC Television Service. In fact, it was too weak as it stood for transmission at all. It was wrong to waste the cost and considerable complication of a studio production on this play. It was also wrong for a costly Regional studio to be wasted on this play.[5]

Although McGivern subsequently absolved Birmingham of responsi-bility for the 'poor quality' of the play, the memo drew forth a response from Denis Morris, Head of Programmes for the Midland Region, complaining about the subordinate role given to Birmingham, as a regional production studio, by the London-based Drama Department:

> We have recently been asked to fill three drama dates for the network. In each case we have sent up one or two scripts which we considered suitable – but were not particularly proud of – which were turned down and were ultimately asked with the blessing of either Script Supervisor or H.D. Tel. [Head of Drama, Television] to put out a play from those in stock in London. By this means we were saddled with (a) an absolute horror in 'Story Conference', (b) a slight script with a very good basic idea in 'The Cobbler's Belle', (c) two slight scripts with good regional justifications in 'The Tattleton Umpire' and 'Fresh as Paint'.[6]

While there may have been 'good regional justifications' for the pro-duction of *Fresh as Paint*, Morris's reference to a 'slight script', together with McGivern's lambasting of the play, suggests that Birmingham, with three network dates to fill, was forced to choose a play from a selection of inferior scripts offered to the Midland Region by London.

The main problem for the BBC Regions was that the structure and development of BBC television as a national service prevented the Regions catering for regional audiences in the way that radio had, or in the way that the ITV companies were able to do from 1956, when the first regionally based ITV company began broadcasting.

In a December 1958 BBC document on 'Television in the Regions' Gerald Beadle noted how, following the introduction of ITV, there were attempts at the BBC to cater for the interests of regional audiences when the regional centres began producing programmes for a local audience, in addition to the national audience. This initiative, as Beadle says, was 'greatly stimulated by the operations of commercial television', but opting out of the network was financially prohibitive for the BBC Regions in the 1950s:

> Since about 1955 there has been some relaxation of the network only policy. It began with a small allowance for each region to enable it to broadcast occasional programmes for the local audience only. This practice, though desirable for social reasons, is expensive because it means opting out of the network programmes which still have to be paid for in full. The urge for regions to increase this practice is now very strong and is greatly stimulated by the operations of commercial television. Commercial television in Britain is organised as a number of operating companies, each independent of the others, and each with a territory of its own. Each has a special obligation towards its own territory and is compelled under the Act to produce a stated percentage of its material locally. This is a wholly different job in theory from that of the BBC which is to provide the national service. However commercial television has, for good business reasons, come to adopt networking on an extensive scale, but the Act imposes limits on this practice which one suspects the companies would be glad to escape. The BBC, on the other hand, would like to do more exclusively regional broadcasting because it believes it to be socially valuable. But the extent of the practice has to be severely limited because of the heavy extra costs it involves. The BBC is unlikely in the foreseeable future to be able to afford to fragment its output regionally to the extent which is obligatory on Commercial television.[7]

Clearly, in the late 1950s, the BBC was trying to find ways to respond to the challenge of ITV, but the Reithian advocacy of a national broadcasting service, with its 'top down' structure, militated against the development of regional television by the BBC along the lines of the new commercial network.

Two years before Beadle's paper, Denis Morris, in his memo to Cecil McGivern, had already drawn attention to the impact ITV was having on BBC drama production. In addition to complaining about the quality of the drama scripts being sent to the Midland Region, Morris warned McGivern that the departure of BBC staff to ITV was likely to restrict severely any initiative by the Head of Television to replace the 'infrequently good' and 'economically wasteful' half-hour television plays with longer plays:

> If this is the case regions will be forced to look for 60 or 90-minute plays if they are to play the part in national broadcasting which their enlarged resources demand. Against this is the fact that our engineering division is considerably diluted through incursions by I.T.A. The capacity of a region to put on a 90-minute play may be prejudiced by the fact that its share of dilution has resulted in a personnel of inexperienced engineering staff and the subsequent necessity to send a considerable proportion of its new recruits for training in London.[8]

By successfully luring trained staff away from the BBC with the offer of more lucrative contracts the ITV companies were not just ensuring they could fulfil their regional and network programming obligations, they were inflicting a severe blow on the BBC's ability to deliver 'quality dramas' in the new competitive environment, especially in the regions where the ITV companies were soon to outnumber the BBC regional production centres.

The ITV network of regional companies, 1955–68

Denis Morris's internal BBC memo was written five months after Associated Television (ATV) began broadcasting as a commercial competitor to the BBC in the Midlands area, the first regional ITV company to follow the London launch of ITV in September 1955 when Associated-Rediffusion began weekday transmissions in the London area, with ATV taking over at weekends. The 1954 Television Act, which authorised commercial television in Britain, required the newly founded Independent Television Authority (ITA) not only to provide a commercial competitor for the BBC but also to ensure there was competition between ITV companies, within the same region:

> The original plan for ITV was that there should be three regional franchises, London, the Midlands and the North, each occupied by more than one contractor. Hence there was to be competition *between* contractors, as well as between the whole ITV system and the BBC. But because of the government's failure to allocate enough frequencies to enable this to happen the ITA adopted another plan. In order to maximize the number of contractors and create as much competition

as it could the Authority split franchises on a weekday/weekend basis. (Crissell, 1997: 84)

While this was not the full competition envisaged in the Television Act it did introduce an element of competition between the ITV companies, as well as providing competition for the BBC. In addition to its London weekend franchise ATV also won the franchise for the Midlands on weekdays. The weekend franchise for the Midlands and the North was initially awarded to the Kemsley-Winnick Group, but the company was unable to take up the contract and was replaced by ABC Television, part of the Associated-British Picture Corporation. The initial pattern of regional ITV coverage was completed by Granada, which was awarded the weekday franchise for the North of England.

As both ATV and ABC were operating in two franchise areas, they were reluctant to build new studios in the Midlands in addition to their studios in London and Manchester, at least not while there was uncertainty about how long their franchises would last. Instead they agreed to share a Midlands studio – a converted cinema in Aston. ATV and ABC each took networked programmes produced by Associated-Rediffusion and Granada (whose operation of the North of England weekday franchise began in May 1956) in addition to producing their own programmes for the Midlands region and for the network.

This network of three ITV 'regions' (including London) was enlarged in August 1957 when Scottish Television began transmitting in central Scotland, followed by TWW in Wales and the West of England in January 1958 and Southern TV in the South of England in August 1958. In 1959 Tyne Tees TV began transmitting in North East England, Anglia TV in Eastern England and Ulster TV in Northern Ireland. The network was completed in 1961–62 with the addition of Westward TV (South West England), Border TV (Cumbria and the Scottish borders), Grampian TV (northern Scotland), Channel TV in the Channel Islands and finally, in September 1962, Wales West and North (WWN) – this latter company being the only one to fail to fulfil its contract, closing down in January 1964, when TWW took over its franchise area.

When the service was fully operational there were seven regionally based ITV companies in England, outside London, plus one, TWW, based in Bristol and Cardiff, serving a dual region of the West of

England and Wales. Clearly, as with the BBC Regions, the ITV regions were established on the basis of the available frequencies and the position and range of the transmitters, with a blurring of regional or national boundaries in the case of TWW and Border (and also in the case of Granada, whose transmission area extended to North Wales, overlapping with the transmission area of WNN – which is one reason why WNN closed down). By September 1962 fifteen ITV companies were operating in fourteen franchise areas – the original three franchise areas being served by four companies (this number was reduced to fourteen companies when TWW took over from WWN).

Through a combination of imported American programmes, such as *Dragnet* (NBC, 1951–59), *I Love Lucy* (CBS, 1951–57) and *Gunsmoke* (CBS, 1955–75), and home-produced programmes, such as Associated-Rediffusion's *Double Your Money* (1955–68), ATV's *Sunday Night at the London Palladium* (1955–67) and ABC's *Armchair Theatre* (1956–68), the ITV network provided a range of popular programming not available on the BBC. Consequently ITV began to lure viewers away from the BBC, gaining a majority share of the audience by mid-1957 (Crissell, 1997: 88). In a July 1956 edition of the *TV Times*, Dennis Vance, Head of Drama at ABC, offered a vision of the kind of service ABC would be offering viewers in the Midlands and the North:

> We have to aim at large audiences, but that doesn't automatically mean low quality programmes. I believe people enjoy good stuff well done – everything depends on how it's presented. And anyway I believe the North and Midlands have good taste – they're terrifically keen musically, their repertory is wonderful. I'm looking forward enormously to giving them the best. And I mean to have new people, young people, and above all Midland and Northern people, helping me . . .
>
> We have many advantages. Our parent company has many stars, and I hope to borrow them occasionally. We shall be using international stars and new ones, too. From September our output of plays will average three or four each month. We will be doing a classic now and again, perhaps once a quarter – the kind of classic ideal for TV, for example something like *The Wild Duck*, or a Galsworthy. (Hynd, 1956: 16)

Vance's ambitions point towards the kind of 'serious' drama programming ABC was to offer, especially in its prestigious *Armchair Theatre* strand on Sunday evenings. The ITV companies proved themselves particularly adept in the art of scheduling, hammocking 'serious' drama between popular light entertainment programmes, and the success of this strategy was clearly illustrated on Sunday evenings when *Armchair Theatre* followed ATV's hugely popular *Sunday Night at the London Palladium* on to the network, inheriting a large portion of its audience.

Armchair Theatre began with a preview on 8 July 1956, an adaptation of a stage play by Dorothy Brandon called *The Outsider*, and was launched as a weekly programme on 16 September 1956 with *Tears in the Wind*, adapted from André Gide's novel *Symphonie Pastorale*. Thereafter the series presented an eclectic mix of plays for television, including adaptations of stage plays and novels, such as Strindberg's *Miss Julie* (23 December 1956) and Henry James's *The Heiress* (5 May 1957), together with original television plays such as Harry Kershaw's *The Hollow Crown* (7 October 1956), Allan Prior's *The Common Man* (11 November 1956) and J.B. Priestley's *Now Let Him Go* (15 September 1957).

In April 1958 the Canadian producer Sydney Newman replaced Vance as Head of Drama at ABC and Newman set about transforming *Armchair Theatre*, reducing the number of adaptations and commissioning more original, contemporary drama, especially plays with regional subject matter. As Philip Purser subsequently observed: 'He knew what he wanted: a school of realism dramatising the social revolution he felt had taken place in Britain after the war' (Purser, 1961: 18). With the assistance of story editor Peter Luke, Newman recruited new writers such as Clive Exton, Alun Owen, Harold Pinter and Ray Rigby to write for *Armchair Theatre* and in 1959–60 a new brand of contemporary regional drama began to appear with plays such as Owen's *No Tram to Lime Street* (18 October 1959), Exton's *Where I Live* (10 January 1960) and Rigby's *The Leather Jungle* (10 April 1960).

Armchair Theatre was both popular and influential. The plays were frequently among the ten most watched programmes on television each week and Newman's predilection for contemporary social realism brought television drama into line with contemporary developments in literature, theatre and the cinema, paving the way for subsequent developments in television drama, on ITV and the BBC, with popular series such as *Coronation Street* (Granada, 1960 to present) and *Z Cars* (BBC, 1962–78) being set in the North of England and featuring regional characters with distinct regional accents. It is significant that this new brand of regional drama on

Armchair Theatre came from an ITV company based in the Midlands and the North, produced at ABC's Didsbury studios in Manchester and shown in other parts of the country via the ITV network. As John Russell Taylor wrote in 1962: 'Newman's brief from ABC's managing director, Howard Thomas, was to continue the development of a programme having its roots in the North and the Midlands, but conceived as family entertainment for a Sunday night viewing circle in homes throughout the British isles' (Taylor, 1962a: 9). As with subsequent developments in 'regional' British television drama, the regional subject matter of these plays was intended not only for the Northern and Midlands audiences which ABC primarily served but for a national audience, courtesy of the network. Unlike regional news programmes, drama was too expensive to be produced only for audiences within the company's franchise area. From the very beginnings of regional drama production on ITV (and the BBC), plays, series and serials were nearly always shown to a national audience, as far as the transmitters allowed.

BBC Midland Region

The impact and popular success of ITV, with its federated regional structure, caused the BBC to rethink its own regional broadcasting policy. Even before ITV came on to the scene, the BBC had been criticised by the 1951 Beveridge Committee for its 'London-centric and metropolitan structure' (Johnson and Turnock, 2005: 19), a criticism that led to ITV being established with a regional structure. Internal BBC policy documents show that the BBC was very conscious of the threat ITV posed to the Corporation, with its regional companies recruiting BBC staff and its popular programming luring audiences away from the BBC. New BBC programmes, such as the popular drama series *Z Cars*, may have shown an awareness of the need to address audiences in the North of England, with a Lancashire-based drama parading a range of non-metropolitan accents, but *Z Cars* was still produced in London, in the studios at the new BBC Television Centre near Shepherd's Bush. In the 1950s and early 1960s the BBC's regional production centres did not have the resources, the budget or the personnel to produce a long-running series like *Z Cars*. Instead the regional studios produced single plays for the national television service, such as Alan Plater's first television plays, *The Referees* (1961) and *A Smashing Day* (1962), plays with a distinctly Northern flavour, which were produced at the BBC's Dickenson Road studio in Manchester.

When the BBC was allocated a second channel some drama production was moved to the regions in order to relieve the pressure on the London studios, as production was stepped up in readiness for the new channel. This is no doubt why the experimental drama series *Teletale* (1963–64) was recorded in different regional studios. Peter Duguid, who had recently completed a BBC Directing Course, directed his first two television plays for the *Teletale* series, at the BBC's Gosta Green studio in Birmingham, and he was full of praise for the production team, which he felt benefited from working in the more intimate environment at Gosta Green:

> They were very good technically, they really were. I mean I had a marvellous camera crew . . . I did have a very strong feeling of family, they all cared about each other and they all cared about each other's work and they were thinking about each other to the extent that you couldn't compare it with London . . . BBC in London is enormous, I can't remember how many camera crews there were but you very rarely worked with the same crew in the same year.[9]

The close-knit 'family' atmosphere Duguid found at Gosta Green was an important feature of regional television production, resulting from the smaller scale of the regional studios and their distance from London. In 1964 BBC Midland Region stepped up its drama production when it produced its first drama serial at the Gosta Green studio. Like the ATV/ABC studio in Aston, the Gosta Green studio was a former cinema which the BBC turned into a television studio in 1955. By the mid-1960s Gosta Green was sufficiently well equipped and staffed to enable it to begin producing twice-weekly, long-running regional drama serials. This marked an attempt by the BBC to compete with ITV's popular twice-weekly drama serials, particularly Granada's *Coronation Street* but also, from November 1964, ATV's Midlands-based soap opera, *Crossroads* (1964–88).

Shortly before *Crossroads* began, BBC Midland produced the twice-weekly *Swizzlewick* (BBC1, August–November 1964) at Gosta Green. This thirteen-week serial was created by the Birmingham writer David Turner, who had previously written single plays with a regional flavour for the BBC. *Swizzlewick* was about the activities of a town council in a Midlands town – hardly a subject likely to challenge the supremacy of *Coronation Street* in the ratings, but an interesting early attempt by the BBC to develop a regional drama serial that was not only set in the Midlands but produced there too.[10]

The following year Midland Region launched two twice-weekly serials. *United!* (BBC1, 1965–67), based around the staff and players at a professional football club, ran for two years and a total of 147 episodes, and *The Newcomers* (BBC1, 1965–69), about a family that leaves London to live in a village in the country, ran for four years and 430 episodes. *United!* was mainly studio-based but included some exterior scenes filmed at Stoke City Football Club, in the North Midlands. *The Newcomers*, set in the fictitious village of Angleton, included exterior scenes filmed at Haverhill in Suffolk, a county that, geographically, is part of East Anglia rather than the Midlands, but which, like the rest of East Anglia, was part of the BBC's Midland Region, indicating the geographical extent of the region in the 1960s. In comparison, ITV had a similar twice-weekly serial called *Weavers Green* (Anglia, April–September 1966), set in a village in East Anglia, which ran for fifty episodes in 1966, but this was produced by Anglia TV, based in Norwich, rather than by the Birmingham-based ATV.

Following the transmission of the final episode of *The Newcomers*, on 13 November 1969, the Midland Region immediately launched a replacement, the twice-weekly *The Doctors* (BBC1, 1969–71), on 19 November 1969. Unlike the previous three serials, however, *The Doctors* was set not in the Midlands but in a medical practice in north London, the BBC seemingly having abandoned attempts to compete with ITV with regionally set long-running serials. *The Doctors* ran for 160 episodes, finishing on 17 June 1971. It was to be another fourteen years before the BBC finally came up with a twice-weekly serial that was able to compete successfully with *Coronation Street* – the London-based *EastEnders* (BBC1, 1985 to present).[11]

ITV regional franchise changes, 1968–81

All fourteen of the original ITV franchises (excluding the failed WWN franchise) were renewed in July 1964, initially until July 1967, although this was later extended by one year until the end of July 1968. The next contract period was to last for six years until 1974 but this was extended in stages until the end of 1981, so that the companies ended up operating for a thirteen-year period to match that of the two original ITV franchises, which operated from 1955 to 1968.

The ITA made three important decisions in the 1968 franchise round. One was to force a merger between ABC and Rediffusion (previously Associated-Rediffusion) which resulted in a new company, Thames Television, taking up the London weekday franchise. The ITA also decided to separate the London weekend contract from the Midlands weekday contract, both previously held by ATV. Consequently ATV took up the new seven-day franchise for the Midlands. Thirdly, the ITA decided to separate the North of England franchise, previously shared by ABC and Granada, into two separate seven-day contracts for Lancashire and Yorkshire. Granada became a seven-day operator for Lancashire and a new company, Yorkshire Television, took up the contract on the other side of the Pennines. The only other changes were London Weekend Television (LWT) taking over ATV's London weekend franchise, and Harlech (HTV) taking over from TWW in Wales and the West of England. Following this reorganisation there were fifteen ITV companies operating in fourteen regions, London now being the only shared region.

From the regional point of view the changes meant that the Midlands became less of a 'poor relation' to the other ITV regions, which it had been when it was served by two companies whose main interests resided elsewhere. With ATV losing its London franchise and gaining the seven-day contract for the Midlands the company was able to commit itself more fully to serving the region and immediately embarked on the building of new studios in the centre of Birmingham. This was still, however, a large region, embracing East and West Midlands, the Black Country, the Welsh Borders and the Potteries (part of which was also within Granada's transmission area). Like the BBC in the Midlands, the ATV region embraced a wide variety of dialects, cultural practices and regional affiliations.

The division of the North of England region into Lancashire and Yorkshire seemed sensible, given the cultural rivalries and separate regional identities of the two communities on either side of the Pennines. The allocation in the first franchise round of the North–East to Tyne Tees, with Border transmitting to Cumbria, had already begun the process of dividing up the huge area of Northern England, and this further division continued the process, creating four regions where the South had three – London, South, and South West. The division of the North into four ITV regions was not entirely determined by technology – it was a tacit recognition that there were distinct regional differences in the North, differences that the BBC, with one amorphous North Region, was soon to acknowledge with its own regional reorganisation.

The reorganisation of BBC regional broadcasting in the 1970s

When the new BBC Television Centre opened in London in 1960 London's hegemony over television drama production was consolidated, so much so that the BBC's foremost response to ITV's regional drama initiatives, *Z Cars*, was produced in London rather than by the North Region. Furthermore, when Sydney Newman became Head of Drama at the BBC in 1963 he decided, according to *Z Cars* producer David Rose, to cut back on regional drama production because he thought the regional studios were not suitably equipped: 'When he arrived he took one look at the Regions and said with the coming of colour, editing and this, that and the other, and the cramped size of the studios, he felt it was not the standard that he was looking for that was coming out of the Regions, and I think that was fair comment, the backcloths did wobble a bit!'[12]

By the end of the 1960s, however, steps had been taken to move away from a centralised 'national' broadcasting service at the BBC with the establishment of a number of local radio stations, partly in response to the popularity of pirate radio stations such as Radio Caroline and Radio London, which broadcast to local rather than national audiences. Following the discussions that had been going on at the BBC throughout the 1960s about regional broadcasting, a BBC policy document called *Broadcasting in the Seventies* was published in July 1969, announcing the intention to expand the BBC's regional broadcasting, both radio and television. *Broadcasting in the Seventies* acknowledged that the regional structure of the BBC in the postwar period had been determined primarily by technical, rather than social, considerations:

> The boundaries were drawn up some forty years ago not on any basis of community interest but to match the range of the transmitters. These are regions devised by engineers rather than sociologists. The Midland Region stretches from the Welsh border to the North Sea. The North Region has to cover Liverpool and Newcastle, Manchester and Hull, Lincoln and Carlisle. The South and West Region serves an area stretching from Lands End to Brighton. Over the years we have sought to meet this problem by creating five additional areas within the regions, but we now feel that the time has come to replace this structure. (BBC, 1969: 7)

The plan was to replace the three English Regions of North, Midland and South West with eight smaller regions. North Region was to be divided into three regions: North East (based in Newcastle-upon-Tyne), North (based in Leeds) and North West (based in Manchester). The Midland Region was to be divided into two: Midlands (based in Birmingham) and East Anglia (based in Norwich). The South and West Region was to be divided into three regions: West (based in Bristol), South West (based in Plymouth) and South (based in Southampton). Also, the production facilities at Manchester, Birmingham and Bristol were to be improved and expanded to enable the North West, Midlands and West regions to supply more programmes to the national television service.

To some extent then, *Broadcasting in the Seventies* proposed a reorganisation of the BBC along the lines of ITV, with eight English regions roughly equivalent to the eight English ITV regions (excluding the London region and Harlech, whose transmission area included the West of England in addition to Wales). The new BBC regional policy gave a certain degree of autonomy to the regions to opt out of the network at certain times, while also requiring the three established regional production centres to provide an increased amount of regional material for BBC1 and BBC2, just as the bigger, regionally based ITV companies provided the bulk of the programmes for the ITV network, with ATV, Granada and Yorkshire emerging to form a 'big five' with the two London companies, Thames and LWT, after the 1968 franchise round.

Surveying 'A Decade in Prospect' in the 1970 BBC Handbook, Director-General Charles Curran described some of the initiatives that were being taken in the expansion of regional broadcasting at the BBC:

> In non-metropolitan radio and television in England there will be some really radical changes. In television we shall have eight new regions which, by 1971, will be producing 400 programmes a year for their own audiences, compared with the 150 a year of the former three English regions ... Through the production centres at Birmingham, Manchester and Bristol regional talent and initiative will continue to flow into network radio and television as fully as or more fully than in the past. (Curran, 1970: 23)

In the 1971 BBC Handbook it was reported that BBC regional broadcasting was reorganised in July 1970, when the three former English

Regions were disbanded and replaced by the eight new regions, with three network production centres:

> The function of the eight English regions and of local radio stations is to provide a local programme service of particular interest to the audience within range of each transmitter, while the task of network production centres is to reflect the character and talent of their part of the country through contributions to the national network. (BBC, 1971: 53)

The use of the term 'local' rather than 'regional' is significant. With the increase in the number of regions came a decrease in the geographical size of each region. While this was not quite a return to the early days of the BBC when nineteen local radio companies served discrete communities, it marked a move towards redefining 'regional' broadcasting as 'local' broadcasting. Subsequently an increased number of BBC local radio stations were to be very successful in catering for local communities based in and around provincial cities such as Leicester, Nottingham and Stoke, while local television was restricted largely to news and sports opt-outs within the eight English regions.

As far as television drama was concerned the most important aspect of the regional reorganisation of BBC broadcasting was the building of the new Pebble Mill studios in Birmingham and the establishment of a new department, BBC English Regions Drama, to be based there with a remit to produce regional television drama for the network. While BBC Pebble Mill was to produce programmes for the network and programmes of local interest for the Midlands region, the purpose of English Regions Drama was not simply to produce Midlands-based drama for the network, as the Midland Region had previously done, but to commission a variety of regional drama from all parts of the country in order to 'reflect the character and talent' of the English Regions to the country as a whole.

Regional theatre and television drama in the Midlands

As an illustration of the relationship between regional culture, specifically the regional repertory theatre movement, and regional television in the 1960s–70s it is instructive to look at the example of the Victoria Theatre Company in Stoke-on-Trent, which was involved in the production of four television plays between 1967 and 1974. Part of the BBC and ITV Midlands region, Stoke is located at the northern limits of the region. Its geographical position in North Staffordshire means it is actually on the border of two broadcasting regions, with parts of North Staffordshire receiving Granada rather than ATV (or Central TV as the company became in 1981). Stoke's geographical position between the North West and the Midlands has contributed to an ambivalence in the area's regional allegiance which has resulted in the Potteries developing a strong sense of independence in their regional and cultural identity. The Victoria Theatre has done much since it was established in 1962 to nurture this sense of a unique social and cultural identity in the Potteries. From 1962 until he retired in 1998 the company's artistic director was Peter Cheeseman. Although born in Portsmouth, Cheeseman lived most of his life in the Midlands and the North and from 1962 he dedicated himself to the production of regional theatre in the Potteries. As Dominic Shellard writes in *British Theatre Since the War*:

> [N]o one in Britain can rival his devotion to a single theatre and its sur-rounding community. Generally following a policy that stuck to three commitments – performances in the round . . ., the juxtaposition of new work and classics and the history and contemporary problems of North Staffordshire – Cheeseman is best known for eleven documentaries on local issues, in the form of 'living newspapers' and in the tradition of Theatre Workshop. These productions have featured the area's ailing mining, steel and potteries industries and have contributed to local political campaigns, as well as helping to keep alive the oral testimony that is so often lost in accounts of local struggles. (Shellard, 1999: 179)

Firmly based in the local community, dramatising local issues and staging plays of particular interest to a North Staffordshire audience, the Victoria Theatre Company was involved with several television productions from the mid-1960s to the mid-1970s, involving all of the Midlands-based television companies and production centres: ABC, ATV, BBC Midland Region and BBC English Regions Drama. An early collaboration came in the form of a BBC documentary, pro-duced by Philip Donnellan for the Midland Region, on the production of *The Staffordshire Rebels* (BBC2, 8 January 1966), a play about the English Civil War which the Victoria Theatre Company staged in 1965. Not only does the documentary provide a unique insight into Peter Cheeseman's method of constructing documentary theatre, it also reveals how the company dramatised historical subjects from a distinctly 'local' perspective.

Not long after this, while the company was staging a production called *Jock on the Go*, adapted from an Arnold Bennett short story called *Jock at a Venture*, Peter Cheeseman became caught up in a dispute with the Victoria Theatre's board of directors concerning artistic policy which led to him being sacked in January 1967 and the company being deprived of a building in which to perform. Cheeseman received tremendous support from the local community and was eventually reinstated as Artistic Director in July 1967 and the company restored to its home, but the period of 'exile' was by no means a fallow period. During those first six months of 1967 Cheeseman received several overtures from television executives wanting to lend support by producing work from the company, and two plays for television were commissioned during this period, one for the BBC Midland Region and one for ABC Television.

Both plays were produced to mark the centenary of the birth of the Potteries writer Arnold Bennett (born 25 May 1867). The first was a television version of *Jock on the Go* (BBC2, 9 September 1967) which the company's resident playwright, Peter Terson, had adapted for the stage and which he and Cheeseman now dramatised for television. The television version (which no longer exists) was directed by Alan Rees and recorded at the BBC's Gosta Green studio on 15 May 1967, with some retakes being recorded on 23 July 1967.[13] *Jock on the Go* was transmitted on 9 September 1967, ironically just a few days after the Victoria Theatre reopened with a Peter Terson play called *The Ballad of the Artificial Mash*.[14] The Saturday evening BBC2 transmission of *Jock on the Go*, from 9.55 to 10.45 pm, followed the final episode of a four-part serialisation of J.B. Priestley's *Angel Pavement*, dramatised for television by the Birmingham writer David Turner. The Priestley serial, however, was a London production, whereas *Jock on the Go* was listed in the *Radio Times* as a production 'from the Midlands . . . adapted from the original stage production at the Victoria Theatre, Stoke-on-Trent' (*Radio Times*, 7 September 1967).

The second play commissioned during the dispute was *The Heroism of Thomas Chadwick* (ABC, 23 September 1967), an amalgam of two Arnold Bennett short stories about the same character, Thomas Chadwick (played by Ken Campbell, who was a member of the Victoria Theatre Company at the time). The play was again adapted by Peter Terson, despite the fact that Terson had an antipathy towards the work of Arnold Bennett, as he explained following a screening of *The Heroism of Thomas Chadwick* at Stoke Film Theatre in

June 2004, when he talked about his time as resident playwright with the Victoria Theatre Company:

> I was a games teacher – a very bad one – I was hauled out of that by Peter Cheeseman – he got me an Arts Council grant to be resident playwright . . . it was a mystery to me. I wrote plays but I didn't know anything about it and when I came here [Stoke] he didn't know what to do with me either . . . so he said 'study Arnold Bennett' – he was crazy about Arnold Bennett – and I was immersed in this bloody Arnold Bennett stuff. I know that there are enthusiasts around but I wasn't one of them, I thought they were very thick books. I spent hours in that museum reading his letters – and what a prolific letter-writer he was – and journals, I really was fed up to the back teeth . . . but I did about three, I did *Jock on the Go*, *Thomas Chadwick* and *Clayhanger* with Joyce [Cheeseman].[15]

Terson's confession was made to an audience of 'Bennett enthusiasts' but he also said how much he enjoyed the 'wordiness' and 'theatricality' of *The Heroism of Thomas Chadwick*, which dated from an era when audiences were more accustomed to discursive, theatrical conventions in television drama:

> In those days people listened to dialogue. It was astonishing that there were so many words in it. If you send a television play off now you get a reject note saying 'too wordy', well, you know, that's what I do, but here there was so much I had to listen to, it was wonderful, and also I liked it sort of being theatrical, instead of all these car chases and whiz-bam and visual effects you had the rattling tram car and the little office, I loved all that.[16]

The Heroism of Thomas Chadwick was commissioned by Leonard White, who was the Executive Producer on *Armchair Theatre* at ABC Television for most of the 1960s, following Sydney Newman's departure to the BBC. White often visited regional repertory theatres in search of new plays that could be adapted for television and he was aware that the Victoria Theatre Company was in dispute with its management at this time:

> Help was needed to keep Cheeseman's company together. ABC Television stepped in to support them . . . ABC always maintained a strong interest and support for the theatres in their franchise regions, the Midlands and the North. So, the ill wind that had driven this Company into exile for some six months did blow some good. Indeed, soon after

this gesture, Peter Cheeseman and his Company were reinstated at the Victoria Theatre, Stoke, under a new independent trust formed of the Arts Council and the local authorities. (White, 2003: 201)

Peter Cheeseman was, in fact, reinstated on 11 July 1967, two weeks before *The Heroism of Thomas Chadwick* began rehearsing on 24 July in the Queen's Hall in Burslem. Further rehearsals took place in Twickenham, near to ABC's Teddington Studios on the outskirts of London, in early August, prior to camera rehearsals on 8 August and video tape recording (VTR) on 9 August: 'From start of rehearsals until recording was seventeen days', as Leonard White recalled.[17] The play was transmitted on the ITV network as a spin-off from the *Armchair Theatre* series – on a Saturday night rather than Sunday which was *Armchair Theatre*'s traditional slot – under the title of *The Story Teller*, referring to Bennett, and presented as a special event to mark the centenary of the writer's birth. Peter Cheeseman was again credited as the producer and Mike Vardy, who later directed episodes of *The Sweeney*, was the director.

Resuming theatre production after the dispute, it was another three years before the Victoria Theatre Company participated in another television production. This time the television company involved was ATV, now operating the seven-day ITV franchise for the Midlands, and the play was another Bennett adaptation, a ninety-minute television version of his 1902 novel *Anna of the Five Towns* (ATV, 28 February 1971). Adapted this time by Joyce Cheeseman and directed for television by Dorothy Denham, *Anna of the Five Towns* was an ATV network production for *Sunday Night Theatre*, transmitted from 10.15 to 11.45 pm (following a screening of the feature film *A Kind of Loving* and preceding an episode of *The Avengers*). Peter Cheeseman had no role in the television version of *Anna of the Five Towns* and was unhappy about the manner in which it was directed for television, especially its slow pace.[18] While *Anna* did have an advantage over the previous two television plays in that it was recorded in colour, following the recent introduction of colour television, the production retained a 'staginess' which *Thomas Chadwick* had sought to avoid. As Leonard White said of *Thomas Chadwick*: 'We did not simply want a photographed "theatre" production. James Weatherup's design helped to make the transformation' (White, 2003: 201). The 1971 television production of *Anna of the Five Towns*, however, was competent but uninspired and constrained by limited set design, although the director did deploy close-ups to good effect, demonstrating an advantage television held over theatre.

In an article in the *TV Times* to accompany the screening of *Anna of the Five Towns* Peter Cheeseman talked about the success of the Victoria Theatre Company in staging plays, in-the-round, for the local community and of the relationship between theatre and television:

> We attract the community because we offer consistent local interest productions, documentaries that use the words of the people. Arnold Bennett was our bonus. *Anna* was our most popular production. You hear the laughter of recognition when they watch Bennett's characters talking about what they know. He's our writer . . .
>
> We don't do Beckett because we don't want to frighten-off the locals. Theatre needs this real community to draw on. It is up to us to find the right stimulus to attract the local community. I think this is happening in a lot of regional theatres.
>
> Television has helped. We have done two Bennett adaptations, *Jock-on-the-Go* and *The Heroism of Thomas Chadwick*, and two documentaries, *The Staffordshire Rebels* and *The Burning Mountain*, about the primitive Methodists. They give an appetite for theatre, but of a particular kind. People want to see actors close-up. The traditional theatre cannot offer this.
>
> Theatre-in-the-round also offers the narrative flow and quick scene-changes that television and cinema have accustomed people to. (quoted in McGill, 1971: 6)[19]

In 1974 Peter Cheeseman tried to emulate the experience of one of the Victoria Theatre's local documentaries when he directed a version of *Fight for Shelton Bar* for BBC English Regions Drama. Made for the half-hour *Second City Firsts* series, *Fight for Shelton Bar* (BBC2, 18 November 1974) was a drama-documentary about the fight to save the local steelworks in Stoke from closure and was adapted from a longer stage version. It was recorded entirely in the studio at Pebble Mill, and Cheeseman tried to retain some of the documentary quality of the original production by using photographs of the steelworks and the local area, together with captions, songs and actors talking to camera. As such it was an unusual production for *Second City Firsts*, but not for English Regions Drama in that it conformed to the policy of commissioning plays representing regional communities and regional issues. *Fight for Shelton Bar* certainly did that, although the need to compress a lot of material into just over thirty minutes inevitably meant that the television version suffered in comparison to the full-length theatre play.

These four television plays, plus the two television documentaries about the work of the Victoria Theatre Company, provide an illustration of how regionally based television companies (ABC and ATV) and regional production centres (BBC Midland Region and BBC English Regions Drama) attempted to 'reflect the character and talent' of one part of their region, the Potteries, by commissioning work from a regional theatre company which was particularly concerned with regional issues, regional culture and regional identity. It is significant that these four productions came in an eight-year period from the mid-1960s to the mid-1970s and that the Victoria Theatre Company was involved in no more television productions after 1974, despite the fact that Peter Cheeseman continued producing local documentaries at the New Victoria Theatre until his retirement in 1998.

The thriving regional theatre movement of the 1960s–70s went into decline in the 1980s, suffering from Arts Council cuts and a political backlash following the 1979 election of Thatcher's Conservative government with its centralising policies and political antipathy towards the regions. The cultural climate in the 1980s was simply not conducive to the kinds of regional collaboration between regional television companies and regional theatre which led to the Victoria Theatre Company working with four different Midlands-based television companies from 1967 to 1974. Of those companies ABC lost its Midlands franchise in 1968 when the ITA forced the company into a merger with the London-based Rediffusion to form Thames Television. ATV continued as the sole ITV operator in the Midlands until 1981 when it became Central Television and in 1994 Central was purchased by the London-based ITV company Carlton Television, which took over the London franchise from Thames Television in 1993. The takeovers and mergers between ITV companies during the 1990s, leading to the eventual consolidation of the ITV network as one company in 2004, served to erode the regional identities of the ITV companies and contributed to a downgrading in the importance of regional broadcasting within ITV.

While BBC English Regions Drama thrived throughout the 1970s it is perhaps significant that there was only one more collaboration with a regional theatre company – Mike Bradwell's Hull Truck Theatre – on a *Second City First* in 1975. BBC English Regions Drama itself went into decline following the departure of David Rose in 1981 (see

Chapter 4) and now no longer exists. BBC Birmingham retains a presence in the Midlands, despite the selling-off of the Pebble Mill studios in 2004, with new studios in the centre of Birmingham and the establishment of a new 'drama village' at Birmingham University's Selly Oak campus, from where the daily serial *Doctors* (2000 to present) and other networked drama series are produced (see Wood, 2004). Whether this initiative will lead to a revival of indigenous regional drama in the Midlands, rather than the regional production of low-cost dramas for the BBC network, remains to be seen.

Notes

1 British Broadcasting Corporation (BBC), 'Regional Broadcasting', 22 December 1958, BBC Written Archives Centre (BBC WAC), T16/230/3.
2 Cecil McGivern, 'Regional Television – Note by D.D.Tel.B.', 6 January 1960, BBC WAC, T16/230/5.
3 Ibid.
4 Ibid.
5 Cecil McGivern, '"Fresh As Paint": One-Act Play, Tuesday July 3rd: 8.45–9.15 p.m. Midland Region', memo to various BBC personnel including Head of Drama and Script Supervisor, 5 July 1956, BBC WAC, T5/2242/1.
6 Denis Morris, 'Plays', memo to Cecil McGivern, 12 July 1956, BBC WAC, T5/2242/1.
7 Gerald Beadle, 'Television in the Regions', 8 December 1958, BBC WAC, T16/230/3.
8 Denis Morris, 'Plays', memo to Cecil McGivern, 12 July 1956, BBC WAC, T5/2242/1.
9 Peter Duguid, interviewed by the author, 28 November 2003.
10 David Turner wrote the first six episodes of *Swizzlewick*. Three other writers contributed to the serial, including Malcolm Bradbury who wrote five episodes.
11 In March 2000 a new daily thirty-minute drama series called *Doctors* was launched on BBC1, once again produced by BBC Birmingham.
12 David Rose, telephone message to the author, 10 October 2003.
13 I am grateful to the late Peter Cheeseman, who died in April 2010, for providing information about the dispute with management and production details about the two Bennett plays recorded for television during this period.
14 *The Ballad of the Artificial Mash* was also subsequently produced for television, dramatised by Peter Cheeseman from Peter Terson's original stage play, but with a different cast (including Stanley Holloway), as

the four-hundredth and last *Armchair Theatre* play produced by ABC Television, on 27 July 1968. On 30 July 1968 ABC merged with the London-based Rediffusion company to become Thames Television.

15 Peter Terson, speaking following a screening of *The Heroism of Thomas Chadwick* at Stoke Film Theatre on 16 June 2004.

16 Ibid.

17 Production information given by Leonard White in his introduction to the screening of *The Heroism of Thomas Chadwick* at Stoke Film Theatre on 16 June 2004.

18 Comments made by Peter Cheeseman following a screening of *Anna of the Five Towns* at Stoke Film Theatre on 11 June 2005.

19 The Victoria Theatre Company's 1969 drama-documentary *The Burning Mountain* was the subject of a BBC2 arts magazine programme, *Review* (BBC2, 17 January 1970): 'At Stoke-on-Trent's Victoria Theatre a new "musical documentary" about the Ranters – primitive Methodists who preached fire and brimstone in the 19th century Potteries – has been worked entirely from old journals, contemporary interviews, hymns, and folk songs. *Review* filmed this lively young repertory company in the last week of rehearsals and looked at the countryside and people who provide much of the source material for artistic director Peter Cheeseman's bid for truly popular theatre' (*Radio Times*, 15 January 1970, p. 21).

3

Granada Television

Granada Television was in many ways the most independent of the ITV companies formed in the mid-1950s. The company was founded as a subsidiary of Granada Group Limited, the parent company Sidney Bernstein ran with his brother Cecil. The Bernsteins took over the family business in March 1922 following the death of their father, Alexander, a Russian Jewish immigrant who came to England from Latvia in the early 1890s. Alexander Bernstein ran his own film business during the silent era and over the next three decades Sidney and Cecil developed the business, establishing Granada as one of the main cinema circuits in the country. It was Sidney who named the company Granada after visiting the Spanish city on a walking holiday in the 1920s, a visit he later recounted in a company booklet, *This Is Granada*:

> En route from Gibraltar I arrived very late at night at the city of Granada. (I saw little of the place until morning – the morning incidentally after the night of the first snowfall that Granada had had for years.) The snow melted early in the day and I then discovered the city. It was wonderful. The Alhambra (the magnificent palace started by King Alhamar in 1238) was a rare, dazzling building in a wonderful setting. I was very impressed and the memory lingered on. I had fallen in love with it. At that time I was searching for a new name for our theatres and I did not want cold initials or the usual names and decided that the word 'Granada' had all the theatrical and exotic feeling I wanted in a name. It represented the gaiety of Spain. So Granada it was. (quoted in Eyles, 1998: 29)

Sidney Bernstein's account of how he decided on the name of the company gives a flavour of his taste for culture and the exotic which would carry over into his business enterprises, including Granada Television, where such attributes were nurtured despite the commercial nature of the enterprise. Bernstein's father, Alexander, owned just three cinemas, but by the 1950s the Granada cinema circuit numbered more than fifty theatres, which were notable for the extravagance of their design, aiming to provide a memorable evening's entertainment, whether it was a film programme, variety show or other form of entertainment.[1]

Under Sidney Bernstein's leadership, Granada played an important part in the growth of the British film industry during the 1930s–40s and Bernstein himself was an active participant in all aspects of the industry, not just the exhibition sector. A committed socialist, he was a founder member in 1925 of the progressive London Film Society and was instrumental in bringing the Soviet film-maker Sergei Eisenstein to Britain to screen *Battleship Potemkin* (USSR, 1925), a film that was banned from public exhibition in Britain because of its revolutionary content. Bernstein was also active in party politics. A member of the Labour Party, which he joined when he was seventeen, he was elected as a Labour councillor at the age of twenty-six, a position he retained for five years. In the 1930s Bernstein became involved in anti-Nazi campaigns and during the Second World War was a member of the Ministry of Information's Films Division, where his connections with film-makers such as Alfred Hitchcock proved invaluable in the production of propaganda films supporting the war effort.

After the war Granada began to develop an interest in television, applying for a licence to operate closed circuit television in Granada Theatres as early as 1948, an application that was rejected. Sidney Bernstein was a great believer in public service television and was initially opposed to the idea of commercial television, but when it became obvious that it was on the way Granada decided to submit an application for a licence:

> In the period of debate leading to the Television Act, Granada was not dedicated to the cause of Independent Television. From the national point of view, in Granada's opinion, the known weaknesses of monopoly seemed less frightening than the thought of competition, or at least some of the likely competitors. But, if Independent Television were to be permitted, Granada would, without question, stake its claim. It would be wrong to leave the field to the big battalions. (Buscombe, 1981: 117)

Bernstein's leftist politics, however, made him an unlikely figure among the applicants for a commercial television licence and when the Conservative government discovered he was in the running for one of the ITV contracts it tried to intervene to prevent Granada being successful. However, the chairman of the Independent Television Authority, Kenneth Clark, who had worked with Sidney Bernstein at the Ministry of Information during the war, resisted this attempt by the government to interfere in the allocation of licences. His son, Colin Clark, who worked at Granada in the late 1950s, later recounted the meeting in which Lord Woolton brought pressure on the ITA Chairman to disqualify Granada on the grounds on Bernstein's political affiliations:

> Lord Woolton summoned the Chairman of the Independent Television Authority to his office. 'Sidney Bernstein is a communist,' he said. 'Now we don't want a communist running our new television network, do we?' 'Certainly not,' replied the Chairman – who also happened to be my Dad, and who loved Sidney. 'You have a copy of his Communist Party membership and all your secret service files on my desk tomorrow morning, and I will see that he is disqualified immediately.' (Clark, 2003: 37)

The attempt to block Granada's application reveals the degree of suspicion with which the company, and Sidney Bernstein in particular, was viewed by the Conservative government presiding over the introduction of commercial television in Britain. Granada's reputation for independence and for having a more liberal stance than the other commercial television companies was to become very apparent over the next few years. The difference between Granada and the other companies became evident on its opening night, when Granada included a tribute to the BBC among its first programmes. As Julia Hallam has noted, Sidney Bernstein's admiration for the BBC and his belief in the values of public service broadcasting ensured that Granada was ideologically different from the other commercial television companies:

> From the outset, Granada set itself the objective of providing high quality popular programmes that would surpass even the BBC's threshold of quality and standards. The company was against cultural segregation and sought to mix its more popular programming with innovative drama, hard-hitting investigative documentaries and pioneering coverage of political events. It quickly earned itself a reputation as the most socially conscious of all the commercial companies. (Hallam, 2003: 12)

'Granadaland'

The Granada TV Network Ltd was awarded the weekday licence for the North of England on 25 May 1955 and began broadcasting on 3 May 1956. Sidney Bernstein claimed that Granada chose to apply for a Northern licence, rather than a London one, after studying maps of population density and rainfall, concluding that Northerners were more likely to spend time watching television because of the inclement climate: 'if you look at a map of the concentration of population in the North and a rainfall map, you will see that the North is an ideal place for television' (Buscombe, 1981: 22). This may indeed be part of the reason behind Granada's application, but a paragraph in the 1980 contract renewal application lists other factors, suggesting that, from the beginning, Sidney Bernstein was looking to establish a different kind of television company, removed from the metropolitan influence of London and the BBC:

> The region contained in the west two great cities, Liverpool and Manchester, also Blackpool – then second only to London as a centre of entertainment – and a famous national newspaper, The Manchester Guardian; in the east the wool and steel towns and the great manufacturing valleys of Yorkshire. The whole represented a part of Great Britain that was independent in character and remote from the metropolitan traditions of the BBC. If any English region could contribute to a change in the face of broadcasting, this was it. (Buscombe, 1981: 121)

The Granada Group was based in London, with offices in Golden Square, but when the company was awarded a Northern television licence the Bernsteins committed themselves to establishing a new television company in the North by building new studios in Manchester – the first purpose-built television centre in Britain.

The region allocated to Granada was based on Lancashire and Yorkshire but also included North Wales and most of Cumbria, while in the south the region embraced Cheshire, the northern parts of Shropshire, Staffordshire, Derbyshire and Nottinghamshire, and most of Lincolnshire. Lancashire and the western part of the region was to be served by a transmitter on Winter Hill in Lancashire, while Yorkshire and the eastern part of the region was to be covered by a transmitter on Emley Moor in the West Riding of Yorkshire. When Granada TV launched on 3 May 1956, however, only the Winter

Hill transmitter was operational. It was not until 3 November 1956 that the Emley Moor transmitter came into operation, which meant that for six months nearly five million people in the east of the region could not receive Granada's programmes. When fully operational the region which Sidney Bernstein dubbed 'Granadaland' embraced a potential audience of over twelve million people, equivalent in size to that of London and the South and considerably larger than the Midland region.[2]

In December 1959, in a paper delivered to the London School of Economics, Sidney Bernstein described the North as 'a closely knit, indigenous, industrial society; a homogeneous cultural group with a good record for music, theatre, literature and newspapers, not found elsewhere in this island, except perhaps in Scotland' (Buscombe, 1981: 22). This was clearly a Southern perspective. While a large percentage of the potential television audience in the North may have been located in the industrial cities of Manchester, Liverpool, Leeds, Sheffield and Hull, to suggest that the inhabitants of these cities formed 'a homogeneous cultural group' reveals Bernstein's lack of awareness of the cultural differences within 'Granadaland'. Even after the 1968 franchise changes, when Yorkshire Television took over responsibility for the eastern part of the region, depriving Granada of five million potential viewers, Granadaland still embraced two large urban populations, in Manchester and Liverpool, with distinct cultural identities and strong local rivalries.

Welcoming the 1968 redefinition of Granadaland as a 'single geographical unit', Granada's Managing Director Denis Forman echoed Sidney Bernstein's homogenising tendency in his description of a 'New Granadaland' which, while it had lost Yorkshire, still embraced the Lake District, North Wales and parts of the Midlands:

> The old Granadaland was a sprawling hegemony of two ancient kingdoms . . . New Granadaland is a single geographical unit stretching back from Liverpool Bay to the mountains of Snowdonia and the Lake District, the Pennine Ridge and the chimneys of the Black Country. Ninety-two per cent of the population live in urban areas, the region is ideal for test marketing; it can reasonably be served with a single local news service; it has the four best football teams in the country; and it rains more on the west than on the east side of the Pennines, which perhaps partly explains why relatively more Granadaland viewers watch television than do Yorkshiremen. (quoted in Wyver, 1981: 11)

When Granada lost Yorkshire in the 1968 franchise round Denis
Forman suggested it was

> a great relief . . . because there are two different indigenous cultures east
> and west of the Pennines and also to look after the regional affairs over
> a region of that size is impossible. So when it was cut in half and we got
> seven days instead of five it was a wonderful deal for us. It sounds in a
> way ungenerous but I was very glad to be shot of Yorkshire.[3]

Contrary to Sidney Bernstein's original equation of Granadaland
with 'the North', after the loss of Yorkshire and the eastern part of
Granada's region in 1968 'Granadaland' was quickly redefined as the
North West, with Lancashire at its heart, in a sleight of hand which
acknowledged the distinct regional and cultural differences east and
west of the Pennines but which also handily described the region
embraced by the signal from the Winter Hill transmitter. Though
smaller than before, the 'New Granadaland' was still a diverse region
which, as Denis Forman subsequently acknowledged, included areas
about which Granada felt less certain:

> Yes well you see we had two transmitters when we were in Yorkshire
> but when we split we only had Winter Hill and again that was a bless-
> ing because the Winter Hill coverage was pretty indigenous, it was
> Cumbria and Lancashire, North Wales and going down some distance
> into the Midlands – that was much stranger territory, I mean we sort
> of lost our identity in the Midlands. But in Wales – we did a lot of Welsh
> programming – and Lancashire and Cumbria we were okay, we knew
> where we were.[4]

The post-1968 conception of Granadaland as a distinct, indigenous
region survived subsequent franchise changes and was resurrected
by Granada presenter Anthony Wilson in his contribution to the
ITC Report on *Television in the Nations and Regions* in 2002, when he
described the boundaries of the region very precisely, suggesting that
having a 'sense of place' was fundamental to the regional identity of
Granadaland:

> Do we have a regional identity in England's north-west? If regional iden-
> tity is sense of self and sense of place, then I can't think of any part of this
> sceptred isle that has more of both. Our boundaries are clear to all: come
> down from Shap Fell into the southern Lakes and you're home; drift
> down through that pine forest on the M6 just before Keele Services and
> you're leaving home. The peat bogs around Saddleworth separate us
> from the tykes, leaving Leeds further away than London (emotionally)

and North Wales is of course part of us though when we devolve, as we
must, we don't get them. The geographical limits I refer to which lie deep
in all hearts, strangely mirror the footprint of Winter Hill.

England's north west, *by chance or design* [my emphasis], just happens
to be Granadaland. How much more subtle and understanding are those
apparatchiks of the IBA and later ITC than the moronic civil servants
who created Merseyside and Greater Manchester, entities that still give
offence to both ends of the East Lancs Road. (Wilson, 2002: 33–4)

Whether 'Granadaland', as an ITV region, is the result of 'chance or
design' is the key issue. The redefinition of the region after the IBA
altered its boundaries in 1968 suggests that the regional concept
of Granadaland was flexible and that the identity of the region was
determined by a combination of both chance – the positioning of the
transmitter which determined the extent of the region – and design
– with the ITA (as it then was) responsible for deciding that a new
company, Yorkshire Television, should take responsibility for nearly
half of Granadaland (in terms of population) from 1968. Thereafter
'the tykes' no longer belonged to Granadaland.

Anthony Wilson's disparaging remarks about the civic regions of
'Merseyside and Greater Manchester' raise another thorny issue about
regional identity within Granadaland, even after the 1968 franchise
changes. While the geographical distance between Liverpool and
Manchester is less than fifty miles, the social and cultural differences
between the two cities are as marked as their strongly differing
accents. With Granada having its headquarters in Manchester,
Liverpool has always felt itself to be the poor relation within the
region. As John Wyver notes, when Granada finally began to imple-
ment plans for a production base in Liverpool in the late 1970s, 'The
inhabitants of Liverpool had been complaining long and hard about
the shabby treatment their city had received from Granada' (Wyver,
1981: 17).

The success of *Coronation Street*, a twice-weekly drama serial closely
identified with Salford and recorded on a purpose-built studio set at
Granada's headquarters in Manchester, was no doubt partly responsible for establishing Granada as a Manchester-based, Lancashire
company. By the time John Finch created *A Family at War* (1970–
72), a popular drama serial about a Liverpool family set during the
Second World War, the association of Granada with Manchester and
Lancashire, rather than Liverpool and Merseyside, was already well
established. Furthermore, whereas a distinctive feature of *Coronation*

Street's regionality was the Lancashire accents of most of its characters, *A Family at War* was not noted for its Liverpudlian accents.
Ironically it was the BBC, rather than Granada, that helped to
promote the Liverpool accent with *The Liver Birds* (1969–79) and
with the production, by BBC English Regions Drama, of work by
Liverpool writers such as Alan Bleasdale, Willy Russell, Neville Smith
and Ted Whitehead (see Chapter 4).

In a section of Granada's 1980 franchise application, on the composition of its Board of Directors, there was a suggestion that the
company had finally acknowledged the cultural differences between
Manchester and Liverpool: 'We have found in particular that over
the years it has been helpful to have a Board member fully conversant
with the affairs of Merseyside, which is unique in being a large con-
urbation with a history and character quite distinct from the rest of
the region' (Buscombe, 1981: 122). This belated acknowledgement,
however, meant that by the time Granada produced Alan Bleasdale's
Scully, in 1984 (a serial screened on Channel Four, not ITV), *Brookside*
had already done more in eighteen months to promote Liverpool
and the Scouse accent than Granada had in its previous twenty-five
years.[5]

Granada drama

Appearing on Granada's opening night programme, 'Meet the People',
it was the ITA Chairman, Kenneth Clark, who proclaimed that drama
would be an important and distinctive feature of Granada's programming. As reported in the *Manchester Guardian* the next day: 'From Sir
Kenneth Clark, chairman of the ITA, looking genial but a trifle out of
his element, came the message of the evening about what independent television can really do for the North. Drama; that's the thing. The
North has a great tradition of drama; a new school of North Country
drama could be started' (Anon., 1956). It took a while, however,
for the company to start producing its own drama. Although a
short play, *Blue Murder* (3 May 1956), was included in the opening
night programme, this was a filmed drama presented under the title
Douglas Fairbanks Presents, a thirty-minute thriller in which Douglas
Fairbanks Junior played a murderous hairdresser. Rather than being
one of Granada's own productions, *Blue Murder* was produced by
the American network NBC as part of the *Douglas Fairbanks Presents*
series, a long-running series of half-hour dramas made in Britain for

the ITV network. The play was not a highpoint of the evening as far as the *Manchester Guardian* critic was concerned: 'The play *Blue Murder* presented by Douglas Fairbanks (on film) was poor stuff; a synthetic thriller which was jerked to a stop by a plea for delicious corn flakes at a crucial point in the build-up, but was none the worse, or better, for the halt' (Buscombe, 1981: 34).

The first television play to be produced by Granada was transmitted nearly six months after the company went on the air. As the *TV Times* announced, *Shooting Star* (31 October 1956) was a play about 'What really happens behind the scenes of professional football in Britain today?' (*TV Times*, 26 October 1956). A ninety-minute, live studio drama, the play was directed by Silvio Narizzano, a Canadian director who was brought over to England to take responsibility for Granada's drama production. The decision to appoint a Canadian as Head of Drama was a deliberate attempt to avoid what Denis Forman later referred to as the 'extravagant practices and bureaucratic notions' that BBC directors might have brought with them to Granada (Forman, 1981: 58). Like other ITV companies, Granada recruited BBC engineers for their technical expertise but wanted to train their own production personnel, rather than use directors and producers who had been trained by the BBC. In a speech at the Edinburgh Television Festival in 1979 Forman explained how

> On the production side . . . BBC influence was thought to be highly dangerous, bringing with it all sorts of extravagant practices and bureaucratic notions. Bernstein's [*sic*] therefore enlisted one American and one Canadian director of experience who trained over two dozen recruits, many from Canada and the rest from British civilian life. By 1959 the trainees had come good and directors like Herbert Wise, Derek Bennett, Jim Ormerod, Claude Watham [*sic*], Max Witts, Mike Wooller, Mike Scott, were carrying the main burden. Amongst the producers were Barrie Heads, Tim Hewat, Jeremy Isaacs, David Plowright and Milton Schulman. (Forman, 1981: 58)

This explains why many of Granada's early television plays were directed either by Narizzano or by another Canadian recruit, Henry Kaplan. Among the many plays Narizzano directed were two by Arthur Miller, *Death of a Salesman* (27 November 1957) and *A Memory of Two Mondays* (27 February 1959), plus J.B. Priestley's original television drama about the H-bomb, *Doomsday for Dyson* (10 March 1958), while Kaplan directed Lillian Hellman's *Another Part of the*

Forest (16 January 1957), Thornton Wilder's *The Skin of Our Teeth* (17 March 1959) and Arthur Miller's *The Crucible* (3 November 1959), among many others. The reliance upon American material is clearly evident in these early plays and the decision to bring in American and Canadian directors, rather than recruit directors from the BBC, may explain this leaning towards American drama in the early years at Granada. Recalling his days as a production trainee at Granada in the early 1960s, the theatre and television director Gordon McDougall recollects the impact of Narizzano's 1957 production of *Death of a Salesman*:

> My next assignment was to assist Silvio Narizzano who was making a series of Feydeau farces adapted by Philip Mackie, called *Paris 1900*. I had always wanted to meet Silvio because he was responsible for the greatest piece of television I had ever seen, *Death of a Salesman* . . . This was the first televisual experience in which one was able to realise the power of the medium to transport one in time, to superimpose a scene from the past upon the present. Yet, Silvio told me, this had been achieved in Studio 2, hardly larger than a shoebox, shot live, with the cameras having to move into the corner of the studio to shoot the captions for the commercials in the ad-breaks. My admiration for the days of steam television and the men who made it increased fourfold. (McDougall, 2003: 79–80)

While it took time for Granada to train its own directors and producers it also took time for the company to find British writers, especially Northern writers, to fulfil Granada's ambitions to put Northern drama on the screen. As Sidney Bernstein explained in a November 1954 newspaper article, several months before Granada went on the air: 'We think the writers are the most important people. We hope to find and develop a team of creative people who will give us the best of their work. We have already had discussions about writers and producers [and] we will deal with them when the time comes' (Bernstein, 1954: 5). Derek Bennett, one of Granada's early directors, started as a floor manager and learnt the craft of directing for television through working on a variety of productions. Shortly before his death, in 2005, Bennett recalled how he came to be taken on by Granada:

> I had been working in the theatre for several years, in various reps, because at that time there were a lot of repertory theatres in the country and I started as stage management and then did some directing. I actually didn't know anything about television at all and I used to practise

judo and one night I was in a club in London and the chap I was practis-
ing with was a film cameraman and we were just discussing vaguely
this sort of thing and he said 'Oh there's this chap called Bernstein, he's
going to start a television station, you ought to write to him' and in all
innocence I just wrote 'Dear Mr. Bernstein . . .' and I had a couple of
interviews and they took me on as a floor manager. This was before they
actually went on the air, several months before, as a completely weird
collection of people. They had some Americans, some Canadians, one or
two people I knew from the theatre here, and we all eventually moved up
to Manchester. They kept the headquarters in Golden Square in London
and messed around for a few weeks and then went on the air and every-
body sort of did everything, because nobody knew what was any good
or who was doing what, and I spent a couple of years floor managing,
drama, because eventually we sorted ourselves out into those people
who were good at light entertainment and those who liked drama and
those people who liked documentaries and things like that, and then
I became a director and immediately went back to doing everything
again, just to go through the mill. I mean everything from quiz shows to
talks and things of that sort.[6]

Bennett got his first opportunity to direct on drama series such as
Knight Errant (1959), a popular series about a modern-day adven-
turer, the children's drama *Biggles* (1960) and *Coronation Street*
(1960), before being given the chance to direct single plays: 'I think
there was a series of really poor half-hour dramas and then possibly
hour dramas, I suppose, and then I suddenly started doing grown-up
stuff, as it were.'[7]

Before *Coronation Street* there was little evidence of the Northern
drama Kenneth Clark referred to on Granada's first night, or even the
'new' drama Sidney Bernstein promised prior to Granada going on
air:

We shall produce new and exciting plays, some of them specifically
written for television. By utilising the wealth of acting talent among the
young and rising band of Northern writers, we aim to develop new ways
of presenting modern variety, to bring interesting people with stories
and abilities to the viewers and to focus the TV cameras onto the history,
legends and folk stories of the people. (quoted in Gaunt, 1955)

Granada's second play was certainly a 'new and exciting' play,
although not one written specifically for television. John Osborne's
Look Back in Anger (28 November 1956) had its premiere at the Royal
Court Theatre in London in the same week that Granada went on the

air. Nearly seven months later a television version of it was transmitted by Granada, featuring most of the original cast and directed by Tony Richardson, the director of the original stage production. Subsequently, plays 'specifically written for television' were produced, such as Priestley's *Doomsday for Dyson*, a play that, according to Philip Purser, was 'very much a special case, or tract . . . But the production attracted much useful attention' (Purser, 2003: 119).

The majority of Granada's early plays were adaptations of novels and stage plays. One important exception was Clive Exton's *No Fixed Abode* (30 January 1959), an original contemporary drama for the *Television Playhouse* series, directed by James Ormerod, one of the Granada-trained directors referred to by Forman. Exton, however, was a Londoner, not a Northern writer, and *No Fixed Abode*, together with *Look Back in Anger*, was one of the few Granada dramas in the mid to late 1950s to contribute to the new wave of social realism prevalent in the arts at the time. It was ABC, with *Armchair Theatre*, which led the way with such 'kitchen sink' drama in the late 1950s and early 1960s, and there were, initially, more Northern writers contributing plays to *Armchair Theatre* than there were writing for Granada.[8]

In the late 1950s and early 1960s Granada did produce a number of plays which were, unequivocally, regional in subject matter. The 'Manchester Plays' of Harold Brighouse, Stanley Houghton and Allan Monkhouse were not transmitted under that title but went out in the *Play of the Week* and *Television Playhouse* anthology series between 1958 and 1962.[9] These were plays from the early twentieth-century Manchester School of playwrights, who had been encouraged by the theatre impresario Annie Horniman to write plays about Lancashire life for the Gaiety Theatre. Horniman established Britain's first regional repertory theatre company in 1907, at the Midland Theatre in Manchester, and in 1908 the company moved to the larger Gaiety Theatre where plays such as Houghton's *Hindle Wakes* (1911), Monkhouse's *The Education of Mr. Surrage* (1913) and Brighouse's *Hobson's Choice* (1915) were performed.

The first Manchester School plays to be produced by Granada were Monkhouse's *Mary Broome* (3 September 1958) and *The Education of Mr. Surrage* (25 January 1959), followed by Houghton's *The Younger Generation* (1 September 1959). Seven more were produced from 1960 to 1962, five of them by Harold Brighouse, including his most famous play, *Hobson's Choice* (25 September 1962). All of these plays dealt with aspects of working- and middle-class provincial life in a realistic manner, often humorously (Monkhouse's plays were comedies) but without patronising their subjects. The Lancashire accent was richly in evidence and provided a strong contrast to the Southern, upper-class or American accents to be heard in other television plays at the time. Distinctly 'regional' in subject matter, Granada's 'Manchester Plays' were produced for the network, but they were only a part of Granada's overall drama production, shown alongside such different 'non-regional' plays as Exton's *No Fixed Abode*, Somerset Maugham's *For Services Rendered* (7 July 1959), James M. Cain's *Double Indemnity* (29 March 1960) and Harold Pinter's *The Dumb Waiter* (10 August 1961), as part of an eclectic portfolio of drama produced by Granada for the network.

In his essay on Granada's early drama in *Granada Television: The First Generation*, Philip Purser suggests that 'Granada never attached as much importance to the single play as did the other companies or the BBC'. He remembers being told early on 'that as an outfit which had always studied the American experience assiduously, Granada was already planning to concentrate on series and serials' (Purser, 2003: 119). Nevertheless, in the first few years Granada's output in single plays was considerable, far exceeding that of its drama series. In the six years from 1956 to 1961 118 plays were produced, nearly all of them for the ITV network anthology series, *Play of the Week* and *Television Playhouse*.

There were also some other interesting early experiments such as *Granada Workshop* (June–August 1957), a short series of half-hour plays shown fortnightly in a late-night slot in the Granada region only. The series consisted of five plays, produced live in the Granada studios, in which new writers and directors could experiment with the form of television drama. The series opened with an adaptation of Lucille Fletcher's novel, *Sorry, Wrong Number* (28 June 1957), a play with a cast of one which had been dramatised as a radio play in America and also made into a feature film in 1948, starring Barbara Stanwyck. A short article in *TV Times* introduced the new series:

Friday's 'live' play from Manchester, *Sorry, Wrong Number*, marks a new development in television drama. It is the first production in a fort-nightly series of half-hour plays which will be presented under the title of 'Granada Workshop'. Only really unusual plays will be included, and new production methods will be tried out. *Sorry, Wrong Number* had a fantastic success as a radio play in America, and was later made into a film. Friday's adaptation is by Leonard Chase. It is a horrific tale with a cast of one – a bedridden woman who, over a crossed telephone line, hears her own murder being planned. Her attempts to summon help make the play a gripping essay of suspense. (*TV Times (Northern Edition)*, 21 June 1957, p. 4)

Other plays in the series included the first television scripts by Michael Hastings and John Hopkins, the latter writing two plays for the series. Hopkins went on to become one of the BBC's leading dramatists in the 1960s, writing over fifty episodes of *Z Cars* in addition to two controversial plays for *The Wednesday Play* and the experimental four-part drama *Talking to a Stranger* (BBC2, 1966). Although short-lived, *Granada Workshop* attests to the enterprising nature of Granada's early drama production, at a time when virtually all drama was transmitted live, before the arrival of videotape, when the only means of recording programmes was the fairly crude system of telerecording (whereby a film camera was set up to film from a television monitor). Consequently none of the *Granada Workshop* plays survives (if they were telerecorded, which seems unlikely, there is no record that any of the recordings were kept).

Granada's television plays were usually sixty minutes in length, in the case of *Television Playhouse*, or ninety minutes if a *Play of the Week*, but occasionally plays were produced outside of these two anthology series, such as Priestley's *Doomsday for Dyson* and a major production of *War and Peace* (26 March 1963) which, at nearly three hours long, was shown in two parts, either side of the evening news. Another major drama production in 1964 was *The Other Man* (7 September 1964), an original play for television by Giles Cooper, directed by Gordon Flemyng and produced by Gerald Savory. The play, featuring Michael Caine, Sian Phillips and John Thaw among a huge cast, also bracketed the evening news, with a running time of almost two and a half hours. *The Other Man* was significant not only for its scale but for being one of the first Granada plays to include location scenes shot on videotape. The epic, ground-breaking nature of the production was highlighted by Alan Blyth in the *TV Times*, although his claim that 'it is the longest play ever to be seen on ITV' overlooked the fact that *War and Peace* was longer:

Including extras, there are 200 people in the cast, 60 with speak-ing roles. Fifty technicians were needed to record roughly 10 hours of tape, which has taken weeks to edit. Two weeks were spent on location . . .

'Until now, epics of this proportion,' said Gordon Flemyng, 'have been the preserve of the films. Now I think we have achieved one for TV. I have tried to open up the medium to show that it is capable of good large-scale, as well as small-scale, work. For the first time, I believe, all outside scenes have been shot outside. To avoid a quality change from film to videotape, all the exterior scenes have been shot on tape, too, also for the first time. I think this adds to the real-life quality of the production. (Blyth, 1964: 12–13)

The decision to use videotape for location shooting in order to enhance the 'real-life quality' of *The Other Man* was especially significant with regard to arguments about the limitations of studio drama at the time. In an influential article published in the theatre magazine *Encore* in March 1964, Troy Kennedy Martin sparked a heated debate among television writers, directors and critics by arguing that naturalism in television drama was outdated and needed to be replaced by a new form of non-naturalistic 'narrative' drama. Many people, including the Granada writer and producer Philip Mackie, interpreted Kennedy Martin's article as a manifesto calling for filmed drama to replace studio drama:

Also blindingly clear is that T.K.M. has started going to the cinema. His notions are splendid, but they are certainly not new: compression, montage, distorted time-scale, personal narrative – all these techniques have been familiar to film-makers (and film-goers) for heaven knows how many years.

Well, why not? Let T.K.M., child of the cinema, kill 'nat' drama his way, and good luck to him. He is barmy to assume that his way is the only way. Television needs a number of adventurers, going off on different explorations in different directions. God forbid we should all go the same way as T.K.M., or his new-old genre would die of a surfeit in a year or so. (Mackie, 1964: 44)

While Mackie was broadly in agreement with Kennedy Martin's argument that naturalism in television drama was outmoded, he took issue with his analysis, especially the suggestion that the television companies were responsible for the perpetuation of naturalism, arguing that at Granada the opposite was true: 'The executives of my acquaintance were involved in giving off cries of rage and despair, as "nat" scripts continued to flood in, from people who hadn't yet learnt that the *genre* was worn out' (Mackie, 1964: 44).

Kennedy Martin's 'Nats go home' polemic was followed in August–September 1964 by an illustration of the theory in practice when *Diary of a Young Man* (BBC, 1964), a six-part non-naturalistic serial written by Kennedy Martin in collaboration with John McGrath, was transmitted on BBC1. Coincidentally *The Other Man* was transmitted on ITV as *Diary of a Young Man* was drawing to a close. Gordon Flemyng's concern to enhance the 'real-life quality' of *The Other Man* by shooting the exterior scenes on videotape suggests the motivation was the quest for greater realism, rather than a rejection of studio naturalism *per se*. Using videotape on location enabled a better visual match to be achieved between interior and exterior scenes, avoiding the change in visual quality which resulted from cutting between studio interiors recorded electronically and location exteriors shot on film. Transitions from studio to film were often jarring because of the mismatch in visual quality and tended to undermine efforts to achieve a convincing diegetic realism as the dramatic action moved between interior and exterior scenes.

While Kennedy Martin's polemic against naturalism in television drama had some short-term impact, mainly within the BBC where it influenced some of the dramas produced for *The Wednesday Play*, such as *Up the Junction* (1965), *Cathy Come Home* (1966) and the early plays of Dennis Potter, the use of mobile video, and subsequently film, for shooting on location was to prove of greater significance in the longer term as filmic realism asserted itself as the dominant form in television drama, gradually replacing the 'theatrical' naturalism of studio drama.[10]

In this respect *The Other Man* was a significant production, especially with regard to Granada's ambitions to portray the region in its drama. However, contrary to Flemyng's claims, *The Other Man* was not the first Granada drama to use videotape for location shooting. That milestone was achieved a few months earlier in *The Villains* (1964–65), an anthology series of Northern crime dramas first transmitted in February 1964. Before considering *The Villains* though, consideration needs to be given to the series which really put Granada on the map as far as Northern drama was concerned.

Coronation Street: social realism and regionality

Before the first episode of *Coronation Street* was transmitted, on 9 December 1960, Granada's regional identity owed more to the production of local news and magazine programmes than it did to drama. The 'new school of North Country drama' Kenneth Clark anticipated on Granada's opening night had really been seen only in a few plays, mainly the 'Manchester Plays', which were hardly contemporary. When *Coronation Street* burst on to the scene at the end of 1960, with its working-class characters and its Lancashire accents, Granada's 'new school of North Country drama' had suddenly arrived, all in one programme. Not that anyone anticipated the impact *Coronation Street* would have, least of all the Granada programme committee, according to executive producer Harry Elton: 'In the autumn of 1960 I screened the pilot of a proposed twice-weekly half-hour serial for the Granada programme committee. It was about the lives of people on a working-class street in Manchester. The committee didn't like it and *Coronation Street* was almost killed before it got on the air' (Elton, 2003: 100).

Elton, a Canadian producer recruited by Granada in 1957, gives an illuminating account in *Granada Television: The First Generation* of how the pilot episode of *Coronation Street* was disliked by everyone on the programme committee. The committee, which included Sidney and Cecil Bernstein, 'reviewed everything affecting programmes at Granada. It decided what went on the air and what did not.' On this occasion, according to Elton, the committee 'with a rare show of unanimity . . . decided this programme was not what we wanted to put on the air'. However this left Elton, and Granada, with a problem, because the company needed to fulfil its commitment to provide two weekly half-hour drama episodes to the ITV network:

> From the earliest days the big four programme contractors (Rediffusion, ATV, ABC and Granada) divided up the time-slots on a network so no one of them had to fill out the schedule alone. The broadcasting act required a total of 85 per cent British content. Although the most popular programmes at that time came from the USA and fitted the 15 per cent allowable foreign content, we had to produce storytelling programmes of our own. Based on the size of our audience Granada was responsible for 40 per cent of the evening schedule from Monday to Friday including two weekly half-hours in the audience-building early evenings . . .
>
> At the time of the dry run, *Biggles*, the current series, had to end in early December. Faced with no alternative the committee reluctantly agreed to let the programme go into the schedule for a *short, limited,* run but I must find a replacement as soon as possible. (Elton, 2003: 101)

Biggles was scheduled on Wednesdays and Fridays at 7.00 pm and these were the slots into which the new series, *Coronation Street*, went, beginning on Friday 9 December 1960, for an initial run of thirteen weeks. However, the popularity of the programme soon became apparent and Harry Elton did not need to find a replacement. In less than a year *Coronation Street* was being watched in over seven million homes and was topping the ratings. Yet, as W.J. Weatherby observed in 1962:

> The irony of *Coronation Street* is that it is an example of becoming top of the pops without meaning to. It had none of the usual inducements, such as top pop names. When Tony Warren created the street and its chief characters and the first episode was produced, the aim apparently was a working class series without any stars. As one of the team put it recently, 'It began very modestly as a local serial without even the prestige value of a fully networked showing'. (Weatherby, 1962: 283)

That it was seen as 'a local serial' immediately highlights the difference between *Coronation Street* and previous Granada series, such as the detective drama *Shadow Squad* (1957–59), which begun life as an Associated-Rediffusion drama before Granada took it over, *Skyport* (1959–60), a spin-off from *Shadow Squad* set in an airport, and *Biggles*, based on Captain W.E. Johns's stories about the famous First World War flying ace. Tony Warren had written episodes of *Shadow Squad* and *Biggles* but developed the idea for *Coronation Street* because, as Harry Elton explained, he wanted 'to write about something he knew':

> I sent him off to find stories about real people who lived in the streets of Manchester and Salford. He returned with the first script and an outline of several further episodes of a serial he called *Florizel Street*. The basic characters, dialogue and style were clearly established. This is what the programme committee saw. Only the name was changed to *Coronation Street* and the characters of Ken Barlow and Albert Tatlock were added. This is what went on the air on 9 December 1960. (Elton, 2003: 102)

The first two episodes of *Coronation Street* were directed by Derek Bennett, who accompanied Warren as he did his research in Manchester and Salford: 'He and I used to sometimes go round pubs at night and observe and listen to people' and while Bennett was responsible for realising Warren's scripts in the studio he maintained that the style of the drama was 'very much driven by his scripts'.[11]

Before *Coronation Street*, representations of the working class in series such as the BBC's *Dixon of Dock Green* (1955–76) and ATV's *Emergency – Ward 10* (1957–67) had been mainly southern and metropolitan in nature. In contrast, *Coronation Street* was set in an industrial working-class district in the North West of England, recognisable not just for the row of terraced houses which provided the main setting for the drama but for the distinctive Lancashire accents of its working-class characters. Furthermore, *Coronation Street* was clearly not a police series or medical drama but a drama of social realism whose nearest equivalent was the 'kitchen sink' films of the British 'New Wave' cinema.

As a continuing serial the nearest television equivalent to *Coronation Street* was the BBC's *The Grove Family* (1954–57), an abortive attempt by the BBC to capture the popular audience it feared it would lose (and did lose) to ITV. Where *The Grove Family* portrayed a lower-middle-class, southern suburban household, *Coronation Street* offered a sharp reminder that not everyone in the television audience resembled the Groves in social class and accent, or even aspired to be like them. In its iconography, characterisation and storylines, *Coronation Street* tapped into the new mode of working-class realism that had been popularised in novels and the theatre since the mid-1950s and which was emerging in the late 1950s in feature films such as *Room at the Top* (1959) and *Saturday Night and Sunday Morning* (1960) and in *Armchair Theatre* plays such as *No Tram to Lime Street* (ABC, 1959) and *Lena, O My Lena* (ABC, 1960).

Noting how social realism had become an 'important, perhaps dominant, mode in fiction' when *Coronation Street* made its debut, Marion Jordan has usefully identified the main conventions of the genre, some of which, she suggests, were adopted by the programme:

> Briefly the genre of Social Realism demands that life should be presented in the form of a narrative of personal events, each with a beginning, a middle and an end, important to the central characters concerned but affecting others only in minor ways; that though these events are ostensibly about *social* problems they should have as one of their central concerns the settling of people in life; that the resolution of these events should always be in terms of the effect of social interventions; that characters should be either working-class or of the classes immediately visible to the working classes (shopkeepers, say, or the two-man business) and should be credibly accounted for in terms of the 'ordinariness'

of their homes, families, friends; that the locale should be urban and
provincial (preferably in the industrial north); that the settings should
be commonplace and recognisable (the pub, the street, the factory,
the home and more particularly the kitchen); that the time should be
'the present'; that the style should be such as to suggest an unmediated, unprejudiced and complete view of reality; to give, in summary,
the impression that the reader, or viewer, has spent some time at the
expense of the characters depicted. (Jordan, 1981: 28)

Many of these conventions are evident in the first episode of *Coronation
Street*. The title sequence – accompanied by a melancholy signature
tune – establishes the world in which the drama is set, opening with
a view of the roofs of terraced houses before descending into the street
to show children skipping and singing outside the local shop. Florrie
Lindley (Betty Alberge) is a new arrival in the area and by this dramatic device the audience is given initial character information as
Elsie Lappin (Maudie Edwards), the shopkeeper, tells Florrie about
some of the street's inhabitants.

The first scene immediately establishes the ordinariness of the situation, with the shop as a focal place in the heart of the community
where chance encounters can take place. The plainness of the decor,
together with the naturalism of the acting and ordinariness of the dialogue, announces this as a drama of the everyday, a drama of social
realism. It also establishes this as a drama in which women will play a
central role and where gossip will feature as a key ingredient, underlining its ordinariness. Some emphasis is put on the unusual married
name of Linda Cheveski (Anne Cunningham) when she comes into
the shop – she has married a foreigner, an outsider – and this provides a link to the next scene in the Tanner household, where Linda's
mother and brother are engaged in an argument. Not only does this
second scene introduce Elsie Tanner (Pat Phoenix), one of the strong
female characters in the serial, it also provides a first glimpse of an
ordinary working-class family home, in which a typical family argument is taking place. Dennis (Philip Lowrie), Elsie's son, cannot find
work, having just come out of borstal, and his situation serves as a
contrast to that of Ken Barlow (William Roache), the scholarship
boy who is introduced in the next scene, in the Barlow household,
where Ken and his parents are having dinner – a cue for some light-
hearted observations about dinner-table etiquette in working-class
households.

The first episode continues in this vein, introducing characters in their homes or in the local pub, The Rover's Return, establishing relationships and local antagonisms. The camera positions and editing (more strictly, vision-mixing) in these scenes indicate that this is a live drama. The staging of the living-room scene in the Barlow's house, for example, is very frontal, replicating the frontal staging of proscenium arch theatre, the model for much live television drama, positioning the television viewer as the 'spectator in the stalls'. If anything, though, the 'intimacy' of live television lends authenticity to the drama of *Coronation Street*, enhancing the realism of the social situation and the naturalism of the dialogue.[12] Even when *Coronation Street* moved over to pre-recording for subsequent transmission this element of intimacy associated with live television was still seen as an important signifier of realism in the serial, and episodes continued to be recorded as a continuous 'live' performance until 1974 (see Paterson, 1981: 56).

As in subsequent episodes, the first episode proceeds by interweaving narratives, and the personal lives of the characters, in a manner that has become a distinctive feature of the continuous serial, or the soap opera, as the form is now more popularly known.[13] The fusion of the conventions of soap opera with those of social realism in early *Coronation Street* resulted in what Marion Jordan describes as soap-opera realism, 'a specific televisual form' (Jordan, 1981: 28). Television soap opera provides 'a narrative of personal events', but not necessarily starting at the beginning with an expectation of arriving at a resolution, in the manner of series drama or the single play. *Coronation Street* was, from the beginning, developed as a continuous serial, with two thirty-minute episodes per week, presenting 'an unmediated, unprejudiced and complete view of reality', a world which the viewer could look in on and spend 'some time at the expense of the characters depicted'.

Following the initial negative response of the Granada programme committee to the pilot episode of *Coronation Street* and the committee's reluctant agreement to its going ahead for 'a short, limited run', Harry Elton solicited the views of other employees at Granada as to the merits of the programme:

> Looking for a way to get some positive feedback for our efforts I arranged a screening for all the Granada staff in Manchester. Monitors were distributed throughout the offices and workshops. Everyone was asked to fill out a questionnaire. Most of them liked it very much! To be sure they were all Northern people and Tony Warren had become a favorite

around the studios. But responses to the casting, the sets and the scripts were very positive and we worked with renewed confidence and energy. (Elton, 2003: 102)

With the programme committee consisting of American and Canadian producers plus Granada executives from London and the South, rather than the North of England, the support among ordinary Granada personnel for a programme created by a Mancunian, Tony Warren, who wanted to write about 'something he knew', suggests that Granada's first successful, contemporary Northern drama was the result of pressure from 'below', rather than the result of policy determined from above, by Granada executives deciding 'what went on the air and what did not'.

At first, *Coronation Street* was only partly networked, both ATV and Tyne Tees initially refusing to take it, but when it became clear that this 'local' serial was proving popular with a national audience ATV and Tyne Tees came on board: 'Five months after the programme went on the air, the midlands and Newcastle completed the line-up. The programme committee was puzzled but pleased with the reaction and decided that it could stay in the schedule longer than they had originally intended' (Elton, 2003: 103). In trying to account for the popularity of *Coronation Street* Harry Elton stresses the role of the writers in creating realistic Northern characters:

[T]he key to the programme's popularity from the beginning was the writing. The genius of the early programmes was Tony Warren who established the characters, their relationships to each other and particularly their use of the north country dialect. These were the very reasons why the programme committee felt that it would not succeed. Clearly *Coronation Street* offered something to the television audience that satisfied a need. Something about watching twice a week helped their lives. And whatever that ingredient is has an appeal far beyond the north of England. It was the work of a group of people who were new to television at a time of great experimentation to find programmes that would be popular. (Elton, 2003: 103)

John Finch was one of the Northern writers recruited early on to provide scripts for *Coronation Street*, once it became obvious that it was going to continue. In an unpublished article on the early development of the *Street* he describes how Northern writers came to form the nucleus of the writing team, highlighting the crucial role played by Harry Kershaw, who succeeded Harry Elton as Executive Producer and was closely involved with the serial as writer and producer for nearly twenty years:

> In the very early days of *Coronation Street* there were not many Northern writers around to be recruited. Novelists like Mercer, Storey and Stan Barstow tended to view Street writers as hacks (some Street writers regarded themselves as hacks!). Writers from the south were unable to accurately adopt the Northern idiom, not so much in terms of the accent, but in general cultural terms.
>
> The burden of getting hold of writers and, if necessary, giving them guidance on the technicalities of writing for television, fell almost entirely on the shoulders of Harry Kershaw. Very early scripts, after Tony Warren largely withdrew from the series, were storied by Harry working in conjunction with the writer of a particular script, or increasingly by groups of writers working in what became the script conference. An early development for which Harry was responsible was the appointment of story writers, whose job was to take away the ideas of the script group and develop them in story form . . .
>
> Harry, myself, Jack Rosenthal, Adele Rose and, shortly, Peter Eckersley, really formed the core of the writing team, together with Driver and Powell. Geoff Lancashire was a fairly early arrival, as was Jim Allen and Les Duxbury. Others came and went. They included some very odd characters whose credits were never, so far as I can remember, ever seen on television again. Reliability was really a major factor in choosing writers. Late delivery was not acceptable in the tight production turn round. Editing time was restricted so that scripts had to be in pretty good shape when they were delivered. But the odd script disaster, when scripts arrived which were not producible, had to be coped with. I was involved in this kind of intensive care throughout my working life on The Street, and the experience served me in good stead in later years.
>
> I can't remember when this tight little team started to disintegrate. I was myself in it for eight years, one as editor and another year as producer. Harry Kershaw stayed with it until he retired many years later. Peter Eckersley ultimately became Head of Drama. Driver and Powell went on to writing comedy. Jack Rosenthal left to become what he called 'a real writer'. Adele Rose stayed the course. Jim Allen departed as soon as he felt able to without penalising his family in terms of financial security. He went on to write one-off plays and films. Geoff Lancashire stayed, but also worked on a number of other series, adaptations, etc . . .
>
> With the departure of writers who had formed the backbone of the team, Harry now had to look around for replacements. It was at this time that more Northern writers emerged from the rank of the would be's. Harry allowed sufficient cash in the budget to finance a few

gambles, and many writers owe him a great debt for the training he gave them on a one-to-one basis. An hour spent with Harry was worth any number of writing courses. He was really responsible in my opinion for the climate of encouragement which enabled writers who were stumbling and uncertain to survive and to go on. Not just in the work which he himself did, but in establishing a kind of tradition which continued for many years.[14]

As Finch indicates, the importance of *Coronation Street* in the 1960s resided not only in its popularisation of regional, working-class voices but in the opportunities the programme gave to Northern writers to develop careers in television. In addition to Finch himself, a number of Northern writers began their careers on *Coronation Street*, including Jack Rosenthal, Geoffrey Lancashire, Jim Allen, Janey Preger and, much later, Paul Abbott and Sally Wainwright. Directors who worked on the *Street* early in their career include Michael Apted and Roland Joffe, and the serial has given opportunities to numerous regional actors who might not otherwise have found work in television.

That *Coronation Street* was designed to introduce a national television audience to Northern working-class life was suggested in a 'mission statement' produced by Tony Warren and Harry Elton to explain what the programme was about:

> A fascinating freemasonry, a volume of unwritten rules. These are the driving forces behind working-class life in the North of England. To the uninitiated outsider, all this would be completely incomprehensible. The purpose of *Coronation Street* is to entertain by examining a community of this kind and initiating the viewer into the ways of the people who live here. (Elton, 2003: 104)

As Harry Elton's account of the beginnings of *Coronation Street* indicates, the serial thrived despite the Granada management, rather than because of it. He adds that he found Granada 'not very warm to popular programmes' (Elton, 2003: 104), a statement suggesting that Granada's considerable single-play output, including the 'Manchester Plays', might have satisfied the cultural tastes of the members of the Granada programme committee more than popular series such as *Shadow Squad*, *Knight Errant* and *Coronation Street*.

There is no doubt, however, that *Coronation Street* did as much as, and perhaps more than, any novel, play or film to alert the nation to Lancashire customs, characters and culture during the 1960s. Riding the 'New Wave' of Northern culture which the theatre, literature and cinema had already promoted, the moment was ripe for a Northern television drama presented in the popular form of a twice-weekly serial, featuring down-to-earth working-class characters, including strong female characters, an important ingredient given the domestic, family-oriented nature of the drama. *Coronation Street* featured characters with whom a working-class audience could identify and this was probably more important when it comes to accounting for its popularity with a national audience than the fact that it was a 'Northern' drama.

Not only did *Coronation Street* prove to be Granada's most successful programme, it became a springboard from which writers, directors, actors and other production personnel could launch successful careers, not just in television but, in some cases, in the film industry as well. Over the next few years, the popular success of *Coronation Street* opened up a range of dramatic possibilities at Granada, paving the way for 'a new school of North Country drama' to emerge on British television.

Group North

That Northern writers were central to the ethos of *Coronation Street*, their local knowledge of Lancashire people and customs helping to guarantee its authenticity, was evident when, in 1963, a number of the *Street*'s writers formed a 'writers' co-operative' called Group North. The founding members of the Group were Cyril Abraham, Harry Driver, Peter Eckersley, John Finch, Harry Kershaw, Vince Powell and Jack Rosenthal. They were joined later by George Reed, the only non-Northerner in the Group. As Derek Jewell wrote in an article on the Group in the *Sunday Times Colour Magazine* in June 1964:

> *Coronation Street*, which in 20 years may be seen as a kind of memorial to the writers of Group North, was in fact the springboard for the organisation. Five of the group's founder-members met on the programme, for which they have written nearly 300 out of 360 episodes; Driver alone, whose memory is the nearest thing Granada has to a card-index system on the history of the Street's characters has provided 320 story-lines for the series. (Jewell, 1964: 12)

Launched as a limited company on 25 April 1963, Group North was intended as a forum for developing ideas for new dramas and a means of providing some security for its members when work was short. To this end they each contributed five per cent of their earnings to a central fund, as Cyril Abraham explained to Derek Jewell: 'It's a safe-guard against illness for any of us, or if the work just doesn't come. Any writer's always terrified of a bad three months' (Jewell, 1964: 12).

In the event, the members of the Group were so successful they did not need to draw on the fund and the main purpose of Group North became that of a forum for generating new ideas for series and serials. It was George Reed, whom Harry Kershaw described as 'an ex-school-master from East Anglia who entered our world by acting as secretary to Harry Driver and who was the first to leave us and go back to his old love, teaching' (Kershaw, 1981: 88), who came up with the title for the only Group North production, a ten-episode series called *Catch Hand* (BBC1, July–September 1964), made not for Granada but for the BBC. 'Catch Hand', according to Reed, was a term used in East Anglia to describe nomadic workers. This became the subject of the series, which featured Mark Eden and Anthony Booth as two casual labourers who are always moving around looking for work. *Catch Hand* replaced *Z Cars* in the BBC1 schedule on 1 July 1964, with the accompanying credit, 'Series created by Group North' (*Radio Times*, 25 June 1964: 43). As Kershaw recalled: 'The formation of Group North had caused something of a flutter in television's executive dove-cotes. Coming as it did at a time when union muscles were beginning to flex within the industry, any co-operative of this kind was bound to be viewed with suspicion' (Kershaw, 1981: 90–1). Yet the sig-nificance of Group North was its role not so much as a writers' union, or even its potential as a writing collective, but as a forum in which the individual members might develop new ideas for programmes: 'We produced the ideas, not collectively, but individually' (Kershaw, 1981: 90). Not only did all of the writers in the Group go on to develop successful careers outside of *Coronation Street* but, as Harry Kershaw noted:

> The diversification practised by the writer-members of Group North has been carried on by subsequent writers for *Coronation Street*. Not only did the show give most of them their first television credit, it demanded that they try their hand at every aspect of their craft. It is not surprising that *Street* writers have since written satire, contemporary drama and comedy in all its varied forms. Writers who started their professional careers on the *Street* have since contributed, in the drama field, to *The*

Odd Men, *The Villains*, *Z Cars*, *Crown Court*, *Village Hall*, *Sam*, *Shabby Tiger*, *Armchair Theatre*, *Play of the Week*, *Play of the Month*, *Fallen Hero*, *All Creatures Great and Small*, *This Year*, *Next Year* amongst a host of others, and in comedy to *Nearest and Dearest*, *The Dustbinmen*, *The Lovers*, *Bless This House*, *Cuckoo Waltz*, *Life of Riley*, *Leave It to Charlie*, *Mind Your Language*, *Selwyn Froggitt*, *Love Thy Neighbour*, *Robin's Nest* and many more. (Kershaw, 1981: 91)

Granada's anthology drama series

From 1960 Granada supplemented its contribution to the two ITV anthology drama series with its own 'themed' anthology series, a genre in which the company specialised throughout the 1960s and 1970s. The first of these was a series called *On Trial* (July–September 1960), ten plays re-enacting famous trials, such as those of *Sir Roger Casement* (8 July 1960) and *Oscar Wilde* (5 August 1960). Described as 'factual dramatisations' by Julia Hallam (2003: 18), this was an early venture by Granada into the realm of drama-documentary, a genre in which Granada subsequently excelled. Like the single plays Granada contributed to *Play of the Week* and *Television Playhouse* not all of these anthology series were 'regional' in subject matter. Anthology series such as *Saki* (1962), based on the short stories of H.H. Munro, *Maupassant* (1963), based on stories by Guy de Maupassant, *The Victorians* (1963) and *The Edwardians* (1965) were all literary adaptations designed to show that Granada was more than capable of producing 'quality' drama and it may not be coincidental that a number of these series were produced in the periods leading up to the renewal of ITV contracts in 1964 and 1968.

Philip Mackie produced many of these literary anthologies in the 1960s, including *Saki*, *Maupassant*, *The Victorians* and the ingenious *The Liars* (1966), another collection of short stories by writers such as de Maupassant, Saki and Wilde in which, as Tise Vahimagi notes, 'producer Philip Mackie fashioned a curious showcase for their presentation. He linked the tall tales through four related narrators who try to outdo each other with their enactment of the outrageous yarns; the "liars" were Nyree Dawn Porter, Ian Ogilvy, William Mervyn, and Isla Blair' (Vahimagi, 1996: 149).

In contrast to these literary adaptations Granada produced a contemporary anthology series of new plays written specifically for television in 1961. *The Younger Generation* was a youth-orientated series comprising eleven new plays by young playwrights and featured a repertory company of young actors specially formed by Granada for the series. The enterprising nature of the venture was reported on in the *North-Western Evening Mail* on 24 June 1961 under the heading 'Interesting Experiment in Television Play Production':

> 'The Younger Generation' series has been planned to give young writers a chance to show us their world through their own eyes.
>
> The search for authors began in July, 1960, when the first of nearly 200 young writers were interviewed. Few of them had ever attempted to write a play for television before, though some of them had novels, poems or magazine articles published. The most promising were invited to submit a synopsis of a play for the series, and eventually were commissioned to write full-length scripts.
>
> These 11 plays are entirely separate, but in each of them the writer has been encouraged to explore a human situation, involving young people, as deeply and truthfully as he can.
>
> For this series of plays, young actors and actresses were chosen to form a repertory group – 'The Younger Generation Players' – and placed under exclusive contract for six months. Each of them will be playing at least one leading part, and a variety of smaller roles, frequently 'against type' – because type casting can be an obstacle to the development of young artists in television.
>
> In 'The Younger Generation,' too, the actors will have the opportunity (unusual in television) of working with the same directors and fellow-artistes over a considerable period.
>
> Each play in the series will be introduced by former factory worker Johnny McDonald, making his first professional television appearance. (Anon., 1961)

The repertory company included Johnny Briggs (who went on to become a long-term member of the *Coronation Street* cast), Judy Cornwell, Bill Douglas (who later turned to film directing), Ronald Lacey and John Thaw (fresh from drama school). Thaw was the leading actor in one of the early plays, *Flow Gently Sweet Afton* (7 July 1961), written by Patrick Garland, 'then still an undergraduate', as director Claude Whatham notes (Whatham, 2003: 131). Recorded in the Granada studios in March 1961, *Flow Gently Sweet Afton* was set in a seaside town during the winter and explored the dilemma of young people trapped in their environment, but unable to leave. Denny (John Thaw) wants to leave but is married to Rose (Mary Miller) who likes the routine of her life. Thematically, the play conforms to the kitchen-sink dramas of the time, the subject of young people (usually men) trapped in their environment being a common theme in plays and films such as *Look Back in Anger* and *Saturday Night and Sunday Morning*.

Not all of *The Younger Generation* playwrights and actors were from the North of England. While John Thaw was from Manchester, Bill Douglas, who played Denny's friend Cowboy in *Flow Gently Sweet Afton*, was Scottish and he affects a very unconvincing Northern accent in the play.[15] Youth was the main theme in all the plays, rather than regionality, and the generational focus places the series within the 'New Wave' of working-class realism prevalent at the time, distancing it from Granada's literary adaptations and adventure series, such as *Saki* and *Knight Errant*. Among the other new young playwrights contributing to *The Younger Generation* were Adrian Mitchell and Roger Smith. Smith went on to work at the BBC as a scriptwriter/adapter and was the first story editor on *The Wednesday Play*, commissioning the first television plays from his friend Dennis Potter:

> The thing that brought me into television was not the BBC, it was Granada Television. They did a new series called *The Younger Generation*, which was new writers, first plays for television. This was end of '60/early '61, it went out '61 . . . the connection that I had there was through Clive Goodwin, who was working at Granada then, and I'd met him because he was the editor of *Encore* . . . It was a play called *Our Ted* [21 July 1961]. I'd seen a young kid, about 16–17, working-class kid, in Earls Court, as a kind of sidekick to the British National Party . . . a fascist . . . and I got fascinated why this kid had got involved in that. That's what the play was about, it was about 'our Ted'.[16]

The Younger Generation was a bold initiative by Granada, highlighting the progressive nature of the company's drama policy. The plays were not all 'regional' in subject matter, nor were all the playwrights from the North, but the project signalled Granada's ambition to nurture new playwrights and to put together a young repertory company to perform their plays.

Later in the 1960s Granada was responsible for a similar initiative when it formed the Stables Theatre Company, a fully fledged theatre company put together by Gordon McDougall to produce plays in a theatre built by Granada (converted from what used to be the stables at the Liverpool Road station in Manchester), with the intention that the plays would also be produced for television. Seven plays by the Stables Theatre Company were televised between August 1969 and July 1970. Granada director Herbert Wise described the project as 'a marvellous concept . . . a glorious generous idea . . . an honourable failure' (Wise, 2003: 72). Like The Younger Generation Players, the Stables Theatre Company gave an opportunity to some young actors and new playwrights, but the venture was not a success. Gordon McDougall, who was both the Artistic Director of the company and Executive Producer of the television plays, explained what it achieved and why it failed:

> The theatre attracted a company of actors who were to stamp their mark on television: Maureen Pryor, Maureen Lipman, Richard Wilson, John Shrapnel, Zoe Wanamaker. The first plays of Trevor Griffiths, Peter Ransley, Bill Morrison and a host of other important writers were performed there, attracting continuously excited reviews . . .
>
> The television side of the operation didn't work so well. 1969 was the worst possible year to start such an operation. Independent television's profits were being decimated by the levy, colour TV was imminent and the unions worked to rule and then struck for several months, and we had a company of twenty actors on salary who couldn't be laid off . . .
>
> [T]he big company pieces didn't work on television because the directors couldn't find a new way of looking at drama under the pressure of having to get the show in the can. And the first company piece we did was the first play in colour in a Granada studio; the technicians were working to rule and it overran by an unprecedented three days!
>
> After two years, Mr Sidney viewed the Stables television output and decided that, although much of it worked, it didn't justify the sums being spent on it. (McDougall, 2003: 81–2)

The significant difference between The Younger Generation Players and the Stables Theatre Company was that the former was created as a television repertory company, rather than as a theatre company which would also produce plays for television. *The Younger Generation* plays were written for television and did not have the theatrical origins of the Stables Theatre plays. By the end of the 1960s, when the Stables Theatre Company was founded, Granada had moved significantly away from the theatrical origins of its early television plays and was producing an increasing amount of drama on location. In this context, the establishment of the Stables Theatre Company in 1969 seems anachronistic, a throwback to an earlier tradition, as far as television drama was concerned, even if it did bring some new writers and actors into television.

A more significant event in the development of Granada's regional drama came five years earlier, in 1964. While Granada had experimented with themed anthology series in 1960–62, producing one per year, in 1963 the company increased production of its anthology series to three (*The Victorians, Maupassant* and *Friday Night*) and in 1964 to six. In that year Granada produced only four plays outside of these series: three for *Play of the Week*, plus *The Other Man*.[17] But as far as regional drama was concerned, the most significant of the six anthology series produced by Granada in 1964 was *The Villains*.

The Villains (1964–65)

This collection of twenty-one crime dramas was transmitted in three series from February 1964 to February 1965. Each drama focused on the lives of villains, rather than the forces of law and order – an innovation in itself at the time – with different casts and different settings in each drama, distinguishing it from a more conventional series such as *It's Dark Outside* (January 1964 to April 1965), a police drama featuring Detective Inspector Rose (William Mervyn), which Granada also produced in 1964–65. As producer Harry Kershaw explained of *The Villains*: 'Our stories will be slanted towards criminal lives rather than crimes. We are, in fact, interested in that part of a criminal's day when he isn't engaged in his particular profession' (Anon., 1964a: 10).

The sixth play to be shown in the first series, *Contraband* (10 April 1964), made extensive use of an Outside Broadcast unit to shoot exterior scenes for a drama about two brothers smuggling a package which they think contains watches on a canal narrowboat, travelling from Runcorn in Cheshire to Birmingham, where three villains are waiting to collect what is, in fact, heroin. In a *TV Times* article, Brian Finch explained how a canal barge worker was enlisted to provide technical advice to the production team and how the actors found him helpful in trying to achieve an authentic regional accent:

> Authenticity and realism are the twin-keynotes of the series. And to obtain these, producer Harry Kershaw moved both cast and production unit down to the Cheshire waterways, lock, stock and barrell [*sic*], to prepare a large slice of the show on location . . .

Ken Nixon, a 31-year-old bargee who has been working the waterways since he was 10 years old ... was seconded to the Outside
Broadcast unit by the British Waterways Commission as a sort of tempo-
rary 'technical adviser.' He turned out to be a lot more than that – particularly to the actors. Jack Smethurst and Derek Benfield, who play the
bargee brothers who fall foul of the law, spent days trying to capture his
accent. 'It isn't anything you can localise exactly,' said Jack. 'A bargee's
accent seems to be coloured by every county he passes through.' (Finch,
1964: 36)

In the play the accents of the two brothers are less pronounced than
those of the three villains to whom they are taking the goods, who
have strong Birmingham accents, indicating the metropolitan destination for the contraband. The younger brother does have traces of
a Birmingham or Black Country accent but the less distinct accents
of the bargees would be authentic if, as Jack Smethurst suggests,
a bargee's accent is 'coloured by every county he passes through'.
Not all of *Contraband* was shot on location – the scenes inside the
barge would have been recorded in the studio – but a significant
amount of the drama was recorded on location, helping to establish
the regional setting for the play as the narrowboat travelled south
through Cheshire and Staffordshire on the Trent and Mersey Canal.

Granada acquired its first Ampex videotape machines in July 1958
and its first mobile videotape vehicle, or 'Scanner', went on the
road a year later. Initially, videotape was used for recording news
and sport, but the documentary film-maker Denis Mitchell started
experimenting with videotape in 1964, first using it at Granada on
The Entertainers (originally scheduled for transmission on 25 March
1964 but not shown until 13 January 1965).[18] Meanwhile, videotape
was first used for recording drama on location in *The Villains*. In the
short second series (June–July 1964), comprising just four plays (one
of which was not transmitted because of an industrial dispute), *Over
the Hill* (10 July 1964), written by series producer Harry Kershaw,
was the first Granada drama to be recorded entirely on location, on
videotape, a fact emphasised in a caption at the end of the episode:
'This programme was made entirely at Nab Farm and in the nearby
village of Pott Shrigley', followed by an end title: 'From the North –
Granada – A Travelling Eye Production', 'Travelling Eye' referring
to the Outside Broadcast unit used to record the drama. The location
shooting received much publicity in local newspapers. This was how
the *Macclesfield County Express* reported the event:

The quiet peacefulness around Nab Farm, Pott Shrigley, one of the highest farmsteads in the district, was shattered during the past week with teams of TV cameramen, producers and players all engaged producing another episode in the Granada series of thrillers 'The Villains,' which is shown on Friday nights.

The entire episode is being shot in the Pott Shrigley area and this is the first time Granada have filmed an episode without having any shots in a studio. An entire team of players, cameramen and technicians will have spent two weeks at Nab Farm by the time the film is completed.

The episode, directed by Dick Everatt [*sic*], is called 'Over the Hill', and Mr. Everatt told the 'Macclesfield County Express' that the story concerns a young farm lad who left home three years previously and travelled to Liverpool, where he went 'bad'. He joined the Army to avoid the police and then came home to his farm in the hills to hide away from them. (Anon., 1964b)

The remote rural location is used to good effect in the drama and the location filming emphasises the remoteness of the location, with one panoramic shot filmed from the top of Alderley Edge, one of the highest points in the area. That the young farm lad, Alan Breck (William Wilde), should choose to return to the remoteness of his parents' farm in order to hide away from the police adds veracity to the drama. Later on, when a villain Breck knew in Liverpool comes to the farm his arrival is announced in a long-distance shot in which Breck is seen as a tiny figure silhouetted on the skyline, running to meet the villain's car before he reaches the farm – a shot clearly designed as a visual metaphor, suggesting the city villain as an intruder arriving to disturb the country idyll. Such a suggestion could not have been made so clearly, with such visual panache, had the drama been recorded in the studio. The arrival of the villain threatens Breck's plans to go straight and Kershaw builds the drama to a dramatic climax by revealing that the villain knows Breck's father from twenty years before, when his father was a villain, a fact of which his son was unaware. Having established the remote farm as a haven from the corrupting influence of the city, Kershaw finally undermines the idea of the country as a sanctuary by revealing the dark secrets lurking beneath the surface of the rural idyll.

In a *TV Times* article announcing the start of the second series of *The Villains*, Kershaw explained how 'It is impossible to tell some stories in the studio because they are so closely bound up with a location ... These episodes were written and developed after we had found a suitable spot' (Anon., 1964a: 10). The location for *Over the Hill* was clearly integral to the drama and it is easy to see how the landscape might have helped shape its development. The *TV Times* article also emphasised that 'Rough, tough Northern realism' was the objective in the series:

> Authentic situations, accurately reported dialogue, and minutely detailed character studies of the criminal elements of Northern society were the factors which made the first series such a success a few months ago . . .
>
> Harry Kershaw and his team will continue their policy of realism in later episodes, they will visit bars, greyhound tracks and dance halls in the North to get background for a story of a young boy whose father is cruelly assaulted in a robbery, and the uneasy romance of a young shop girl and a crook. He said of the series: 'We are sticking to our policy of localising stories in the North and its cities. If it is Deansgate, in Manchester, or Leeds, then we use these names and locations. We don't invent place names.' (Anon., 1964a: 10)

Just as Birmingham had been cited in *Contraband* as the canal boat's destination, so Liverpool, Macclesfield and Birmingham are invoked in *Over the Hill*, lending regional credibility to the drama.

There were two more location-based dramas in the third series of *The Villains* (December 1964 to February 1965). *Hideaway* (18 December 1964), as the end title announced, was 'made entirely at Alderley Edge, Cheshire', while *Red Hot in Winter* (22 January 1965) was filmed 'in genuine Pennine surroundings'. Both were written by John Finch, who was seeking other outlets for his dramatic ambitions outside of *Coronation Street*, on which he had become established as one of the regular writers. Finch recalls how his script for *Hideaway* was adapted during production to suit the location at Alderley Edge, illustrating how the process of location shooting could provide a different kind of challenge for the director, compared to the more instrumental process of studio dramatisation: 'The director on *Hideaway* was, I seem to remember, a chap called Peter Plummer. We went to the proposed location in Alderley Edge with a scribbled story I'd done and fitted it to the various sites Peter found interesting and viable. Cameras being what they were then the viability was very important.'[19]

While the interiors in *Red Hot in Winter* were recorded in the studio, most of the drama was recorded in the bleak moorland surrounding an old house in the Pennines, where the villains hide out after knocking down and killing a man while driving a stolen car. In her review of the programme, the *Guardian* critic Mary Crozier noted how the bleak Pennine landscape added to the intensity and coldness of the drama, illustrating once again the advantage of filming on location:

> The setting was a remote house in the terribly bleak moorland country which was filmed around Saddleworth; the villains were a young man and an elderly man just out of prison who had stolen a car and killed a man in making their getaway.
>
> The play was concerned with their extraordinary clumsy and panic stricken efforts to get rid of the car, complicated by the presence of a disapproving crippled brother, a pretty wife, and an inconvenient visitor . . . The northern settings, bleak, bare, cold, and windswept, were enough to strike a chill to the bones of the fireside viewer (Crozier, 1965)

Apart from John Finch, several other *Coronation Street* writers also wrote for *The Villains*, including Harry Kershaw, Jack Rosenthal, Harry Driver and Vince Powell. Another Northern writer who contributed to the third series of *The Villains* was Alan Plater, whose *Three to a Cell* (15 January 1965) was both complex in its plotting – considering that it revolved around three men locked up in a prison cell – and surprisingly fast-paced for a studio drama. Jack Rosenthal's *Bent* (11 December 1964) was also a well-plotted studio-based episode, about a corrupt policeman who repents when he discovers that his daughter, on whom he has brought pressure to succeed in her exams because he wants her to go to university, has turned to drugs because of the pressure. Her supplier, it is revealed, gets his drugs from a nurse whose illegal activities the bent copper knows about, but condones for a share of the profits. Although *Bent* was recorded entirely in the studio, the Lancashire accents of the characters indicate the regional setting of the drama, illustrating that a play did not need to include location scenes to convey regionality.

City '68 (1967–68)

The number of themed anthology series produced by Granada increased during the 1960s as anthologies of literary adaptations, such as *A Choice of Coward* (1964), *The Edwardians* (1965) and *The Liars* (1966), alternated with anthologies of original drama, such as *A Question of Happiness* (1964), four plays by different writers on the theme of happiness, including one by Alan Plater called *Fred*

(18 May 1964), and *Triangle* (1964), where each episode comprised three short plays by Robin Chapman, Michael Hastings and Hugh Leonard. Some of the literary anthologies were 'northern' in flavour, such as *The Stories of D.H. Lawrence* (1966–67), but perhaps the most significant, and certainly the most original, regional anthology series produced by Granada in this period was *City '68* (1967–68), a series of thirteen dramas set in a fictional Northern city called Fylde.

City '68 was devised by John Finch who, in 1967, was in his seventh year as a writer on *Coronation Street* and seeking to do something different. He put forward an idea for an issue-based documentary-drama series which would explore social problems in large cities – issues which a popular entertainment-based serial like *Coronation Street* was unable to address. The renewal of Granada's franchise in July 1967 (to take effect from July 1968) led to an expansion in production when Granada was asked to provide a seven-day service for the North West (taking over the weekend schedule from ABC). An increase in transmission from forty to sixty hours per week meant that Granada needed more programmes to fill the schedules, and *City '68* was one beneficiary of this development. In personal correspondence John Finch explained his original idea for the series and how the concept altered when Harry Kershaw was appointed as producer:

> I had just finished a spell as producer of *Coronation Street* when I was asked to put any ideas I might have into a drama conference at Granada. I considered I had done my duty by *The Street* by then and wanted to do my own thing so I jumped at it.
>
> At the time there was a lot of interest in the problems of big cities, such as Newcastle where they had what was called a City Manager (the Newcastle bloke finished up in jail). In my time on *Coronation Street* I had tried to introduce more realism, but only with moderate success. (I pushed for the introduction of a coloured family as early as 1963 but didn't get anywhere.) *The Street* hardened somewhat when Jim Allen came in during the mid Sixties, but the original formula was so successful that it was obvious that if you wanted to do anything else you would have to do it elsewhere.
>
> My intention with *City '68* (then called *Big City*) was to do what would really have been documentary drama. However, although they liked the idea and gave it the go-ahead they appointed a producer, Harry Kershaw, who put more emphasis on entertainment at which he was very good. What I had intended as a drama documentary series with national significance became basically an anthology of plays with some sort of tenuous connection with city life.[20]

While Finch had great respect for Harry Kershaw, describing him as his 'mentor' at Granada,[21] his ambitions for *City '68* were clearly at variance with the qualities that Kershaw, as producer, brought to the series. The plays, two of which were written by Finch, one by Kershaw and one by Geoffrey Lancashire, with several other *Coronation Street* writers also contributing to the series, were an eclectic mix of dramas addressing contemporary social issues such as football hooliganism, juvenile delinquency, racism, the education system, homelessness, employment, housing, traffic problems and prostitution. Although a variety of approaches and styles were adopted by the different writers and directors (including Michael Apted, who directed four episodes), the common element was the setting, the fictional Northern city of Fylde which, according to an article by Harry Kershaw in the *TV Times*, was located on 'the north bank of the Ribble between Preston and Blackpool' (Kershaw, 1967). In fact, as Kershaw pointed out in the article, Fylde was not entirely fictional because it existed as a 'district of Lancashire extending from the Wyre estuary in the north, to the Ribble estuary in the south'. However the city of Fylde which provided the setting for the thirteen plays in the series was entirely fictional, a necessary dramatic construct enabling a variety of issues to be explored within the same fictional setting: 'Fiction often demands a larger canvas than fact can provide – and *City '68* needs that large canvas. It has a wide variety of stories to tell' (Kershaw, 1967).

In addition to producing the series, Harry Kershaw also wrote the first play to be transmitted, *The Shooting War* (8 December 1967), directed by Michael Apted.[22] This opening episode highlighted the issue-based nature of the series with a story based around football hooliganism. It opens with a rowdy group of Fylde United supporters wrecking a train carriage on the way home from a match. One of the group throws a bottle through the carriage window and, unbeknown to them, it hits and seriously injures a man on the railway embankment. The incident is followed up by a journalist on the *Fylde Evening News* who telephones the club for a comment, 'in view of the violent soccer climate in general and the unfortunate record of our club in particular'. One of the club's board members also expresses concern about the issue, suggesting that the violence is perhaps 'the greatest danger the game has ever faced'. It is quickly established, therefore, that football hooliganism is the social problem to be explored in the episode.

The line that the journalist pursues is that violence on the pitch causes violence on the terraces and it so happens that the club's star striker, Len Huskisson (Kenneth Cranham), who is hero-worshipped by the young 'hooligans' who support the club, has a reputation for getting into fights on the pitch. The club chairman, who has clearly bought his way in to the club and is concerned about its image, wants to suspend Huskisson, but the manager persuades him to change his mind – on the basis that the player is crucial to the club's success. At a subsequent match, however, Huskisson gets into a fight with an opposing player and fighting breaks out on the terraces. A policeman goes into the crowd and the 'hooligan' who had thrown the bottle through the train window pulls a knife and stabs him. The death of the policeman raises the dramatic temperature of the episode, but the killer's mates are shown to be appalled by what he has done. Eventually the culprit betrays himself when he boasts to Huskisson, in the pub, that he has killed a copper 'for him'. Huskisson is dropped for the next match, which is preceded by a spontaneous minute's silence for the dead policeman – the resolution suggesting that the violence was caused by one 'bad apple' rather than being a widespread social problem.

The Shooting War is very successful in dramatising the issue of football violence, providing different points of view on the subject as different characters voice their opinions, and doing it without seeming didactic, underlining John Finch's point that Harry Kershaw was very good at 'entertainment'. The implication that the problem comes down to one 'bad apple' among the supporters, rather than being 'the greatest danger the game has ever faced', might suggest that the need to individualise characters in order to create effective drama worked against the investigative documentary impulse which was apparently Finch's original intention for the series. On the other hand, *The Shooting War* enabled the series to begin with a dramatic and contentious subject, whereas some of the other episodes, which engage with the politics of city institutions in a more earnest and discursive manner, might have discouraged some viewers from returning for subsequent episodes. Harry Kershaw's mixture of drama and social commentary in his opening episode was clearly intended to entertain as well as investigate.[23]

This dual objective to entertain and investigate was a key aspect of Granada's 'serious' drama programming, illustrating the extent to which Granada combined its public service commitment to inform and educate, derived from Sidney Bernstein's ambition to emulate the public service function of the BBC, with a more commercial, showbiz instinct towards entertainment, a view with which John Finch concurs:

> I suspect Granada wanted it both ways. They wanted something with apparent serious intent which would still get the big audience. At the time I believed Derek Granger's dictum that 'the battle for higher standards will be fought in the area of mass entertainment' so I believed it was possible to be what T.C. Worsley called 'good and popular'. In fact, I achieved this later, but not with *City '68* except in a fragmented way perhaps.[24]

With its Lancashire accents and Northern settings *City '68* was not that far removed from the social realism of early *Coronation Street*. In fact the links between the *Street* and other Granada series in the 1960s were close, as John Finch points out: 'Many series at Granada used actors who had been in *The Street*, largely because their regional authenticity was already well known, so far as accent etc was concerned. There is nothing worse from a writer's point of view than a "phoney" northern accent.'[25] The main football hooligan in *The Shooting War* was played by Geoffrey Hughes (Eddie Yeats in *Coronation Street*) and the pub scenes look very much like the set for The Rover's Return. The designer on *City '68*, Denis Parkin, was the first designer on *Coronation Street* and the casting director, Jose Scott, was also the casting director for the *Street*, while most of the writers and directors on *City '68* had previously worked on *Coronation Street*.

The major difference between *City '68* and *Coronation Street* was the opportunity to explore an issue over nearly an hour in the form of a self-contained single play, but *City '68* was different also in the extent to which it used location shooting in order to foreground its regionality and to lend the series a greater realism than it might otherwise have achieved as a studio-based drama. The documentary aspect of *The Shooting War*, for example, is helped enormously by the exterior scenes filmed on location at a real football ground, and other episodes use location filming in a similar way, to enhance the documentary realism of the series. For example the second episode, *Son of the City* (15 December 1967), which was also directed by Michael Apted, made extensive use of location shooting, occasionally on film, but mainly through the use of a mobile video unit. Through the means of location filming, *Son of the City* – which features George Leese (Martin Shaw) as a teenage victim of Fylde's social care policies, whose strict

upbringing in children's homes prevents him from developing relationships and leading a normal social life – is able to show the consequences of confinement in repressive social institutions as Leese tries
to make the transition to public life. Had *Son of the City* been made
as a studio-based drama this ability to show the teenager's difficulties in adjusting to social reality would have been inhibited by the
artificiality of the studio setting.

Son of the City illustrates the way in which location shooting is
used to open out the drama and give it a documentary quality. The
play begins with a pre-credits sequence shot at a swimming pool (on
film – presumably because shooting with an Outside Broadcast unit
in a public swimming baths was not possible) where George Leese, the
young attendant at the baths, attacks a young woman, apparently
because he thought she was flirting with him. After the title sequence
the play cuts to a studio scene, recorded on video, in which two men
discuss the attack and Leese's record of psychiatric disturbance. A
social worker, Carol Wellin (Anna Cropper), tells the men that Leese
was brought up in care from the age of six months. She goes to see
him at his lodgings (studio set) and they go to a local café (also a studio
set). The police decide to charge Leese for the attack on the girl and
on returning to his digs he sees a police car outside and runs away
(location recording on video, with a high-angle shot showing Leese
running up the street). With Leese on the run from the police much
of the remainder of the play is shot on location. Apart from one scene
showing Carol Wellin driving a car, which is shot on film, probably
because it was not practical to record with video inside the car, video
recording predominates. Leese goes back to the children's home where
he was brought up, hiding out in an old treehouse he had built when
he was there. This is where the social worker finds him. Leese tells her
about his strict upbringing at the home and about being caned by the
matron. Eventually the police track him down and he is taken before
a court, where he is given a twelve-month prison sentence. The social
worker's argument that Leese has been 'most efficiently institutional-
ised' and that prison, as yet another institution, will not help him, is
ignored.

Son of the City sets up an opposition between Carol Wellin's liberal
stance on social welfare and the punitive position of the police and the
courts. This is the issue which the play explores and it is illustrated
through the case of George Leese, a 'son of the city' who has experienced a number of city institutions in his young life. Most of the play is

spent exploring the background to the incident portrayed at the beginning, through the sympathetic mediation of the social worker, and it is clear whose side the audience is encouraged to take in this debate.

The imperative to shoot on location, albeit using an Outside Broadcast (OB) unit rather than film, was motivated by the same quest for social realism that prompted Ken Loach and Tony Garnett to escape from the confines of the television studio at the BBC two years earlier with *Up the Junction* (BBC1, 1965). This ground-breaking *Wednesday Play* undoubtedly set a precedent for Granada directors such as Michael Apted and Mike Newell to follow. However, nearly all of the exterior scenes in *City '68* were shot on video, using an O.B. unit, rather than film, the latter being much more expensive to shoot with. The advantage of using video for location shooting, however, was that the difference in quality between studio-recorded interior scenes and exterior scenes was less marked, whereas when film was used for exterior scenes the juxtaposition when cutting from interiors to exteriors could be disarming. Apart from this aesthetic advantage, the mobile video unit, or 'scanner', to use the technical name by which the OB unit was sometimes known, also had an obvious financial advantage, as John Finch explains:

> There is, of course, a significant time (and therefore cost) difference in the technique. With a scanner on location and two or three video cameras, you can set up and light a whole sequence, cut between the different cameras on the spot and shoot it in a fraction of the time. Directors hate it because it means compromise and robs them of the chance to make changes in the cutting room. They much prefer the film technique where each angle is lit and shot separately and so the sequence takes about five times as long. [. . .]
>
> From a technical point of view I was very keen to use the outside units as much as possible. I was helped in this by a young director, Michael Apted who (though I suspect he would have preferred film) worked very hard to do as much as possible outside. This was not just to 'show' the city, but to introduce a more realistic atmosphere. We achieved it mostly, I think, with a two hander where the exteriors were largely shot at night! One useful aspect was that by having the scanner on site we could watch a shot and then accept or reject it on the spot, and not have to wait for the film to be developed before we knew what we had got.[26]

Given that shooting entirely on film would have been financially prohibitive, mobile video provided the opportunity to achieve 'a more realistic atmosphere' while also ameliorating the difference in visual quality between interiors and exteriors, a difference which might have undermined the ambition to achieve verisimilitude in *City '68*. As in *The Villains*, where shooting on location was important in creating a sense of place in certain episodes, the use of OB units on *City '68* enabled the fictional world of Fylde to be turned into a visual reality, providing a visual guarantee of 'the real' by placing the characters and the stories in the landscape of the industrial North.

What the episodes in *City '68* attempted to do was to explore various aspects of life in a Northern industrial city, through the fictional example of Fylde, using the technology of mobile video in order to enhance the realism of the drama. The opening sequence of episode six, *In Memoriam* (12 January 1968), provides another illustration of the advantages of location shooting, using the OB unit. Following the modernist graphics of the *City '68* title sequence, which, combined with the ominous chords of the title music, is clearly intended to denote a 'serious' drama, the episode begins with an exterior scene on industrial wasteland, a panning camera revealing a bleak Northern industrial landscape, where the issue to be explored is introduced. Desmond Maverley (Noel Johnson), born and bred in Fylde and the owner of Maverley Electronics, has entered into an agreement with Fylde city council for a factory to be built on land he has bought because, as he pragmatically puts it, 'We need the capacity, Fylde needs the employment'. However, his son Paul (Neil Stacy) represents a new generation of capitalist entrepreneur and is sceptical about the deal. He feels no allegiance to the city and sees the factory as an 'old fashioned, labour intensive plant. It's a monument to all that's wrong in industrial development and it is not the slightest good for us', to which his father responds, benevolently, that it is 'good for Fylde'. Surveying the industrial landscape, Desmond Maverley asks his son what he sees and Paul replies: 'Smoke, grime, waste' as the camera reveals, in long shot, the iconography of the industrial North: huge smoking chimneys, factories, an enormous electricity pylon and a steam train bellowing smoke as it traverses the scene. This iconic shot is followed by a close-up of the father as he responds to this negative assessment: 'There's people, nine hundred of them, going to waste. We can bring them up here, give them jobs.'

The scene is set for a debate between the old and the new, between the industrial past of cities like Fylde (and, by extension, its real-world Northern counterparts of Liverpool, Manchester, Preston, Sheffield) and the need to regenerate in a new economic climate. The episode deals with city politics in a discursive manner, with much of the discussion about the issue of the proposed joint venture between Maverley Electronics and the city council taking place in the Fylde council offices or, in one contrasting scene, the lavish London office of Paul Maverley. The opening scene is crucial for establishing the reality of the situation at the heart of the drama. Being able to show a real industrial wasteland, rather than simply refer to it in a studio-based scene, emphasises the regional reality of the drama, underlining its drama-documentary quality. The linguistic and ideological differences between father and son which are established in this opening scene also hint at a North/South divide, which is confirmed when a Fylde MP goes to visit Paul Maverley in his London office, high up in a modern skyscraper overlooking the city.

Although several of the episodes deal with city politics and feature city councillors who appear in more than one episode, there is considerable variety in the series. Donald and Derek Ford, who wrote *In Memoriam*, also wrote *Son of the City* and *Freedom of the City* (9 February 1968), the latter taking a similar approach to *In Memoriam*, only this time the issue is the funding of a new office block by a multi-millionaire in exchange for him being given the 'freedom of the city'. Anthony Skene wrote two episodes, including *Love Thy Neighbour?* (2 February 1968), a drama about a car-sharing scheme (introduced as a result of traffic congestion in the city) which is much lighter in tone, almost a comedy. This was the only episode, according to John Finch, to get into the weekly top twenty viewing figures, which would give it an audience of at least fifteen million. Apart from that one episode, *City '68* 'was not a high-rating series', according to Finch, although even an audience of eight to ten million would have been impressive given the 'serious', issue-based nature of the series.

Some episodes were clearly more 'authored' than others, in that they displayed evidence of an authorial signature beyond the thematic concerns of the series. The two episodes by John Finch have a distinct identity of their own, while taking an oblique perspective on the city of Fylde. *The Visitors* (5 January 1968) takes as its subject a homeless family who arrive in Fylde from Lancaster where, it is revealed, they were evicted from their house. A Fylde city councillor gives them refuge in his own house, in return for the woman acting as housekeeper, but they take advantage of his hospitality and when he reports them to welfare services they leave. The final shot shows them on the road again. Finch's other episode, *It's Dearer After Midnight* (23

February 1968), was essentially a two-hander involving a woman (Sian Phillips) who is picked up by a taxi driver (Keith Barron) late at night on the outskirts of the city. She asks to be taken to an address in the city, which turns out to be a strip club. All of the action takes place during the course of one night, with a lot of exterior night-time filming (shot on video), including the opening scene up on the snow-covered moors outside the city. The episode, which was directed by Michael Apted, was a more intimate drama, much less focused on city politics than some of the other episodes, exploring the 'dark side' of the city at night through the relationship between the two characters. According to Finch:

> *It's Dearer After Midnight* was my attempt to compensate for what I felt we had lost from the original conception and to do at least something that was my own 'thing'. Myself, Mike Apted, and the two actors virtu-ally lived in each other's pockets throughout. I can remember a good response to this one, and that we found the experience of working so closely together very worthwhile. As a result, in my next series I wrote another two hander (though also to avoid dire budget problems) and was again closely involved with equally gratifying results. It was also a good learning process.[27]

While *It's Dearer After Midnight* is quite different from other episodes in the series, it does show another side to the city, with most of the second half of the play set in a seedy nightclub. At the end, after a high-angle shot looking down on a city street as the woman leaves in a taxi, the camera tilts up to present a panorama of the city at night. The episode could well have been a self-contained single play, perhaps a *Theatre-625* or *Wednesday Play* had it been on the BBC, whereas some of the other episodes in *City '68* really work only within the context of the series.

A *Question of Priorities* (26 January 1968), written by Geoffrey Lancashire, another *Coronation Street* writer, is probably the most discursive episode in the series. The episode is about the need for more housing in Fylde. Having had a proposal to build on green-belt land turned down, a city councillor proposes building on the five hundred acres of the cemetery. This initiates a series of debates about the ethics of building on burial ground, which are played out in several long scenes. Eventually it is revealed that the councillor's proposal was a ploy to force the planning commission to agree to the council's request to build on land outside of Fylde, thereby expanding the city's boundaries. Like other episodes in the series, *A Question of Priorities* is clearly an issue-based drama and its discursive strategy illustrates the investigative, drama-documentary nature of the series.

Although John Finch felt that *City '68* did not completely fulfil his original intention, the series is interesting for several reasons. Firstly, it represented an attempt to reaffirm Granada's commitment to the North West – specifically Lancashire – at a time when 'Granadaland' was about to be reduced in size, losing Yorkshire and five million viewers. Secondly, it was an early example of a drama-documentary series, a genre for which Granada was to become well known in later years, although here the emphasis was more on drama than in other examples of the genre and there is an absence of documentary conventions such as voiceover and captions.[28] Thirdly, the extensive use of location shooting, made possible by the more cost-effective mobile video unit, was important in helping to establish a regional identity for the series. Finally, not only did *City '68* help to establish Granada as a company with links to its region (by setting the series in a fictional Lancashire city), it also demonstrated Granada's ambitions to engage, through its drama, with national debates about housing, education and other social issues. In this respect *City '68* might be seen as a regional ITV response to the issue-led plays screening in the BBC's *Wednesday Play* series (e.g. 'race' in *The Fable*, abortion in *Up the Junction*, homosexuality in *The Portsmouth Defence*, homelessness in *Cathy Come Home*). That *City '68* was conceived as more than a provincial drama series was suggested by John Finch in a *TV World* article introducing the series: 'Fylde is northern only in geography. It could be a city anywhere in Britain' (Finch, 1967: 5).

The System (1968)

Soon after *City '68* John Finch was instrumental in putting together another anthology series: *The System* (July–September 1968). Loosely themed around 'the constant clash between individuals and society' *The System* was conceived as a sequel to *City '68* but with 'a wider framework'.[29] Using many of the same personnel from *City '68*, three of the six plays in the series were written by Finch himself, with one each by Anthony Skene, Julia Jones and Hugh Forbes. Although rather a mixed bag, *The System* continued the exploration of aspects of provincial life initiated in *City '68*.

Anthony Skene's opening episode, *The Flea Pit* (30 July 1968), most obviously relates to the theme of 'the clash between individuals and society'. The story concerns the abduction by students of a military General who is visiting the city to receive an honorary degree from the university. He is taken to an abandoned cinema – the eponymous 'flea pit' – where he is 'interrogated' by the students and finally dumped in a city square, blindfolded, without trousers and wearing a mortar board. Clearly picking up on the rebellious mood of the time, coming shortly after the student protests in Paris and anti-Vietnam demonstrations in London and elsewhere, *The Flea Pit*, which was directed by Michael Cox, introduced contemporary politics into a Granada anthology series and was described in the *Sunday Times* as 'Not at all a pleasant play, of course, but a play about actual issues, vividly and forcefully developed' (4 August 1968).

In contrast, *Penny Wise* (6 August 1968), was a more personal drama about an elderly man living on his own in a typical Northern terraced house who is visited by Penny Slim, a middle-class woman from Hampstead recently moved to the North with her husband, who is working as a volunteer for Social Services, taking meals to the elderly. Where *The Flea Pit* and the subsequent episode, Hugh Forbes's *Keep Out of Sight* (3 September 1968),[30] were more overtly 'political' (*Keep Out of Sight* explored the educational policy of the local Labour Party, specifically its plans to replace independent schools with comprehensives), *Penny Wise* was more 'personal', exploring the issue of social welfare through the human drama of the relationship between the elderly, working-class Northerner, Nathaniel Prescott (Billy Russell), and the middle-class Londoner, Penny Slim (Katherine Baker), their contrasting characters enabling the social and cultural divide between North and South to be highlighted. Significantly, *Penny Wise* was written by Julia Jones, one of the few women writers working in television in the 1960s. Jones had previously written a *Wednesday Play* and two *Thirty-Minute Theatre* plays for the BBC but *Penny Wise* was her first play for Granada and the issue-based nature of the series clearly appealed to her:

> Whenever I wrote a play, comedy or otherwise, I felt I must have an underlying theme which had something relevant to say about the times. Also to give women a fair crack of the whip. *Penny Wise* was the first piece I wrote for Granada and I enjoyed working in the North, where I grew up, with John Finch the producer of the series under the umbrella title *The System*. These series of one-off plays by different authors under umbrella titles were a way, I understand, of keeping the single play alive.

I remember being told that it was easier to sell abroad a series than single plays on their own.[31]

Jones highlights how, even in 1968, there was a concern that the single play on television was an endangered species. At the same time she provides a reason for the increase in anthology series at Granada during the 1960s and 1970s, because they provided a means of 'keeping the single play alive', an explanation which would account for the corresponding decline in the production of single plays made outside of these series. Her concern to write plays 'which had something relevant to say about the times' was clearly pertinent to the issue-based nature of the anthology series devised by John Finch.

Like *Penny Wise*, *Victims* (10 September 1968) was an intimate, character-based drama, written as a studio two-hander by John Finch to counterbalance the cost of the more expensive filmed drama that would close the series (see below). Directed by Michael Cox, *Victims* features a husband (Anthony Bate) and wife (Libby Glen) whose marriage is on the verge of breaking down. All of the action is played out on one studio set, yet the claustrophobic atmosphere of the confined setting is entirely conducive to the examination of a disintegrating relationship. We discover, through the discussion that unfolds, that the tragic, unspoken death of their young daughter, early in the marriage, is the root cause of the breakdown and the source of much resentment, with the wife blaming the husband for the daughter's death. Learning that his wife is preparing to leave him for someone else he tries desperately to persuade her not to go, telling her, in an allusion to the theme of the series, that he can't cope with 'the system, the whole bloody jungle we live in'.

John Finch also wrote the fifth drama in the series, but *The House that Jigger Built* (17 September 1968) was in marked contrast to the other two episodes he wrote for the series, being more light-hearted and comedic in tone, a consequence perhaps of Jigger being played by Harry H. Corbett and his father being played by Wilfred Pickles, the latter's strong Yorkshire accent giving the drama a genuine regional flavour.[32] The upwardly mobile Jigger has made money through dodgy property deals, but his family take advantage of his 'system' of stashing money in the house, and the drama becomes increasingly farcical as Jigger dashes around the house looking for his money, with light-hearted music emphasising the comic nature of the situation. Jigger's upward mobility – he drives a Jag and wears a cream suit with tie and pocket handkerchief – is in marked contrast to his working-class father, a miner who talks about growing up in the neighbour-hood that Jigger wants to develop. *The House that Jigger Built* was clearly satirising the modern-day property developer and it may be no coincidence that Jigger's surname is Barrett.[33]

The final play shown as part of *The System* was a landmark drama for Granada. John Finch's *Them Down There* (24 September 1968) was the first all-film drama to be transmitted by the company. Directed by Mike Newell, who had previously directed episodes of *Coronation Street* and one of the *City '68* plays under the name of Cormac Newell,[34] *Them Down There* was filmed at a remote farmhouse in the Pennines, which may explain why it was shot on film as the location may have been too remote for an OB unit to get to – certainly some of the interior scenes would have been difficult to film with the larger video cameras in use at the time. As with Finch's thematically similar *Villains* episode, *Red Hot in Winter, Them Down There* depended on its remote location for much of its atmosphere, as one reviewer noted at the time:

> An isolated farm cottage situated in the middle of the Yorkshire moors, many miles from the nearest town or village, is inhabited by three people, two men and a woman. One of the men is confined to his room having been crippled by an overturned tractor many years before. The other man works on the farm, and loves the woman, who, it later tran-spires, is married to the cripple, the owner of the farm. Into the ménage comes a carpenter and his mate, hired by the woman to do some unspec-ified task. During the course of their week-long stay, the events of *Them Down There* occur . . .
>
> The characters are all well-drawn, and the dialogue sounded, to me, very authentic. But the great interest of this play, was that it was shot entirely on location, on the Yorkshire moors, and in the actual cottage which was the inspiration for the play.
>
> The exterior scenes were entirely successful, the actors and the cameras capturing perfectly the feeling of isolation, and the relationship of the characters to each other and to the countryside which surrounded them. (Phillips, 1968)

A brooding, menacing atmosphere was successfully created in the drama, enhanced by the more cinematic *mise en scène* which shoot-ing on film, in a remote location, made possible.[35] In contrast to the light-hearted tone of *The House that Jigger Built, Them Down There* was a tragedy, ending with the invalid husband, Cuff (Morris Perry), shoot-ing Baxter (Michael Turner), the other man on the farm, who is having a relationship with Cuff's wife, Sheila (Patricia Haines), before turning the gun on himself. 'Them down there' was the expression used by Sheila Cuff to refer to the villagers further down the valley, whom she viewed with some disdain, immersed as she was in her moorland isolation. The regional setting for the play was especially commended in reviews, including this one from the *Oldham Evening Chronicle*:

> *Them Down There*, latest in the ITV drama series, *The System*, achieved that rare distinction of being a really worthwhile play. A fascinating and moving story from the pen of author-producer John Finch was matched by faultless acting and a perfect setting – poignant tragedy amid the silent, enigmatic moors. Basically, it was the story of a woman's consuming devotion to the bleak hillside farm where she had lived as a child, a farm that was decaying for want of a man, for her husband was bedridden following a tractor accident . . .
>
> There were no histrionics in this tragedy, though; no brave speechifying or noble gesture. But feeling, yes. The dialogue may have been presented in monosyllables, roughly spoken, yet one could really understand the inspiration and determination that the woman drew from her moorland solitude. (Anon., 1968)

As *The System* came to an end another, quite different, Granada series was starting. Philip Mackie's *The Caesars* (September–November 1968), a series of six historical dramas about the lives of the Roman emperors, was entirely studio-based, yet the duplicity and intrigue of the Roman Senate was enhanced by the claustrophobic and intense atmosphere generated in the studio, in a production directed by Derek Bennett. A much underrated and overlooked series, partly because it was made in black and white whereas the later, more popular BBC series *I Claudius* (1976) was in colour, *The Caesars* represented the polar opposite to the issue-based, regional contemporaneity of *City '68* and *The System*. Yet these series, together with the boisterous *Rogue's Gallery* (1968–69), the gangland drama serials *Spindoe* (1968) and *Big Breadwinner Hog* (1969), Tony Warren's trilogy about a 1940s black marketeer, *The War of Darkie Pilbeam* (1968), and *Judge Dee* (1969), a 'detective' drama set in seventh-century China, testify to the diversity and originality of Granada's drama in the late 1960s.

Filmed drama in the 1970s

Them Down There was not the only filmed drama Granada produced in 1968. Jack Rosenthal's *There's a Hole in Your Dustbin, Delilah* (30

September 1968), a ninety-minute *Playhouse* production directed by Michael Apted, was screened within a few days of *Them Down There* being transmitted and was Granada's first feature-length filmed drama.[36] The subject matter and mood of the two dramas, however, could not have been more different, the contrast largely resulting from the different authorial styles of John Finch and Jack Rosenthal.[37] The nicely observed comic scenario of Rosenthal's play, involving a team of garbage collectors who try to outwit a new inspector (Frank Windsor) from the Corporation Cleansing Department, was in marked contrast to the psychological realism of Finch's *Them Down There*. Filming on location in the urban environs of Manchester, however, was as essential to the realism of *There's a Hole in Your Dustbin, Delilah* as filming on the Yorkshire moors had been to the atmospheric dynamic of *Them Down There*. Rosenthal subsequently developed *There's a Hole in Your Dustbin, Delilah* as a popular situation comedy, *The Dustbinmen* (1969–70), which ran for three series, although Rosenthal wrote only the first series.[38]

   The directors of *Them Down There* and *There's a Hole in Your Dustbin, Delilah*, Mike Newell and Michael Apted, were clearly at the forefront of Granada directors seeking to get out of the studio and film on location (it is not surprising that both directors subsequently pursued careers in the film industry). Granada producer Peter Eckersley, who rose in the ranks to become Head of Drama at Granada (as did Philip Mackie), was supportive of the development of filmed drama, recruiting Ken Trodd on a short-term contract in 1970 in order to tap into Trodd's experience of producing drama on 16mm film.[39] Trodd had been part of a progressive group of writers, producers and directors in the 1960s at the BBC, where he was a script editor on *The Wednesday Play*, working alongside Tony Garnett, Ken Loach, James MacTaggart, Dennis Potter and Roger Smith. In 1968 Trodd left to set up Kestrel Films with Garnett, Loach and MacTaggart as 'British TV's first independent drama production company' (Cook, 1995: 62). In addition to producing feature films such as Loach's *Kes* (1969), Kestrel signed a contract with the new ITV company London Weekend Television to provide the company with single plays, although, for 'economic and logistic' reasons, many of these were 'recorded on videotape within the confines of LWT's studios' (Cook, 1995: 63). Three exceptions were Colin Welland's *Banglestein's Boys* (18 January 1969), directed by John Mackenzie, Julia Jones's *Faith and Henry* (6 December 1969), directed by Jack Gold, and Neville

Smith's *After a Lifetime* (18 July 1971), directed by Ken Loach, each of which was shot on film.

Eckersley's 'head-hunting' of Trodd was an acknowledgement of Granada's lack of experience in producing filmed drama, but Trodd was a political radical and the experience and personnel he brought to Granada resulted in a clash of ideologies which caused his stay at the company to be relatively short. During his two-year residency Trodd produced three plays and a serial: *Roll On Four O'Clock* (20 December 1970), a filmed drama written by Colin Welland and directed by Roy Battersby, *Paper Roses* (13 June 1971), Dennis Potter's only play for Granada (also shot on film), *Square* (27 June 1971), and *Home and Away* (February–March 1972), a seven-part serial written by Julia Jones which was part-studio and partly filmed on location in Eastern Europe.

According to Bob Millington, who has researched the making of *Roll On Four O'Clock*, while Eckersley hoped Granada would benefit from Trodd's experience of filmed drama, Trodd and Battersby found Granada's existing film capability inadequate when they began work on *Roll On Four O'Clock*:

> Peter Eckersley had seen the cinematic Welland material on LWT and recognising its strength invited Trodd to Granada to shift the whole shooting match forward at the organisation in 1970. They [Granada] may have undertaken work on film before this programme but it was all 'taxi filming' according to Trodd, i.e. done quickly and lit for mixing as an insert between two studio scenes. This applies even to work that was for logistical reasons shot entirely on film, e.g. when there are many locations and outdoor shots. Battersby found his camera crew weak (even incompetent) and needed to import a specialist lighting cameraman (cinematographer) to achieve the precision 'realistic' lighting effects he was looking for. On the set training was a key feature of the project.[40]

Roll On Four O'Clock was one of Granada's first dramas to be filmed in colour.[41] Given the personnel involved, it is not surprising that the film was in the documentary-drama, social-realist tradition exemplified by the work of Loach, Garnett and Jim Allen at the BBC.[42] Colin Welland had been an actor in *Z Cars* and had a leading role in Loach's *Kes* in the same year that his first script, *Banglestein's Boys*, was produced by Kestrel for LWT. It was while he was working on *Kes*, in which he played a progressive secondary school teacher, that Welland was commissioned to write *Roll On Four O'Clock*, a play which is also set in a secondary school, this time in Lancashire rather than Yorkshire. *Roll On Four O'Clock* was clearly influenced by *Kes*, focusing on a pupil who, like Billy Casper in *Kes*, is an outsider, a victim of bullying and homophobia. Director Roy Battersby adopted a similar naturalistic style in shooting the film to that used by Ken Loach on *Kes*, filming in a secondary school in a working-class district of Manchester, but he also included some non-naturalistic montage sequences in order to reinforce the socio-political message of the drama, within an overall realist structure.

Three months after the transmission of *Roll On Four O'Clock*, Arthur Hopcraft's *The Mosedale Horseshoe* (23 March 1971) was shown as part of the ITV *Playhouse* series and these two filmed plays provide contrasting representations of the region among Granada's drama output in the early 1970s. Welland, a Yorkshireman schooled in the BBC social realist tradition, produced a socially committed drama with *Roll On Four O'Clock*, whereas Hopcraft, who grew up in the Midlands and moved to Manchester when he got a job as a journalist with the *Daily Mirror*, produced a more lyrical, melancholic portrait of a group of ramblers in Cumbria. Hopcraft first worked for Granada on *Scene at 6.30*, a current affairs programme, before being asked by Gordon McDougall to have a go at writing a play for the Stables Theatre Company. His first script was not produced but after the Stables closed Peter Eckersley encouraged Hopcraft to write another:

> [W]e had agreed I should write a play about hill-walking in the Lake District, because I'd done a lot of that and Peter wanted to get the camera out of doors. He didn't go much for my first suggestion involving a climbing club's annual dinner dance. Forty-five actors sitting round a table? Then forty-five actors spread all over the mountainside? He was much more sympathetic to a tale about four people. So I wrote *The Mosedale Horseshoe*.
>
> I delivered it, I think, around October/November in 1970. The read-through was on 14 January 1971. Filming began up at Wastwater four days later and finished on 5 February. The play was transmitted on the 23 March. It was directed by Michael Apted. (Hopcraft, 2003: 111)

The subject, characters and Lake District setting of *The Mosedale Horseshoe* were in complete contrast to the urban setting and emphasis on youth, education and homophobia in *Roll On Four O'Clock*. Owing to an industrial dispute, *The Mosedale Horseshoe* was filmed in black and white rather than colour, giving the drama a more sombre tone than it might otherwise have had. Nevertheless, the Lakeland landscapes of *The Mosedale Horseshoe* provide a romantic contrast to the urban setting of *Roll On Four O'Clock* and the story of four old friends meeting up for their annual walk around the 'Mosedale Horseshoe' unfolds at a leisurely pace. In one scene, for example, there is a lengthy recitation of a poem by one of the characters as they sit on a hillside eating lunch, played partly for humour as the listeners patiently wait for the orator to conclude. Featuring middle-aged characters, or characters approaching middle age in the case of the two women, the theme of the play is about growing older, with an awareness, especially in the case of the two women, of living unfulfilled lives.

With its pastoral Northern setting and air of melancholia, *The Mosedale Horseshoe* seems a more typical Granada project than does *Roll On Four O'Clock*, where there is an echo of the 'agitational contemporaneity' that was central to the issue-led dramas produced at the BBC in the 1960s for *The Wednesday Play* (see MacMurraugh-Kavanagh, 1997). The writer/producer/director team of Hopcraft/Eckersley/Apted on *The Mosedale Horseshoe* was more immersed in the Granada ethos than were Welland/Trodd/Battersby and although the latter did start work on another project at Granada, about a strike in the clothing industry, set in Leeds, Granada never committed to it and Trodd eventually took the project to the BBC, where it was made as a *Play for Today* entitled *Leeds – United!* (BBC1, 1974):

> For us the story had everything – northern setting, heart-tearing and pyrrhic struggle by little people against mighty bosses; it was real and very recent, and there was a sharp political tang to our take on the story. But mysteriously the project did not thrive . . . It is still the film I am most proud of and it still feels like a Granada programme, not just because its stars include Lynne Perrie, Liz Dawn and half the future cast of *Coronation Street*. (Trodd, 2003: 130–1)

For whatever reason, the more overtly political approach of Welland/Trodd/Battersby seemed to be viewed with some suspicion by Granada, whereas the more benign politics of *City '68* and *The System* was less threatening, perhaps because the plays produced for those series involved storylines which were more 'personal' than 'political'. *Roll On Four O'Clock* was acceptable to Granada because it foregrounded the personal dimension of the story, even if the broader context was the education system. *Leeds – United!*, on the other hand, was a project involving a more confrontational engagement with a political subject, the kind of political drama for which the BBC and *Play for Today* was well known, but which was less common on the commercial network. This may illustrate a fundamental difference between Granada and the BBC as 'public service' broadcasters at the time. While Granada saw itself as a liberal company it was, nevertheless, part of a commercial network which needed to deliver large audiences to advertisers. Consequently there was always a tension between Granada's public service ambitions and its commercial obligations. The difference between the 'personal' drama of *Roll On Four O'Clock* and the 'political' drama of *Leeds – United!*, which was destined to be a more expensive project as well as a more overtly political one, indicates where Granada felt it needed to draw the line.

Not that 'political' drama was absent from the Granada schedules. In 1974 Jack Gold directed a studio drama for Granada called *I Know What I Meant* (10 July 1974), about the American President Richard Nixon and the Watergate Tapes. The play was dramatised, by David Edgar, from public statements and tapes recorded at the White House, using captions, voiceover, photographs and archive footage, intercut with studio scenes featuring Nicol Williamson as Richard Nixon. Although *I Know What I Meant* was shown as a *Late Night Drama* this was clearly a drama-documentary in the tradition of *World in Action*'s dramatised documentaries and Leslie Woodhead's drama-documentaries about real events, such as *Three Days in Szczecin* (21 September 1976), about a shipworkers' strike in Poland, and *Invasion* (19 August 1980), about the 1968 Soviet invasion of Czechoslovakia. The difference between these 'political' drama-documentaries and the political drama of *Leeds – United!* was that the drama-docs were about world events, often seen from a historical perspective, whereas *Leeds – United!* was a play about contemporary class politics in Britain.

Granada's 'international' drama-documentaries were in marked contrast to the more parochial regional dramas written by Granada's Northern writers, such as Jack Rosenthal, whose *Another Sunday and Sweet F.A.* (9 January 1972), about a provincial Sunday morning football team, was also made as a filmed drama, directed by Michael Apted. Like John Finch, Rosenthal learnt the craft of television drama on *Coronation Street*, writing 129 episodes for the serial in the 1960s, while also contributing to series such as *The Odd Man* (1962–63), *The Villains* and the anthology series *Friday Night* (1963), for which he wrote his first two plays, *Pie in the Sky* (8 November 1963) and *Green Rub* (22 November 1963). Rosenthal also wrote for and devised comedy series such as *Bulldog Breed* (1962), *The Dustbinmen* (1969) and *The Lovers* (1971), all for Granada, and much of his drama was characterised by a distinctive Northern humour, evident in another filmed drama, *Ready When You Are, Mr. McGill* (11 January 1976), an affectionate study of a day in the life of a film extra, directed by Mike Newell, which Rosenthal wrote for the anthology series *Red Letter Day* (1976), a series which he also devised.[43]

Four of the seven dramas in the *Red Letter Day* series were shot on film and by the end of the 1970s an increasing amount of Granada's drama was being filmed on location, rather than recorded in the studio. The reasons for this were partly to do with changing audience expectations. The BBC increased its production of filmed drama in the 1970s, especially on *Play for Today*, and Thames Television founded Euston Films in 1971 especially to produce filmed drama for the ITV network. The financial incentive for producing drama on film was that it was easier to sell abroad than studio drama, but the increased costs of filmed drama had a detrimental effect on the production of the single play and it was significant that *Red Letter Day* was one of the last anthology series Granada produced. As Granada entered the 1980s a new, more competitive era was dawning in British television which would see a decline in the production of parochial Northern drama and an increase in the production of filmed series and serials, with high production values, that were more international in flavour and, therefore, more marketable overseas.

Granada and the 'telenovel': *A Family at War, Sam* and *The Spoils of War*

While the single play went into a gradual decline during the 1970s, series and serials emerged to take up prominent positions in the schedules. In addition to *Coronation Street*, by now firmly established at the top of the ratings, there were long-running series such as *Adam Smith* (1972–73), about a clergyman in a Scottish village, *Crown Court* (1972–84), a thrice-weekly daytime courtroom drama, *Village Hall* (1974–75), a studio-based anthology series, the spy series *The XYY Man* (1976–77), *Cribb* (1980–81), a Victorian police drama, and *Ladykillers* (1980–81), an anthology of real-life murder cases. In addition to these were a number of literary adaptations, including *Country Matters* (1972–73), an anthology of stories by H.E. Bates and A.E. Coppard which Philip Purser cherished as 'the finest literary anthology series ever' (Purser, 2003: 121), the seven-part *Shabby Tiger* (1973), adapted by Geoffrey Lancashire from the novel by Howard Spring, *A Raging Calm* (1974), a seven-part adaptation by Stan Barstow from his own novel, *The Stars Look Down* (1975), adapted from the A.J. Cronin novel by Alan Plater, Arthur Hopcraft's four-part adaptation of Dickens's *Hard Times* (1977), *Brideshead Revisited* (1981), adapted by John Mortimer from Evelyn Waugh's novel, and Stan Barstow's ten-part *A Kind of Loving* (1982).

These were all major productions, some of them shot on film or including significant amounts of filmed material, and many of them engaging with regional subject matter, especially the Northern-based serials *Shabby Tiger*, *The Stars Look Down* and *A Kind of Loving*. Even an anthology series like *Country Matters*, where the stories were not necessarily set in the North, used Northern locations because, as designer Roy Stonehouse notes, 'we rarely went more than 30 miles from the studio for drama productions'. His account of designing for a location shoot on *Country Matters* problematises the definition of 'regional' television drama:

> In 1972 I was asked to design *Country Matters*, a series based on short stories by A.E. Coppard and H.E. Bates to be shot on film. One particular story was set in the south of England and called for the creation of a working farm in the 1930s, which was difficult as we rarely went more than 30 miles from the studio for drama productions. The stockbroker belt of Knutsford in Cheshire was selected because it had unspoilt views of the countryside and looked very much like Kent. (quoted in Finch, Cox and Giles, 2003: 269)

Stonehouse's account raises the question of whether regional identity is determined by the ostensible setting of a drama, even if it is actually filmed in a different region altogether, or whether regionality is dependent on a complex of other factors, such as authorial input (from the writer and/or director and producer), regional subject matter, characters, or linguistic specificity (accent and dialect).

Ed Buscombe notes a similar anomaly in relation to the popular drama series *The Darling Buds of May* (Yorkshire, 1991–93). A rural drama, like *Country Matters*, set in the South of England, in Kent, *The Darling Buds of May* was also produced by a Northern ITV company, Yorkshire Television: 'The question of what *exactly* is meant by local content is never an easy one. There is clearly something a little ersatz about the authenticity of *The Darling Buds of May*'s sense of place if it is made by a company based at the other end of the country from its ostensible setting' (Buscombe, 1993: 34).

Most of Granada's drama serials, though, were more firmly rooted in the North, in terms of both their physical setting and their representation of Northern culture and identity. The most sustained expression of this came in the long-form serials, or 'telenovels', created by John Finch: *A Family at War* (1970–72), *Sam* (1973–75) and *The Spoils of War* (1980–81). The narrative of *A Family at War* spanned the six years of the Second World War and featured the middle-class Ashton family in Liverpool, the city where Finch was born (although he grew up in a Yorkshire mining village). The serial ran for fifty-two one-hour episodes, shown in three series from April 1970 to July 1972. Michael Cox, one of several directors and producers who worked on it, explains how *A Family at War* came about as a result of the success on the BBC of *The Forsyte Saga* (BBC2, 1967), which Denis Forman had earlier tried to persuade the Bernsteins to do:

Denis Forman had always regretted that the Bernsteins would not support his idea of dramatising *The Forsyte Saga*. He was told that costume pictures never made money and besides it would necessarily have been a serial. Then in 1967 the BBC tackled Galsworthy's novels in twenty-six episodes and brought the nation to a standstill on Sunday nights. He could not resist drawing attention to this at a drama conference and the point was made: the television audience would accept a serial, even if it was a period piece.

At the same conference, to which we all had to submit ideas as the price of admission, John Finch floated a notion with the working title of *Conflict* about the experiences of an ordinary family in the Second World War. That working title encapsulated the reasons for its eventual success. We all know that successful drama is about conflict of some kind; John's brilliant thought was to run two conflicts on parallel lines. We were to see the personal clash of emotions within a family against the backdrop of the most frightening confrontation of nations in living memory. The proposal won the day and was called – with winning simplicity – *A Family at War* . . .

All of us who worked on *A Family at War* can look back and see that John Finch had created a new narrative form: the television novel. This was long before Frederick Raphael delivered *The Glittering Prizes* for the BBC or Alan Bleasdale celebrated *The Boys from the Blackstuff*. This was the original breakthrough which established the television playwright as a person with his own unique voice, recording the human condition but writing in a popular form just as Dickens had done in the previous century. (Cox, 2003: 98–9)

John Finch was not the sole author of *A Family at War* – several writers, including Alexander Baron, Stan Barstow and Harry Kershaw, contributed to the serial – but he was undoubtedly its guiding light. Having worked for several years as writer, editor and producer on *Coronation Street*, before creating *City '68* and *The System*, Finch was eager to develop a portrait of Northern life on a larger scale. His previous scripts for television had shown not only his concern to write about aspects of Northern life but a dedication to popular forms of writing. In this respect Michael Cox's comparison to Dickens, who also wrote in a popular serial form, was not inappropriate. In a short memoir, recalling his time with the Merchant Navy during the Second World War, John Finch wrote about his literary influences:

When I sailed from Liverpool in December 1941 my only education of any practical use was a modest proficiency in Morse code, but there was a tea chest in the corner of the mess the contents of which probably influenced the whole future course of my life. It contained books, collected by the WVS and supplied to all ships sailing from the UK.

From that first treasure chest came the works of writers as diverse as Chandler, Shakespeare, Mrs Beeton, Priestley, Hemingway, Professor C.E.M. Joad and, blessed above all, Charles Dickens in the shape of David Copperfield. Later in life, faced with a major operation, I started to re-read Copperfield as a sort of pre-med, and it was the first thing I reached for when I came out of the anaesthetic which had temporarily come between us.

On the long, boring radio watches, surrounded by the grey sea of war, I devoured other writers: Hemingway, Wells, Steinbeck, a feast of poets, the Brontes, Lawrence and numerous others whose names but not their influence have, alas, been forgotten. I acquired what thirteen schools had not been able to give me, which was an abiding love of the English language. I had no formal education in grammar, and at no time did I actively seek one; basically I learned what I felt I needed to learn by example . . .

I am not a novelist, though I have written one novel. I am a scriptwriter. Much of my work has been on a broad Dickensian canvas, which is as close to Dickens, alas, as I will ever get. My move from early, unsuccessful prose writing to drama I owe to the radio play. Long before television I listened to plays on Saturday Night Theatre which was then an occasion. Chekhov, Ibsen and, nearer home, Priestley inspired me to go on. There was a time when my greatest ambition was to become the Sean O'Casey of Yorkshire. Dream on! (Finch, 2004: 33)

Finch's literary influences, especially that of Dickens, are revealing, and *A Family at War*, with its pantheon of characters and epic narrative sweep, is, thematically and structurally, firmly within the tradition of the nineteenth-century realist novel. At the time, it was the most expensive drama Granada had produced and the investment paid off because it proved to be very popular, not just in Britain but also abroad. As Michael Cox notes: 'It usually achieved the highest viewing figures and several times reached first or second place in the charts.' Furthermore, 'It opened up overseas markets for British drama, particularly in Scandinavia where it was enormously popular' (Cox, 2003: 99). *A Family at War* showed that a British drama serial, taking a provincial Northern family as its subject, could succeed both at home and overseas, although the historical context of the Second World War undoubtedly broadened its appeal.

John Finch followed *A Family at War* with another serial drawn from his own experience. The semi-autobiographical *Sam* was set in a South Yorkshire mining village and followed the life of the eponymous hero from the 1930s to the 1970s. Whereas *A Family at War* was notable for its lack of Liverpool accents, perhaps because its focus was on a middle-class family, rather than a working-class one, *Sam* was replete with Yorkshire accents and dialect, arguably the primary signifier of 'regionality' in the serial. Visually, the production combined studio interiors, showing the austerity and poverty in which the villagers lived, with filmed exterior scenes, enabling the iconography of the Yorkshire mining village and surrounding landscapes to be shown. Michael Cox was the producer on *Sam* and describes how the serial was made on the same traditional production pattern as *A Family at War*:

[F]or an hour episode we had two or three days of location filming, a week of rehearsal and then two days in the studio with electronic cameras. Because it's a story about mining we spent a lot of time filming in collieries which had to be found near to our base in Manchester. We seldom went back to Yorkshire where the story is set but we did manage to get there for the opening titles.

It's a basic imperative for producers to find locations which do not demand too much time or money spent on travelling. Those are expenses which show in the budget but do not show on the screen.

When the script demands the seaside or the country, however, as in the episode called A Day to Remember, the cost of travelling is money triumphantly well spent because the results do show on the screen.

At the time of production in the 1970s mining was an industry which had not changed much from the 1930s in which the first series takes place. So scenes at the pit head were not too difficult to recreate. The pit villages were different: an improved standard of living had altered the appearance of them considerably. But eventually we found one, called Gin Pit village, just outside Manchester. It seemed, like Brigadoon, to have been stuck in a time warp and come to life just for us. With some minimal changes, removing television aerials and motor cars, we were back in the Thirties.[44]

John Finch wrote all thirty-nine episodes of *Sam*, a huge undertaking which is unlikely to be repeated. Yet, despite the austerity and parochial nature of the serial, Granada was openly receptive to his proposal. Responding to accusations from critics that his work was 'dour' or 'glum', which, as he says, was 'inevitable I suppose since most of my writing has been about poverty or war' (2003: 108), Finch emphasised that Granada never expressed similar concerns:

In some twenty-five years of writing for Granada the company never attempted to censor anything I wrote and never complained that I was 'dour'. At the end of *A Family at War* Denis Forman, then managing director, asked me what I would like to do next. We spent half-an-hour chatting about my early experiences in a mining community, and at the end, without asking for a pilot or even an outline, he simply said, 'Go and do it.' Trust was a major factor in Granada's creative approach to drama. (Finch, 2003: 109)

Despite the often bleak nature of its narrative, *Sam*, like *A Family at War*, was popular with audiences. As John Finch notes on his website, the serial 'had a varied international audience and was repeated three times in New Zealand. It won a number of major awards and was very warmly received by the critics. It was in the top UK ratings throughout, and knocked *Coronation Street* from its number one position.'[45] Among a number of positive quotations from critics on the same page of the website, this one from Philip Purser, writing in *The Sunday Telegraph*, highlights the literary quality of the dialogue: '"You're honest beyond the need" could be Shakespeare. In fact it's John Finch again in Granada's *Sam*.'[46]

In comparison to *Sam*, John Finch's next serial, *This Year Next Year* (1977), about a Yorkshireman who leaves the Yorkshire Dales to go and live in London, was a more modest production, yet it still extended to thirteen episodes, confirming Finch's mastery of the long-form serial. In the same year, Arthur Hopcraft's adaptation of *Hard Times* was a mere four episodes, less than a third of the length of *This Year Next Year*.

The Spoils of War was John Finch's last 'telenovel', in which he returned to the theme of *A Family at War*, only this time the action began at the end of the war, in 1945, continuing through to 1952. Shown in twenty one-hour episodes, in three series from January 1980 to August 1981, *The Spoils of War* explored the effects of the war on two families living in the Lake District. With one working-class family and the other middle class, the serial dramatised the relationship between the classes in postwar Britain, following the election of a Labour government in 1945, within the microcosm of the fictional town of Whitstanton. Once again combining studio interiors with filmed exterior scenes (shot on location in the Cumbrian town of Millom) *The Spoils of War* represented the end of a tradition of historical, long-form regional drama production at Granada, in which stories about the people and culture of the North West of England were unraveled in the form of the 'telenovel'.

While *The Spoils of War* was in production, work was also under way on a more lavish (and far more expensive) drama serial: *Brideshead Revisited* (October–December 1981). Whereas *The Spoils of War* was an original, regional drama, set and produced within the boundaries of Granada's own transmission area, *Brideshead Revisited* was an international production, from a well-known novel, filmed in locations around the world, featuring a star-studded cast. At the beginning of a more competitive era in broadcasting, which would see the arrival of a fourth terrestrial channel within a year and satellite television before the end of the decade, *Brideshead Revisited* marked the beginnings of a shift at Granada towards the production of more costly, non-regional drama which was more marketable abroad, whereas *The Spoils of War* represented the kind of indigenous 'regional' drama which would struggle to get made in the new era of 'global' television.

While the perennially popular *Coronation Street*, together with Stan Barstow's ten-part serial *A Kind of Loving* (1982), adapted from his own novel, and Geoffrey Lancashire's six-part *Foxy Lady* (1982), about the female editor of a Northern newspaper, continued to fly the flag for Northern drama in the early 1980s, expensive filmed dramas such as *Staying On* (1980), adapted by Julian Mitchell from the novel by Paul Scott, *Brideshead Revisited*, *The Jewel in the Crown* (1984), adapted from Paul Scott's *The Raj Quartet*, and *The Adventures of Sherlock Holmes* (1984–85) signalled a new departure in Granada's drama policy in the 1980s as the company began to reposition itself as an international broadcaster with an eye on overseas markets. In this new broadcasting environment indigenous regional drama, of the type discussed in this chapter, began to go into decline.

Notes

1 See Allen Eyles, *The Granada Theatres*, Cinema Theatre Association / British Film Institute, 1998.
2 A timeline in *As Others See Us*, a booklet produced by Granada in 1981 to mark the company's twenty-fifth anniversary, gives a precise date for the naming of the North West region as 'Granadaland': 9 November 1960 (exactly one month before transmission of the first episode of *Coronation Street*), but there is no explanation as to why the term came into parlance on this date.
3 Denis Forman, interviewed by the author, 4 May 2006.
4 Ibid.
5 *Brookside* was produced by Mersey Television, an independent production company established by Phil Redmond in the early 1980s. In 1992, when the contracts of the ITV companies came up for renewal, the Liverpool-based Mersey Television made an audacious bid for the North West region, partly on the basis of Granada's historic neglect of Liverpool. Although Mersey TV's bid exceeded that of Granada's, the contract was awarded to Granada on the basis that the Liverpool company had failed to achieve the 'quality threshold', a clause written into the 1990 Broadcasting Act in an attempt to ensure the continuation of 'quality' programming on ITV.
6 Derek Bennett, interviewed by the author, 21 April 2005.
7 Ibid.
8 For more on 'kitchen sink' theatre see Lacey (1995) and Taylor (1962b). For more on *Armchair Theatre* see ABC Television (1959) and Cooke (2003: 37–42).
9 Six of the 'Manchester Plays' were published in 1962 by Manchester University Press, on behalf of the Granada TV Network, under the title: *Granada's Manchester Plays: Television Adaptations of Six Plays Recalling the Horniman Period at the Gaiety Theatre*.
10 For more on Troy Kennedy Martin's 'Nats go home' polemic and the debates about naturalism versus realism and video versus film in 1960s

television drama see Caughie (2000: 92–102), Cooke (2007a: 69–79), Hill (2007) and Sexton (2003).

11 Derek Bennett, interviewed by the author, 21 April 2005.

12 For more on the 'intimacy' of live television drama see Jason Jacobs, *The Intimate Screen: Early British Television Drama*, Oxford: Oxford University Press, 2000.

13 According to Harry Elton, one member of the Granada programme committee – the American light-entertainment producer Eddie Pola – did refer to *Coronation Street*, disparagingly, as 'a soap opera' following the screening of the pilot episode, telling Elton, for good measure: 'You don't put that crap on at seven o'clock at night. That should play in the afternoon' (Elton, 2003: 100).

14 John Finch, 'Coronation Street', short unpublished (and undated) article, sent to the author by email, 22 October 2005.

15 Bill Douglas pursued a career as an actor before enrolling at the London Film School in the late 1960s. In the 1970s he made a highly acclaimed trilogy of films about his childhood in Scotland and then spent eight years trying to realise his ambitious three-hour film about the Tolpuddle Martyrs, *Comrades* (1987). *Flow Gently Sweet Afton*, in which Douglas is one of the main characters, is one of only two plays to have survived from *The Younger Generation* series.

16 Roger Smith, interviewed by the author, 26 April 2000.

17 By 1964 *Television Playhouse* had been discontinued, to be replaced by *Playhouse* in 1967.

18 *The Entertainers*, which was directed by John McGrath and produced by Denis Mitchell, was initially banned by the ITA because of a striptease sequence. Videotape was also used to record the prize-winning documentary *A Wedding on Saturday* (Granada, 1 April 1964), about a wedding in a Yorkshire mining community, produced by Mitchell and directed by Norman Swallow.

19 John Finch, email to the author, 25 May 2006.

20 John Finch, email to the author, 4 June 2004.

21 John Finch, email to the author, 24 October 2005.

22 Dates and times of transmission varied according to region. In the Midlands and the North the series was transmitted on Fridays, 9.00–10.00 pm, beginning on 8 December 1967. In London and the South of England, however, the series was relegated to a late-night slot on Fridays, 11.10–12.10 am, beginning four weeks after it started in the North, on 5 January 1968. The order in which the episodes were shown was also different in the South, although the first three episodes were the same.

23 *The Shooting War* was not the first episode in the series to be recorded and is listed as episode four in the Granada catalogue, suggesting it was brought forward to open the series because it was thought more likely to

win an audience than some of the other episodes. Or maybe the producer, Harry Kershaw, simply exercised his authority to get his episode shown first!

24 John Finch, email to the author, 4 June 2004.

25 Ibid.

26 John Finch, from two emails to the author, both 4 June 2004.

27 John Finch, email to the author, 4 June 2004.

28 For more on the use of documentary codes and conventions in drama-documentary see Derek Paget, *No Other Way to Tell It: Dramadoc/ Docudrama on Television*, Manchester: Manchester University Press, 1998.

29 John Finch, quoted in a *Daily Mirror* review of the first episode of the series, 30 July 1968.

30 There was a four-week gap between episodes two and three of *The System* being transmitted owing to an ITV industrial dispute.

31 Julia Jones, email to the author, 5 April 2005.

32 Harry H. Corbett was best known at the time for the BBC sitcom *Steptoe and Son* (1962–74); Wilfred Pickles had been an announcer on the BBC's North Region radio service before becoming the first newsreader on the National service to speak with a regional accent. After the war Pickles was best known as the host of the long-running radio show *Have a Go* (1946–67).

33 Barratt Developments, one of the largest residential property development companies in the UK, was founded in 1958 and was listed on the London Stock Exchange in 1968, the year in which *The System* was transmitted.

34 Cormac is Mike Newell's middle name. His later credits as a film director include *Four Weddings and a Funeral* (1994) and *Harry Potter and the Goblet of Fire* (2005).

35 The credits list a camera operator, sound recordist, dubbing mixer, unit manager and film editor – not credits normally associated with television drama at the time.

36 The actual length of *There's a Hole in Your Dustbin, Delilah* was seventy-eight minutes. The play was scheduled from 8.30 to 10.00 pm, including three commercial breaks. It followed *Coronation Street* at 7.30 pm and *World in Action* at 8.00 pm in a Monday evening programme which shows the importance of Granada's contribution to the ITV schedule at the time.

37 That John Finch was also the producer on *There's a Hole in Your Dustbin, Delilah* illustrates the extent of his contribution to Granada's drama at the time.

38 The original play featured Jack MacGowran as the leader of the garbage crew and the actor-playwright Henry Livings as one of the dustbinmen. Neither appeared in the subsequent series.

39 I am grateful to Bob Millington for information about Ken Trodd's Granada contract.

40 Bob Millington, email to the author, 14 June 2005.

41 One drama in the 1970 *Confession* anthology series, *The Fell Sergeant* (21 August 1970), was shot on film, in colour, and three dramas in the 1970–71 anthology series *The Sinners* were also filmed, in colour. Information obtained from *The Trodd Index* (1977), reprinted in Pilling and Canham (1983: 56).

42 After writing 36 episodes of *Coronation Street* in 1965–66 Jim Allen's first full-length television play was *The Lump* (BBC1, 1 February 1967), produced by Tony Garnett and directed by Jack Gold, followed by *The Big Flame* (BBC1, 19 February 1969), produced by Garnett, directed by Ken Loach – both were filmed dramas (although *The Lump* did contain some studio scenes – see Chapter 4, n. 14).

43 Jack Rosenthal finished writing a new version of *Ready When You Are, Mr McGill* as a critique of the television industry in 2003, but the new version wasn't transmitted until September 2004, on Sky Movies 1, four months after Rosenthal's death. It was transmitted by ITV on 26 December 2005. For a comparison of the two versions see Sue Vice, *Jack Rosenthal*, Manchester: Manchester University Press, 2009, ch. 6.

44 Michael Cox, 'The Production of *Sam*', www.johnfinch.com/ProductionofSam.html, accessed 31 March 2006.

45 John Finch, '*Sam*', www.johnfinch.com/Sam.html, accessed 31 March 2006.

46 Philip Purser, quoted on www.johnfinch.com/Sam.html, accessed 31 March 2006.

4

BBC English Regions Drama

BBC English Regions Drama emerged out of the regional reorganisation within the BBC at the beginning of the 1970s (see Chapter 2). The proposals announced in *Broadcasting in the Seventies* (BBC, 1969) were confirmed in the 1970 BBC Handbook when Director-General Charles Curran described the initiatives the BBC was taking in regional broadcasting, including a major investment in new studios in the Midlands:

> In non-metropolitan radio and television in England there will be some really radical changes. In television we shall have eight new regions which, by 1971, will be producing 400 programmes a year for their own audiences, compared with the 150 a year of the former three English regions . . . Through the production centres at Birmingham, Manchester and Bristol regional talent and initiative will continue to flow into network radio and television as fully as or more fully than in the past. Birmingham, for instance, will eventually have at its disposal a £6 million television complex at Pebble Mill. In each place there is a senior executive whose terms of reference include responsibility for nourishing creative talent in his part of the country. (Curran, 1970: 23)

The new studios at Pebble Mill were officially opened on 10 November 1971, having eventually cost £7 million. Phil Sidey was appointed Head of Network Production Centre, Pebble Mill, and David Rose was appointed Head of English Regions Drama, a new department, with a brief to commission and produce regional television drama for the network. Having worked at the BBC for a number of years, in the Drama-Documentary Department and as the first producer on Z *Cars*, Rose was well qualified to be Head of English Regions Drama. Furthermore, he was a firm believer in the authority of the writer in the creation of original drama:

One of the reasons I think we kept the original Z-*Cars* on the road for four years retaining, I hope, some of the qualities of January '62 through to '63, '64, '65 and '66 was because we always venerated the writer. If there was a quality for that series of Z-*Cars* it was to do with our respect for the writer . . . The first and last thing is the writing as far as I'm concerned. (quoted in Millington and Nelson, 1986: 25)

With Barry Hanson as script editor, Rose set about commissioning drama from writers 'who either live in or who have particular concern for the regions' (BBC, 1972: 73). Hanson had been working at Hull Arts Centre as the Artistic Director, having previously worked at the Royal Court Theatre, and the connection with regional writers and the repertory theatre movement was to be crucial to the success of English Regions Drama at Pebble Mill:

> I was working with Alan Plater in the new theatre and arts centre in Hull when David Rose hired me as a script editor. Working with him was exciting because, although I knew little of the practicalities of television, we shared an interest in, and a commitment to, many of the writers with whom he had worked on Z *Cars*. Also, we were both determined to make Birmingham's mark with, as far as possible, regional writers new to television. (Hanson, 2000: 58)

Together, David Rose, whose television experience went back to the 1950s, and Barry Hanson, new to television but conversant with contemporary regional theatre and regional playwrights, formed an ideal partnership.

The advantage of the new department being based in Birmingham was twofold. Firstly, with the infrastructure of new, well-equipped studios and trained BBC staff already in place, Rose and Hanson were able to concentrate on commissioning regional writers and working with them to produce new plays for television. Secondly, their Birmingham base meant they were removed from the controlling influence of the main BBC drama department in London. To a large extent they were able to operate independently, as Hanson explains:

> The important factor about Birmingham in 1971 was that there was talent, craft and technical infrastructure of the highest, BBC-trained order: the situation was akin to that of Manchester in the early 1960s when Vivian Daniels produced the first plays of John Hopkins, John McGrath and Alan Plater.
>
> In the late 1950s and early 1960s, Peter Dews, the eminent theatre

director, had run a one-man drama department in Birmingham where, along with contemporary plays, he produced the magnificent Shakespeare history cycle, *An Age of Kings*. As the 1960s progressed, Birmingham generated several notable productions, such as Zola's *Germinal*, adapted by Midlands writer David Turner. It also hosted many successful series and serials from London. But 1971 was the first time that the regions had gained complete autonomy from the 'Centre'
. . .

It was around this time that David Rose hung a map of the British Isles on his office wall with black-inked arrows pointing to which region was to be blessed next with our Medician beneficence. The feeling that it was the rest of the country against London was strong. (Hanson, 2000: 58–60)

Hanson's account of the setting up of English Regions Drama as a relatively autonomous BBC department, with an apparently free hand to commission regional writers, many of them from regional theatre and new to television, highlights the progressive nature of the new venture. His account is corroborated by David Rose who, as head of the department, had the most contact with the 'Centre', being required to attend occasional meetings in London. Rose, however, declined an invitation from the Head of Plays at the BBC to attend regular meetings in London, wishing to maintain an artistic distance, and an autonomous identity, for his regionally based department. This decision to keep a distance from the 'Centre' extended to avoiding, as far as possible, going to London for rehearsals, even though many actors were based in London and there were financial implications involved in bringing actors to Birmingham for rehearsals:

Christopher Morahan was Head of Plays, he extended a very generous invitation to me to join their weekly Plays Department meeting and I declined, I hope courteously, to say that, you know, I'd rather not, I don't really want to know what you're doing and I don't want you to know what I'm doing. I thought it was healthier not to be sharing in their sort of thinking and we avoided London writers, we tried to engage writers who were still living in the regions. We tried to avoid ever going to London as a setting or a location and I had a hell of a battle to insist that rehearsals took place in Birmingham because this is where we were working and living, rather than London, but the obvious thing was most actors were based in London and it was cheaper, so sometimes we had to do some rehearsal in London but we did our damnedest and I tried to get the budget to enable us to have actors living in Birmingham, which I think was a real bonus; it was like being on film location or something, you're remote, you're a team, you're sort of working to one end together.[1]

In order to create a 'regional ethos' Rose felt it was important not only to live in the region (he moved to live near Stratford-upon-Avon while he was Head of English Regions Drama) but to strive to operate independently, secure in the knowledge that the department was financially supported by the BBC with ready access to purpose-built facilities.

Thirty-Minute Theatre and Second City Firsts

The first English Regions Drama productions were transmitted in February 1972 as *Thirty-Minute Theatre* plays. *Thirty-Minute Theatre* had been running on BBC2 since 1965, largely as a training-ground for new writers (one of Dennis Potter's first plays was for *Thirty-Minute Theatre*), so it was logical that English Regions Drama should 'nourish creative talent' in the regions by commissioning half-hour plays from regional writers. The fourteen *Thirty-Minute Theatre* plays the department produced in 1972 were from regionally based (mostly Northern) writers, but by no means were they all new writers. Among those contributing to *Thirty-Minute Theatre* were John Hopkins, Alan Plater, Jack Rosenthal and David Rudkin, all experienced writers who had been writing for television, and other media, since the early 1960s.

The department's *Thirty-Minute Theatre* plays ranged in kind from Arthur Hopcraft's drama about a 'progressive' Methodist preacher, *Said the Preacher* (BBC2, 6 March 1972), a studio-based drama directed by Michael Apted featuring Victor Henry as the preacher, to John Hopkins's non-naturalistic filmed drama, *That Quiet Earth* (BBC2, 28 February 1972), written and directed by Hopkins and featuring his wife, Shirley Knight Hopkins. *That Quiet Earth* was an example of Hopkins's more experimental television work, in the tradition of his ground breaking *Talking to a Stranger* (BBC2, 1966), and was too obscure for many viewers, according to the BBC's Audience Research Report on the play.[2]

That Quiet Earth was the only filmed play among the fourteen *Thirty-Minute Theatre* plays produced by English Regions Drama in 1972, only five of which have survived. Of the other surviving plays, Ted Whitehead's *Under the Age* (BBC2, 20 March 1972), directed by Alan

Clarke, was a play about homosexuality, set in a bar in Liverpool, and featured the Scouse dialect of Paul and Michael Angelis; *Scarborough* (BBC2, 12 October 1972), by Donald Howarth, was about the relationship between three young people fruit-picking near Scarborough, all of the action being set in the barn in which they are sleeping; while *You're Free* (BBC2, 16 November 1972), by Henry Livings, was a two-hander featuring Rachel Roberts and Colin Blakely as a couple living in a farmhouse in the south of France which they have bought on the proceeds of the husband's win on the football pools. Of these five plays only *Under the Age* and *Scarborough* are clearly set in the regions, although as both were single-set studio plays their regional setting was not readily apparent. The claim to 'regionality' in these plays largely resides in the fact that their authors were regionally based writers. The writers commissioned by English Regions Drama were not asked to engage specifically with regional subject matter in their plays – although Rose and Hanson no doubt hoped that a regional sensibility would emerge in the writing, whatever the subject matter.

The *Thirty-Minute Theatre* plays were transmitted in two seasons, from February to April 1972 and from October to November 1972. All except *That Quiet Earth* were recorded in the studio and this continued to be the pattern with the half-hour plays produced by English Regions Drama. Of the 73 half-hour plays the department produced from 1972 to 1978 nearly all were studio plays, recorded in the new studios at Pebble Mill – only eight were shot on location, on either film or video. Film tended to be reserved for the longer plays the department contributed to *Play for Today*.

When a third series of half-hour plays was transmitted in February–March 1973 the *Thirty-Minute Theatre* title was dropped. Although the department had close links with the theatre, drawing on writers, directors and actors from regional repertory companies, it had no intention of simply transposing theatre plays to television. By abandoning the *Thirty-Minute Theatre* title the department was seeking to distance itself from any association with 'televised theatre', as David Rose confirms: 'I didn't like the title *Thirty-Minute Theatre*, I didn't think television was theatre, shouldn't be, and thirty minutes I thought people could pop out and put the kettle on, so we found another rather clumsy title, *Second City Firsts*.'[3]

The untitled series of six plays transmitted in February–March 1973 was the stepping stone between *Thirty-Minute Theatre* and *Second City Firsts* (the first series of which was screened in October–

November 1973). To highlight the fact that the department did not want to be associated with 'televised theatre', and also to emphasise the regional content of the plays, the first drama in the new series was shot entirely on film, on location, in an Asian district of Birmingham. Tara Prem's *A Touch of Eastern Promise* (BBC2, 8 February 1973) tells the story of a young Indian man who fantasises about an Indian film star he learns is coming to Birmingham and whom he determines to meet. Filming on location enabled the region to be shown in a way that was not possible in a play recorded entirely in the studio. In studio plays 'regionality' could be expressed through the story, characters and dialogue, and regional accents were sometimes the primary signifiers of regional identity in studio plays, but filming on location afforded the opportunity to show the regional setting in all its verisimilitude, in a way that a studio-based play could not hope to do, although studio plays did sometimes use filmed sequences in order to establish the regional setting before cutting to the studio set for the majority of the play. Few half-hour plays were shot on film because filmed drama was far more expensive to produce. Filmed drama also required the skills of a film director, film cameraman and film editor, specialised roles drawing on a different repertoire of skills to those of their studio counterparts. *A Touch of Eastern Promise* was directed by Michael Lindsay-Hogg, who had previously directed the Beatles documentary *Let It Be* (1970) and who went on to direct several feature films, plus episodes of *Brideshead Revisited* (Granada, 1981).

Not only was *A Touch of Eastern Promise* set in Birmingham, it featured the indigenous Indian community of the city, and the use of regional locations is complemented by the distinctive Birmingham accents of some of the younger Indian characters, while others speak Punjabi. *A Touch of Eastern Promise*, therefore, shows the concern of English Regions Drama not only to go out and film in the region but also to represent the multicultural communities of a provincial city like Birmingham.

In contrast, the third play in this series of half-hour plays was a studio drama featuring just one actor and minimal studio sets. *You and Me and Him* (BBC2, 22 February 1973) was written by David Mercer and featured Peter Vaughan as Coster, a man with three separate personalities. Imaginatively directed by Barry Hanson, in a departure from his usual job of script editor at Pebble Mill, *You and Me and Him* uses three studio sets to show Coster in his living room, bedroom and office. Through clever use of eyeline matching, and the skilful editing of videotape editor John Lanin, Coster is seen holding conversations with his other selves, in an exploration of divided personality, a familiar theme in David Mercer's work.[4] Clearly *You and Me and Him* could not have been recorded live, although this would have been possible with other studio dramas in the series, such as David Cregan's *I Want to Marry Your Son* (BBC2, 8 March 1973), which was recorded on one studio set in a conventional naturalistic studio style. According to Peter Ansorge, who joined English Regions Drama as a script editor in 1975, 'We didn't shoot them live, but you shot great chunks, if not the whole piece occasionally, in a multi-camera set up, continuously.'[5] While shooting on location, on film, was more time-consuming and more expensive, studio recording was equally demanding, requiring different skills, and in studio production the role of the director was central, as Ansorge explains:

> Studio drama is almost a lost form now. It wasn't theatre, although obviously it's quite close to theatre in some ways, and it wasn't film, but we did think of these little studio dramas as mini-films, if you like. And it was always, in the end, in the hand of the director of the day, because it was all rehearsed and recorded in a single day and quite often you'd rehearse from ten o'clock until the supper break, you'd have a lunch break, a tea break, and then after the supper break you would go in and you would have two hours to record . . . In some ways it was much harder than making a first film, where you have a DoP [Director of Photography] generally telling a first-time director what he shouldn't do. It was quite a demanding skill that and so the director in the day of recording and rehearsal became the pivot of the whole thing and his or her imagination and how well he dealt with the multi-camera set-up, the realisation of it, was part of the excitement of the whole process.[6]

Following *A Touch of Eastern Promise*, Tara Prem joined English Regions Drama as a script editor and she came up with the title of *Second City Firsts* for the next series of half-hour plays, transmitted from October to November 1973. Whereas some experienced regional writers had been commissioned to submit plays for *Thirty-Minute Theatre* the intention with *Second City Firsts* was to premiere work by new writers, hence the 'firsts' in the series title, produced by English Regions Drama in Birmingham, England's 'second city'.

The first play to be shown in the *Second City Firsts* series was *The Medium* (BBC2, 15 October 1973), written by the Sunderland-based writer Denise Robertson. Its subject was spiritualism: a group of women gather in the house of Beattie (Norah Fulton), whose husband has recently died, to have their fortunes told by a drunken clairvoyante (Winifrede Shelley). Beattie's daughter (Valerie Georgeson) sees that the clairvoyante is a fraud but she pretends otherwise to her mother so as not to destroy her faith in the afterlife. *The Medium* was recorded entirely in the studio, with no telecine sequences to establish the location, but the accents of the characters immediately announce this as a regional drama set in the North East, showing that regional identity could be established even when a play was entirely studio-based.

Other plays in the first series of *Second City Firsts* included *If a Man Answers* (BBC2, 29 October 1973), by the Yorkshire actor and writer Brian Glover, and *King of the Castle* (BBC2, 12 November 1973), the first play for television by the Liverpool playwright Willy Russell. *King of the Castle* was shot on location in an industrial setting, using an OB unit, an alternative means of achieving a sense of place, without the expense of shooting on film. Pebble Mill had recently acquired a new Lightweight Mobile Control Room (LMCR), a two-camera OB unit, using lightweight cameras, which was more flexible than the larger five-camera OB unit, and this was the first time that the new lightweight unit was used on a drama production at Birmingham. Unfortunately, recording on videotape made the drama equally vulnerable to being erased as studio plays, and the recording of *King of the Castle* no longer exists. Reflecting on it thirty-seven years later, Willy Russell felt that the play had suffered from being cut down from the longer version he had originally written and was not too concerned that it no longer existed, but he retained some affection for it as the first of three television plays written for English Regions Drama:

> The production had to bear the weight of a number of compromises – an hour script had to be cut so that it would fit into the thirty minute slot, a number of the actors were cast very much against accent and it was shot in a disused factory in Birmingham, not Liverpool . . . I'm not too distressed that it's been wiped – the production was not the best – although I always think back to it with some degree of affection because it began my association with the Drama department at Birmingham and in particular with David Rose.[7]

The 'new writers' qualification for *Second City Firsts* was not always strictly followed. The first play shown in the second series, *Humbug, Finger or Thumb?* (BBC2, 18 February 1974), was written by Arthur Hopcraft, who had already written *Said the Preacher* as a *Thirty-Minute*

Theatre play for English Regions Drama and whose *The Mosedale Horseshoe* (Granada, 23 March 1971), filmed on location in the Lake District, was an important precursor of the filmed dramas produced by BBC English Regions Drama. *Humbug, Finger or Thumb?* was followed in the *Second City Firsts* series by *Girl* (BBC2, 25 February 1974), the first of four plays written for English Regions Drama by James Robson and the first of several controversial dramas the department was to produce. The controversy surrounding *Girl* concerned the portrayal of a lesbian relationship between Jackie (Alison Steadman), a young army recruit, and Chrissie (Myra Frances), a corporal with whom Jackie has an affair. Jackie is leaving the army because she is pregnant and Chrissie comes to see her before she goes. She tells Chrissie her pregnancy is the result of being raped and that she still loves her. The drama takes place in one room, but includes a flashback to show Chrissie and Jackie in bed together. At one point Chrissie puts a Dusty Springfield single, 'This Girl's in Love', on the record player, referring to the song as being 'top of the gay girls' hit parade' and they dance together, singing along to the song. While the record plays, the volume of the music increases, introducing a moment of heightened melodrama during which their illicit relationship is celebrated. *Girl* contains what is probably British television's first lesbian kiss, and the sensitivity of the project caused the Controller of BBC2 to preview the programme and to rewrite the introductory announcement to it.[8]

The second series of *Second City Firsts* included two plays shot on location. *The Actual Woman* (BBC2, 11 March 1974), written by Jack Shepherd, was filmed on location outside Birmingham by Philip Saville, using the LMCR, while *Match of the Day* (BBC2, 18 March 1974), written by Neville Smith and directed by Stephen Frears, was shot on film. A comparison between these two location-based dramas, shot on different formats, might have been illuminating but, once again, the recording of *The Actual Woman* no longer exists. However, a very complimentary review of the drama shows that the recording was still available eighteen months after its first transmission for a repeat screening in October 1975:

> *The Actual Woman* is the second play in the last series of *Second City Firsts* which the BBC considered to be worth repeating (BBC-2, October 11, 10.15 pm) before they embark upon their new series. And, certainly, producer Barry Hanson has every reason to be pleased with this vivid tour de force.
>
> It is, to begin with, remarkably literate. Author Jack Shepherd has a

fierce flow of dialogue that bites and glows, together with a perception of human beings living precariously on the edge of their emotions, and Philip Saville is a director who has a particular gift for the presentation of words, balancing them against the visual aspects of a production in a way that gets the best out of both. (Holt, 1975: 13)[9]

Although no recording is available to make possible an analysis of the visual style of *The Actual Woman*, a viewing of *Match of the Day* shows that the drama was clearly liberated from the constraints of the studio by being shot on film, making extensive use of flashbacks and voiceovers in addition to a variety of interior and exterior locations. The title has a double meaning, referring to the wedding which forms the basis of the story and the obsession with football (in particular Everton FC) of its central character, Chance (Neville Smith). Chance narrates the events, seen in flashback, leading up to the wedding of his sister, as well as those which occur on the day of the wedding, including his attempts to chat up a woman at the reception while he is also trying to get the football scores. The entertainment value of the drama is considerably enhanced by some lively dialogue and Liverpudlian humour. It is clear from the accents alone that *Match of the Day* is a regional drama, but its regional identity also emerges from the fact that Neville Smith is writing about people with whom he can identify and situations with which he is clearly familiar.[10] As with Denise Robertson's *The Medium*, the regional authenticity of *Match of the Day* arises from the writer's regional affinity, fulfilling the objective of David Rose to place the writer at the centre of drama production at Pebble Mill.

While many of the writers commissioned by English Regions Drama had regional theatre connections, one of the plays in the third series of *Second City Firsts* directly acknowledged the special relationship the department had with regional theatres. *Fight for Shelton Bar* (BBC2, 18 November 1974) was a thirty-minute version of a longer stage play produced earlier the same year by the Victoria Theatre Company in Stoke-on-Trent, dramatising, in documentary style, the struggle to prevent the local steelworks in Shelton from being closed down (see Chapter 2). In the event the television version of *Fight for Shelton Bar* formed part of a successful campaign to keep the steelworks open.

The *Second City Firsts* series enabled a number of now very well-known writers to have their first television scripts produced. Alan

Bleasdale made his television debut in 1975 with *Early to Bed* (BBC2, 20 March 1975), shown in the fourth series of *Second City Firsts*. The drama tells the story of Vinny (David Warwick), an eighteen-year-old student, who is having a sexual relationship with Helen (Alison Steadman), the young married woman living in the terraced house next door. Like *Match of the Day*, *Early to Bed* was shot on film, which again enabled the drama to achieve a greater sense of place and regional identity than some of the studio dramas were able to achieve. It begins, for example, with a shot of a pit head, establishing the location as that of a Lancashire mining community, and the scenes filmed in the small town help to illustrate the limited opportunities there for Vinny, establishing his need to get away. *Early to Bed* was an apprentice work for Bleasdale and he acknowledged the contribution of the film's director, Les Blair, who 'made a script of some promise, but no great quality, into something worth watching' (quoted in Millington and Nelson, 1986: 27).

Also in the fourth series was *The Permissive Society* (BBC2, 10 April 1975), the first of two *Second City Firsts* by Mike Leigh, both studio productions and the only studio dramas, apart from *Abigail's Party* (BBC1, 1978), that Leigh has ever produced. The scenario is typical of Leigh's work: a slice of working-class life, set mainly in a living room, featuring a rather mismatched young couple and the boy's older sister, who goes out on a date only to return at the end of the play having been stood up. Nothing much happens and like most of Leigh's work *The Permissive Society* (the title is clearly ironic) is a character study. But the claustrophobic studio set suits the drama well, reinforcing the sense of the characters being trapped in lives with limited horizons. Once again *The Permissive Society* illustrates that it is not essential to film on location in order to convey a sense of characters being trapped in their environment.[11]

As with the plays for *Thirty-Minute Theatre* and *Play for Today*, the primary objective of *Second City Firsts* was to commission regional writers rather than regional drama. The distinction is important because it meant that not all of the plays produced by English Regions Drama were obviously 'regional' in subject matter. For example, Ian McEwan's *Jack Flea's Birthday Celebration* (BBC2, 10 April 1976), shown in the sixth series of *Second City Firsts*, was a studio drama about a young man who is writing a novel called 'Jack Flea's Birthday Celebration', the content of which, it transpires, is remarkably similar to the subject of the play. Thematically the drama is typical of

McEwan's first collection of short stories, *First Love, Last Rites* (1975). In fact McEwan saw the play 'as really belonging in that volume' (McEwan, 1981: 10–11). *Jack Flea's Birthday Celebration* is not particularly 'regional' in subject matter but the fact that the play was produced in Birmingham did have a distinct advantage, according to McEwan:

> At the end of a day's rehearsal the four actors – who all came from far away – could not go home. They had to hang about together in restaurants or in the hotel bar. No one could quite escape his or her part. By the end of ten days a very odd and gratifying level of controlled hysteria had been reached and this suited the claustrophobic nature of the play perfectly, as did the detached quality of Mike Newell's camera script. (McEwan, 1981: 11–12)

McEwan's remarks bear out the intentions of David Rose to have the actors, whenever possible, based in Birmingham for the course of a production in order to replicate the conditions of being 'on film location . . . you're remote, you're a team, you're sort of working to one end together'.

The director of *Jack Flea's Birthday Celebration*, Mike Newell, is now better known for feature films such as *Four Weddings and a Funeral* (1994) and *Harry Potter and the Goblet of Fire* (2005), among many others. He is one of several *Second City Firsts* directors who went on to have successful careers in the film industry, others being Les Blair, Alan Clarke, Stephen Frears, Roland Joffe, Mike Leigh, Michael Lindsay-Hogg and Philip Saville, all of whom directed half-hour plays at Birmingham in the 1970s. While English Regions Drama may have privileged the writer, directors made an important contribution, as indeed did set designers, given that most of the productions were studio plays.

By no means all of the *Second City Firsts* were successful. *The Frank Crank Story* (BBC2, 17 April 1975), screened a week after Mike Leigh's *The Permissive Society*, was one of the less successful productions. A debut play by a machine minder and jazz fan, Alan Taylor, *The Frank Crank Story* might, on the evidence of the recorded drama, have benefited from more work at the script editing stage and it is difficult to see why this particular play was preserved for the archive when others by Mike Leigh, Alan Plater, David Rudkin and Willy Russell have been wiped.

Yet the importance of the *Second City Firsts* series was that it gave writers an opportunity to experiment and to have original work produced, rather than having to conform to the more formulaic strictures of the continuous drama serial, which is what most new writers are obliged to do today.[12] It also gave an opportunity to an unprecedented number of new writers. Forty-two writers contributed to the nine series of *Second City Firsts* over a period of six years, while another seventeen writers contributed to the two series of *Thirty-Minute Theatre* plays and the untitled series of six half-hour plays from 1972 to 1973. While not all of these writers were making their television debut, most of those who wrote for *Second City Firsts* were. Some of them went on to write other work for television and a couple (Bleasdale and Leigh) have since contributed to the 'canon' of British television drama with work such as *Boys from the Blackstuff* (also produced by English Regions Drama) and *Abigail's Party*.[13] The chief significance of *Second City Firsts*, however, is that it provided a forum in which regional writers could try their hand at television drama, without having to write a full-length *Play for Today*.

From the plays that survive, it is clear there was a considerable diversity in the work produced in the nine series of *Second City Firsts*. They include naturalistic studio plays as well as social realist dramas; intimate personal dramas as well as campaigning agit-prop dramas like *Fight for Shelton Bar*; plays about the West Indian community in Birmingham (Barry Reckord's *Club Havana*) and about lesbians in the army; plays about football, journalism, dogs, clairvoyantes, strikes and politics. The fact that the plays were only thirty minutes long and mostly recorded in the studio may have limited what they were able to achieve, but the writers were given the freedom to do what they wanted within that limited canvas.

In many cases the limitations of the confined studio set placed more emphasis on the writing and the performances, but in the hands of a creative director like Philip Saville a studio drama like *Rotten* (BBC2, 13 May 1978), the last *Second City First* to be transmitted, could be transformed into something extraordinary, in this case an experimental drama using electronic effects, split-screen, montages and superimposition to tell the story of a boy who lives a childhood fantasy life in the 1960s, inspired by the music of The Beatles, growing into a rebellious teenager by the time punk explodes on to the scene in the mid-1970s (the title refers to Johnny Rotten of the Sex Pistols). Written by Alan Brown, *Rotten* was both a contemporary 'state of the nation' drama and a testament to the creative ingenuity that English

Regions Drama and the *Second City Firsts* series inspired. Like most of the drama produced at Pebble Mill under David Rose, the *Second City Firsts* series extended the range of dramatic representations in the 1970s, providing a televisual forum for regional writers, many of them writing for television for the first time, while encouraging a spirit of adventure, originality and diversity in British television drama.

Single plays: creating 'a sense of place'

The production of seventy-three half-hour plays by English Regions Drama from 1972 to 1978 was matched by an equally prolific, diverse and original output of seventy-four full-length plays between 1972 and 1982. Where the half-hour plays were shown as part of an existing BBC anthology series (*Thirty-Minute Theatre*) and a new anthology series (*Second City Firsts*) devised by English Regions Drama, most of the full-length plays were shown as part of existing BBC anthology play series (BBC1's *Play for Today* and BBC2's *Playhouse*) and a new anthology series which started on BBC2 in 1977 (*Play of the Week*), although English Regions Drama did develop a short anthology series of its own in 1979 (*The Other Side*). There were also a number of single plays produced by the department which were screened outside of these anthology series (see Appendix 2 for a full list of the plays produced by English Regions Drama from 1972 to 1982).

It is significant that nearly all of these plays were original television plays, rather than adaptations of novels or stage plays, mostly written by regionally based writers, some of whom had made their television debut with a half-hour play for English Regions Drama. With a remit to 'nurture creative talent' in the regions the department encouraged original contemporary drama, rather than adaptations, although there were some significant exceptions to this, such as Henry Livings's adaptation of Harold Brighouse's *The Game* (BBC2, 3 January 1977). It is also significant that, unlike the half-hour plays, the majority of the full-length plays – certainly those made for *Play for Today* – were filmed on location. English Regions Drama produced three or four plays for *Play for Today* each year and, in order to emphasise the regionality of each play, it was felt to be very important to be able to use film for shooting on location, as David Rose explains:

> [B]ecause of where we were and my desire to reflect regional life, the landscape and the community, we tried to make as many of those

four *Play for Todays* on film as possible, to somehow get a feeling of the
outlook of the regions. Film has a particular strength and the film itself
creates an atmosphere. Writing a studio play and writing for film are
two different things. In the studio you are dependent on words. There's
a limit to the imagery that can be conjured up in the studio. Film can say
so much else. Space is created! (quoted in Millington and Nelson, 1986:
25–6)

The impulse behind getting out of the studio to film on location, in
order to 'reflect regional life, the landscape and the community', is
similar to that which motivated Loach and Garnett in the mid-1960s
when they broke with tradition to film *Up the Junction* and *Cathy
Come Home* in real locations. There may have been less emphasis on
'agitational contemporaneity' in Rose's desire to reflect regional life
but, coming from a drama-documentary background and having produced the early *Z Cars*, where filmed inserts were very important for
lending realism to the drama, it is clear that Rose shared a belief that
film enhanced verisimilitude, whereas studio drama was restricted by
being confined to artificial sets and a dependence on words.

It is interesting that, apart from a few experiments with lightweight video cameras, most significantly on *Boys from the Blackstuff*
(BBC2, 1982), English Regions Drama did not make extensive use of
mobile video for shooting on location, unlike Granada in the 1960s.
When Granada was first making use of OB units, in 1964, to record
episodes of *The Villains* on location, the BBC was also making its first
location-based drama using an OB unit – Philip Saville's dramatisation of *Hamlet at Elsinore* (BBC1, 19 April 1964). Saville's production, however, seemed to set a theatrical precedent for the use of
video on location which was precisely what Troy Kennedy Martin,
John McGrath, Ken Loach, Tony Garnett and others at the BBC were
arguing against in the debate sparked off by Kennedy Martin's 'Nats
Go Home' article (Kennedy Martin, 1964). While Granada was using
OB units on *City '68* and *The System* in 1967–68, directors such
as Jack Gold, Ken Loach, John Mackenzie and James MacTaggart
were shooting plays such as *The Lump* (1967), *In Two Minds* (1967),
The Voices in the Park (1967), *An Officer of the Court* (1967) and *The
Golden Vision* (1968) on film.[14] The tradition of filmed drama at the
BBC was well established by the time Granada took its first tentative
steps towards filmed drama in 1968–70, hence the recruitment of
Ken Trodd by Granada in 1970 in order to tap into his experience of
producing filmed drama.

Following John Hopkins's filmed drama *That Quiet Earth* (BBC2, 28 February 1972), one of the first English Regions Drama productions, made for *Thirty-Minute Theatre*, the first full-length filmed drama to be produced by the department was Peter Terson's *Play for Today, The Fishing Party* (BBC1, 1 June 1972). Terson worked mainly in the theatre in the 1960s and was playwright-in-residence with Peter Cheeseman's Victoria Theatre Company in Stoke-on-Trent from 1966 to 1968. In 1967 (as noted in Chapter 2) he adapted *Jock on the Go* (BBC2, 9 September 1967) and *The Heroism of Thomas Chadwick* (ABC, 23 September 1967) from stories by Arnold Bennett as his first television plays, both performed by the Victoria Theatre Company. Terson then adapted two more plays for the BBC's *Wednesday Play* series, *Mooney and His Caravans* (BBC1, 2 October 1968) and *The Apprentices* (BBC1, 29 January 1969), before writing his first original script for television: *The Last Train Through the Harecastle Tunnel* (BBC1, 1 October 1969), also as a *Wednesday Play*. All of these were studio dramas, with some filmed inserts. *The Fishing Party*, however, was Terson's first screenplay and the decision to film the drama on location fulfilled David Rose's desire to 'reflect regional life, the landscape and the community'. The advantages of location filming are evident from the opening titles.

The Fishing Party opens with three Yorkshire miners arriving, by bus, in Whitby, on the North Yorkshire coast, laden with fishing tackle in anticipation of 'a blameless weekend fishing the cod' (*Radio Times*, 25 May 1972). A jolly brass band theme over the opening titles accompanies their arrival, signalling a light-hearted, entertaining drama. The opening shot provides a vista of the town of Whitby across the river as the miners make their way to the dockside, stopping at a kiosk advertising 'Teas' where they take some refreshment before seeking accommodation for the weekend. The opening banter with the tea man introduces the comic tone that pervades the drama, suggesting this will be no earnest drama of social realism, an impression which is enhanced by the play being filmed in colour (rather than the black and white of Ken Loach's 1971 *Play for Today, The Rank and File*):

Tea man (John Comer): 'Fishing are yer?'
Art (Brian Glover): 'Aye.'
Tea man: 'Season's over, you know that do yer?'
Ern (Ray Mort): 'We know that but fish is still there.'

Tea man: 'Off the end are yer?'

Art: 'End?'

Tea man: 'Of the pier ...'

Art: 'Boat!'

Tea man: 'Season's over.'

Ern: 'Season's over he says, season's over!'

Tea man: 'Aye aye aye, no truculence.'

Art: 'He's right, you know, the season is over. We'll find it difficult to catch fish, right?'

Tea man: 'You'll find it difficult to find owt, let alone fish. Funny 'ats, candy floss, sticks o' rock, anything, even ice creams.'

Abe (Doug Livingstone): 'E's taking us for trippers'.'

Ern: 'You taking us for trippers?'

Abe: 'E is though, taking us for trippers'.'

Tea man: 'Look if you tripped 'ere, then yer trippers'.'

Art: 'Look, look, let me be the peacemaker.' [To Abe and Ern]: 'What my friend means, that we aren't trippers in a derogatory sense of the word. You get me meaning.' [To the Tea man]: 'You'll get me meaning don't you?' [To Abe and Ern]: 'We aren't funny 'ats and kiss-me-quicks'.'

Tea man: 'Aye no offence lads, no offence. I mean I wasn't insinuating anything of the sort.'

Ern: 'No, no, no, no offence at all mate, that's alright.'

Abe: 'That's alright.'

Tea man: 'I mean if yer fishermen, well that's not trippers. You see trippers isn't fishermen as a rule.'

Art: 'That's alright then, great.'

Tea man: 'Well best o' luck when you get out there lads. If you can find any fish.'[15]

Two of the main signifiers of regionality are evident in this opening sequence, one linguistic and the other visual: dialect and setting. The Yorkshire accents of the three miners and the tea man would be sufficient, if this was a studio drama, to locate its regionality, but the filming of the scene on location in Whitby confirms the regional setting, providing a guarantee of verisimilitude in a way that studio drama is unable to do. As David Rose says: 'There's a limit to the imagery that can be conjured up in the studio. Film can say so much else. Space is created!' This is immediately evident in the opening scene when the miners walk down to the quayside to the teas kiosk, framed in long shot to reveal the harbour behind. Then in the shot/reverse shot exchange between the miners and the tea man the placing of the camera inside the kiosk frames the miners with the spectacular panorama of the entrance to Whitby harbour behind them, providing a constant visual reminder of the setting and the reason for their visit. After a comic interlude when they book into a guest house, they will shortly be seen leaving the harbour on a fishing boat as they embark on their fishing trip. Not only does Michael Williams's cinematography emphasise 'space' in these opening shots, it also emphasises the 'sense of place' that David Rose felt was so crucial to regional television drama:

> That was why we tried to up the stakes in film as opposed to studio. Within *Play for Today* we had a higher percentage of film as opposed to studio than London had and I thought that was necessary in the regions because it was about people, but it was about where they lived. I keep on saying: 'a sense of place'. It's difficult to realise it in the studio.[16]

What the opening scene also emphasises is that *The Fishing Party* is going to be a character-based drama, with a strong emphasis on sharp, witty dialogue. This emphasis on character and caustic dialogue is typical of Peter Terson's writing.

Terson repeated the formula in the second *Play for Today* for English Regions Drama, *Shakespeare – or Bust* (BBC1, 8 January 1973), in which the same three Yorkshire miners (again played by Brian Glover, Ray Mort and Douglas Livingstone) go on a pilgrimage to Stratford-upon-Avon, by canal boat. According to BBC Audience Research, *Shakespeare – or Bust* was even more favourably received than *The Fishing Party* with 93 per cent of the audience research group finding the play 'thoroughly entertaining' (compared to 82 per cent for *The Fishing Party*). The filming of the play on location was clearly appreciated by most of the audience who 'had nothing but praise for a very "natural" production with a nice varied pace, the scenery along the canal and the shots of the Royal Shakespeare Theatre at night (all beautifully photographed) being thought to have enhanced the true to life atmosphere of the play'.[17]

English Regions Drama had clearly hit on a popular formula with Terson's plays. The BBC Audience Research Report for *Shakespeare – or Bust* also noted a number of viewers expressing a desire 'to see more of the lads and their adventures'. Terson duly obliged with *Three for the Fancy* (BBC1, 11 April 1974), another *Play for Today* featuring the same three characters who were this time seen entering their prize pets for the Bradford Championship Show.[18]

Terson's comic screenplays illustrate the difference between the plays English Regions Drama contributed to the *Play for Today* series and the dominant tradition of social realism in BBC drama, established in the early 1960s with *Z Cars* and evident in plays such as *Cathy Come Home*, *The Lump*, *The Big Flame*, *Edna, The Inebriate Woman* (1971) and *Hard Labour* (1973). Despite his long association with *Z Cars* and *Softly, Softly* in the 1960s David Rose was intent on English Regions Drama offering more than social realism and welcomed imaginative drama of all kinds:

> I was looking for something . . . that people did remember because it really touched them and made them aware of something a little bit more than a story . . . to give them a social awareness was part of it, yes; but I hope that doesn't reduce the opportunity that was given for imagination, because sometimes when you mention social awareness it can get a bit 'grey' and I wanted it to be bright! – for there to be bright lights shining through as well! (quoted in Millington and Nelson, 1986: 24)

Consequently the drama produced at Pebble Mill in the 1970s and early 1980s traversed the dramatic spectrum, from comedy to fantasy, domestic drama to thrillers, soap opera to social realism, and included both historical subjects and contemporary drama.

Following *Shakespeare – or Bust* the third English Regions Drama *Play for Today* to be screened was Alan Plater's *Land of Green Ginger* (BBC1, 15 January 1973). By the 1970s Plater was an established playwright, writing for television, radio and the theatre. One of his most 'regional' plays, *Close the Coalhouse Door* (BBC1, 22 October 1969), about a mining community in the North East of England, was produced as a musical for the theatre before being made into a *Wednesday Play* and his *Tonight We Meet Arthur Pendlebury* (BBC2, 19 October 1972) was produced as a *Thirty-Minute Theatre* play by English Regions Drama shortly before *Land of Green Ginger* was screened.

Plater, who was born in Newcastle but grew up in Hull from the age of three, described in a 1977 article how a remark by Joan Littlewood – 'You can walk the streets of Hull and hear the people talking poetry' – provided him with the impetus to start writing from his own experience: 'I discovered what as a native Geordie I should have known all along – that in everyday speech there is a richness and music that makes the voice the most powerful and sensitive instrument for human emotion: and that this exists as a tool for the dramatist at its most useful when the voice speaks with a local accent or dialect' (Plater, 1977: 38). Plater applied this wisdom to his scripts for radio, television and the theatre throughout the 1960s but it was not until *Land of Green Ginger* that he had the opportunity to place his characters in authentic regional locations, instead of the artificial sets of the theatre or television studio. Like *The Fishing Party*, *Land of Green Ginger* was filmed on location, in Hull, and Plater was able to place his characters in their environment, to extend his drama beyond having his characters speak 'with a local accent or dialect' to the extent of having the environment itself feature in the drama:

> [W]hen you move outside the studio the power of the visual image is much greater, because there's more to look at. You can go out into the streets of Hull, down to the dockside or some place, you can stand up a character and you point a camera at him, and behind him there'll be a ship and behind him some cranes and behind him the river and behind him the other bank of the river and then some clouds and perhaps an aeroplane flying over, and you've got five, six, ten layers of significance. It's a very basic thing about the job that not many people understand or appreciate. If I'm writing for film I give little drawings. If I'm writing for studio I just write the words. (quoted in Hunt, 1981: 137)

Plater might have been describing the opening sequence of *The Fishing Party* here, as well as *Land of Green Ginger* – the sentiments apply equally to both, as indeed they do to all of the filmed drama produced by English Regions Drama. Regionality could certainly be conveyed in studio drama – through the words, the accents, the story – but film enhanced the possibilities for conveying a 'sense of place', adding, as Plater puts it, 'five, six, ten layers of significance'.

The opening shots of *Land of Green Ginger*, accompanied by a folk song about a 'north country maid' returning to 'her north country home', introduce the two central characters and establish the theme of the play. The first shot is of a trawler at sea, which will become associated with Mike (John Flanagan), the fisherman boyfriend of Sally (Gwen Taylor), the 'north country maid' whom we see in the second shot hurrying to catch a train from London's King's Cross station to take her home to Hull. On the train she has a conversation with a journalist who is 'writing a series about the regions'. He asks her if she knows 'The Land of Green Ginger'. She says, 'It's a street isn't it?' – but she's not sure. We never find out if there is a street in Hull called 'Land of Green Ginger' – although Albert Hunt quotes from Plater's 'scripted suggestions' for the opening sequence: 'If it's a little misty and magical that's all to the good. You don't expect cold reason in a town that calls a street the Land of Green Ginger' (Hunt, 1981: 138) – but it becomes clear that the title is a metaphor for a 'misty and magical' city which, like many towns and cities in the 1970s, was changing as old industries and ways of life declined and young people sought new horizons. Sally has left the city of her birth and is returning for the weekend to visit her mother. She also looks up her old boyfriend, who is more firmly wedded to his birthplace, with a job on a fishing trawler and a chance to skipper his own boat.

Land of Green Ginger has a melancholy quality to it which the cinematography – lyrical shots of the city and the sea – and the evocative folk songs of The Watersons help to reinforce. The fact that the city is changing is emphasised on Sally's arrival when she visits her mother who has moved (or been moved) to a high-rise block of flats on a new housing estate: 'Is this it?', Sally asks the taxi driver uncertainly. 'Homes for heroes, love . . . That's what the planner's say. Alcatraz me brother calls it.' Afterwards Sally goes to see her old house and finds it has been knocked down and is just a pile of bricks in a wasteland of demolished houses.

After meeting up with Mike, her boyfriend, they go to see where the new bridge over the Humber is due to be built, a sign of the new prosperity which is supposedly going to transform the city, but Mike is cynical about the prospects. Later Sally tells Mike she is not going to take the job abroad that she has been offered and that she intends to return to Hull, but she is not happy about him continuing to work on the fishing boats, because of the danger. This is not a drama where the happy couple are to be reunited and get married. In fact there is no clear resolution to the drama, which ends with Sally returning to London on the train, where she meets the same journalist who asks her if she found the Land of Green Ginger: 'No, we didn't look hard enough.' The final shots of fishing trawlers setting off to sea, of the docks and the city, are accompanied by a reprise of the Watersons song heard at the beginning, a lament for a time 'when the oak and the ash and the bonny ivy tree, all flourish and bloom in my north country'.

Not only is *Land of Green Ginger* firmly placed in its locality, there is a lyrical, melancholy quality to the play which derives largely from Alan Plater's script, but is reinforced by the evocative, traditional folk music of The Watersons. The 'regionality' of the drama is illustrated visually by Michael Williams's sparkling cinematography ('sparkling' not being a word usually associated with studio drama) which helps to create the 'sense of place' so important to the filmed plays produced by English Regions Drama. This air of regionality is reinforced by the authentic, naturalistic performances of the cast, with some parts being played by local, non-professional actors.[19]

The theme of separation from Northern roots was continued in the next *Play for Today* from English Regions Drama, David Halliwell's *Steps Back* (BBC1, 14 May 1973). Also filmed on location, with photography again by Michael Williams, *Steps Back* was also about a character returning to their home town after a long period away. In this case, Gerry (David Hill) is returning to Brighouse in Yorkshire with his fiancée, Nita (Harriet Harper): 'Fifteen years since I was forced t'leave, forced t'leave me roots, the territory of me heart' (*Radio Times*, 14 May 1973). In tandem with Peter Terson's comedies, a theme was clearly emerging in these early plays from English Regions Drama. Not only was each clearly 'regional' in its setting, subject matter, character and dialect, there was a recurrent theme of loss, of separation from (Northern) roots, with an accompanying discourse about the impact on Northern communities of social and economic change. It was evident also in Barry Collins's *The Lonely Man's Lover* (BBC1, 17 January 1974), only this time the story concerned the impact that an outsider, Daniel (David Bailie), has on a Yorkshire village and on one person in particular, Lizzie (Jan Francis), who is intrigued by him and finally gets pregnant by him. Once again there is a melancholy tone to the drama which is underlined by Lizzie's voiceover and the use of music by the Yorkshire folk group The Oldham Tinkers.

While each of these plays had contemporary settings their themes evoked the past and the impact of social change on Northern communities. However, another play produced by English Regions Drama in 1973 was clearly far more 'historical', dealing with the subject of the Great Plague of the seventeenth century and its impact on a village in Derbyshire. Written and directed by Don Taylor, *The Roses of Eyam* (BBC2, 12 June 1973) was first produced as a stage play in 1970 and it became English Regions Drama's first full-length studio drama, transmitted on BBC2 as a two-hour production. Taylor was a great advocate of studio drama, arguing, against the grain of the prevailing trend towards filmed drama in the late 1960s and 1970s, that studio drama had its own distinct aesthetic and was the only 'true television drama':

> Is there any kind of television drama that can be described as indig-
> enous, in the sense that it is not available in any other form, and cannot
> be produced by any other medium? Only one kind of work answers the
> definition: the original studio television play. This is the true television
> drama, the form that cannot be produced in any other way, that only
> works in the lounges, drawing rooms and bedrooms of the nation. For
> genuine television a cinema screen is too big, and a cinema ambience
> not sufficiently intimate. Studio television is the only genuine and
> irreplaceable TV drama. (Taylor, 1990: 254)

Taylor had long cherished an ambition to be a playwright – in his autobiography he records that he began writing *The Roses of Eyam* as early as 1961 (Taylor, 1990: 17) – but his first play was not produced until 1967, by which time he had been directing the work of other television playwrights for seven years, numbering among his productions the early television plays of David Mercer, plus plays by N.J. Crisp, Hugh Whitemore and the Birmingham writer David Turner. Having seen *The Roses of Eyam* produced in the theatre in 1970 (directed by Anton Rodgers), Taylor adapted the play for television in 1973, directing it himself. Its production marked a distinct departure for English Regions Drama from the contemporary subjects of the department's previous plays. As a dramatisation of a three-hundred-year-old historical event, *The Roses of Eyam* was clearly no 'play for today' and, although it was produced by David Rose, its production as a studio drama seemed to run counter to Rose's advocacy of filmed drama because of its ability to create a 'sense of place'. Yet at two hours in length, compared to the fifty to seventy minutes of the filmed dramas made for *Play for Today*, *The Roses of Eyam* would have been a very expensive drama to produce on film, even if Don Taylor had wished to do so.

The issue of its merits and limitations as a studio drama came up at the BBC Television Weekly Programme Review meeting the day after its transmission, when the various BBC executives present discussed what the play might have lost by being recorded in the studio as opposed to being filmed on location:

> C.P.S.Tel. noted astonishingly good make-up in this dramatisation of
> the story of plague in a Derbyshire village in 1665, but he felt the pro-

gramme had cried out to be done on film . . . Shaun Sutton (H.D.G.Tel.) welcomed a major regional offering, produced by David Rose (H.E.R.D.) and set in a theatrical key. He understood C.P.S.Tel.'s point about film but the expense of finding a seventeenth century village and taking the whole cast to film in it would have been prohibitive.

C.BBC-2 whilst commending the production, accepted one or two weaknesses which had made the fact that it was a stage setting rather obvious, with no birds in the village, and an absence of audible silence, so that the drama seemed to be taking place in a vacuum.[20]

BBC executives were clearly conscious of the aesthetic consequences of recording *The Roses of Eyam* in the studio but the question of budget, given the historical setting of the play and its large cast of forty-two actors, was obviously a determining factor in its production as a studio drama.

According to BBC Audience Research the fact that the play was recorded in the studio did not adversely affect the response of most of the audience, with only a few people commenting that the studio sets 'at times detracted from the illusion of reality':

> This 'grimly realistic' account of the 1665 plague in the Derbyshire village of Eyam was exceptionally well received, many viewers acclaiming it as one of the most impressive and compelling television broadcasts they had ever seen . . . The sets, costumes and production as a whole were generally commended and said to be 'realistic'. The make-up for the plague victims was 'remarkable', and horribly convincing. A small group, however, were somewhat disappointed that the village houses were 'obviously a studio job'; while appreciating the impossibility of discovering an 'unspoilt' location, they found that the sets at times detracted from the illusion of reality.[21]

Around ninety per cent of the BBC Viewing Panel thought *The Roses of Eyam* was 'thoroughly entertaining' with an 'excellent plot' and was 'definitely out-of-the ordinary'. English Regions Drama, it seemed, could do no wrong, whether it was producing contemporary filmed plays such as *The Fishing Party* and *Land of Green Ginger* or historical studio dramas such as *The Roses of Eyam*: clearly there was an appetite for 'regional' drama of all kinds.

Although the vast majority of the department's plays were contemporary, *The Roses of Eyam* was by no means an aberration. In fact the next English Regions Drama production to be transmitted was a studio version of Nikolai Gogol's 1835 short story *Diary of a Madman* (BBC2, 23 August 1973), featuring Victor Henry in a virtuoso role that he had been performing on stage in a touring show produced by Michael Wearing, who was soon to join English Regions Drama as a script editor:

> Victor and I toured that around the country, which sort of grew out of our joint experiences with 7:84, John McGrath's company. Anyway we did that out of the back of a van really and David [Rose] saw it in Wolverhampton, I think, somewhere like that, somewhere in the Midlands – we played it in all sorts of strange venues: art schools, fire stations, the occasional theatre – and he decided to do it for television. So that's actually when I first met David and then . . . this vacancy occurred so they asked me to do it . . . my impression always was that Shaun Sutton had set David up with this little department in Birmingham and I always thought that what the BBC as a whole probably expected out of that department was the dramatic equivalent of *Gardeners' World* . . . but of course he fell into it . . . David was gradually expanding the basis of that department with, I suspect, a lot of backstage help from Shaun Sutton.[22]

Like many BBC English Regions Drama recruits, Wearing worked in the theatre before joining the department, illustrating once again the close links between English Regions Drama and regional/community theatre. *Diary of a Madman*, however, was not a typical production for the department, not just because of its transposition from stage to screen but because it was an adaptation of a piece of nineteenth-century Russian literature. Part of the attraction in producing it for television may have been the virtuoso performance of Victor Henry, an exciting actor who had been in one of English Regions Drama's first productions, Arthur Hopcraft's *Thirty-Minute Theatre* play *Said the Preacher*.[23]

While the majority of English Regions Drama productions were contemporary there was another significant historical drama produced in 1976. *The Witches of Pendle* (BBC2, 19 June 1976) was written by the author of *The Lonely Man's Lover*, Barry Collins, but this time Collins's subject was the historically documented persecution of a number of Lancashire women as witches in the seventeenth century. Unlike Don Taylor's *The Roses of Eyam*, *The Witches of Pendle* was shot on film, enabling the play to be set in authentic Lancashire locations. That the play was not as long as *The Roses of Eyam* (seventy-five minutes compared to two hours) may have made possible the use of film, despite the increased cost, but by 1976 English Regions Drama had proved itself an accomplished and economical department and the amount of drama it was producing, on film and in the studio, was steadily increasing.

Among the plays that helped to forge Birmingham's growing reputation for original, innovative drama with a strong regional flavour was David Rudkin's *Penda's Fen* (BBC1, 21 March 1974). Rudkin had previously written and adapted plays for radio, the theatre, television and the cinema, prior to writing two short experimental plays for English Regions Drama in 1972–73. He had a reputation as a highly original writer, interested in classical and mythical themes, and his work for English Regions Drama provides an illustration of how far the department was prepared to go in producing dramas of the imagination, as well as dramas of social realism. In an illuminating study of Rudkin's work David Ian Rabey describes how

> Rudkin's drama works through intensely poetic language and similar stage images to create moral landscapes which uniquely externalise inner turmoil. His plays are not naturalistic: rather, they are reinterpretations of narratives from cultural history or new-forged creation myths which assault disturbingly the settled priorities of self-possession as achieved through political 'rationalities' which are exposed as essentially sanctifications of self-obsession, fixation and fear. (Rabey, 1997: 11)

Penda's Fen provides an exemplary illustration of this. It is a complex, non-naturalistic drama focusing on a middle-class teenage boy, Stephen Franklin (Spencer Banks), growing up in the Malvern Hills in Worcestershire. Stephen loves the music of Edward Elgar, a quintessentially English composer whose music was inspired by the same landscape, and the play opens with Elgar's *The Dream of Gerontius* playing over panoramic images of the English countryside, accompanied by Stephen's voiceover: 'Oh my country, I say over and over: I *am* one of your sons, it is true. I am. I *am*. Yet how shall I show my love?' Stephen's love of Elgar's music is bound up with his patriotism and love of the English landscape, but it is also complicated by a growing awareness of his own homosexuality.

Rudkin takes this complex of emotions as the focus for an exploration of mythological themes, expressed partly through the symbolic imagery of Stephen's imagination. As Stephen wakes from a troubled dream a demon appears on his bed, representing his suppressed sexuality; sheltering from the rain he meets an elderly, wheelchair-bound Edward Elgar in a derelict cottage; an angel appears in the English countryside; the aisle of a church cracks open as Stephen plays music on the church organ; and towards the end of the drama the pagan English King, Penda, appears on a hillside. Narratively and ideologically these elements form part of Stephen's contemporary experience as he negotiates both his adolescence and his sense of 'Englishness'. As Rabey observes:

> Stephen Franklin comforts himself with a sense of his own participation in the English myth of historical harmony and social continuity; he contemplates the rural Midlands landscape shared by Elgar and himself, proud in his own potential beckoning into the generational succession of an English elect, capable of reading the mythological dimensions of a landscape in terms of Heaven and Hell, angels and devils. (Rabey, 1997: 63)

It is a sign of Rudkin's success in creating a convincing narrative world in *Penda's Fen* that his iconography of angels, demons and pagan kings does not appear anachronistic or ridiculous, although credit must also be given to Alan Clarke's 'realistic' direction (treating the supernatural elements as naturalistic) and also to Michael Williams, once again, for his fine cinematography. No opportunity is lost to 'show the region' in the play and *Penda's Fen* again illustrates the importance of filming on location for conveying a 'sense of place'. In this case, shooting on location was essential in order to realise fully the creative vision of the writer, as David Rudkin indicated in an article in the *Radio Times*:

> I think of *Penda's Fen* as more a film for television than a TV play – not just because it was shot in real buildings on actual film but because of its visual force . . . It was conceived as a film and written visually. Some people think visual questions are none of the writer's business – that he should provide the action and leave it to the director to picture it all out. For me, writing for the screen is a business of deciding not only *what* is to be shown but *how* it is to be shown. (Rudkin, 1974: 12)

When *Penda's Fen* was repeated on Channel Four in 1990 a new introduction by David Rudkin (filmed against the backdrop of the Worcestershire landscape in which the drama is set) highlighted the importance of history, landscape and identity to the dramatic mythology of *Penda's Fen*:

> This is Three Choirs country, landscape of the great Anglican cathedrals of the Severn and the Wye. Though Severn and Wye were those rivers'

native names long before Angle or Saxon or Christian, or Roman soldier even, came. Behind me there is Bredon Hill, Housman country. And westward, nearer than they seem, the Malvern Hills, of Langland, Piers Plowman, of Edward Elgar, *The Dream of Gerontius*, introduction and allegro, quintessential, visionary England. But Bredon isn't an English name either. That's ancient British, or Celtic, Brey Doon, 'hill of the fort'. As for Malvern there, well, that name has been pure Welsh, or British, for a good two thousand years, 'Mawl Vryn', 'bare hill', layer upon layer upon layer of inheritance. What's in a name? The devil of a lot. Or, in the light of this film, the demon of a lot.[24]

Apart from giving an insight into the history and mythology inform-ing the drama (as well as providing a flavour of Rudkin's writing – many of the characters share his own rather arcane form of linguistic expression) Rudkin's reference to the 'layer[s] of inheritance' to be found in the place names echoes Alan Plater's description of the addi-tional 'layers of significance' made possible by filming on location, as opposed to recording in the studio. In *Penda's Fen* Rudkin's evocation of Englishness and his unique linguistic style is perfectly comple-mented by the expansive and imaginative visual style brought to the drama by the director and cameraman.

Penda's Fen was directed, somewhat surprisingly, by Alan Clarke, one of the leading television directors of the 1970s and 1980s, best known for his work on contemporary realist film and television drama such as the controversial *Scum*, banned by the BBC in 1977, ostensi-bly because of its violence, and remade by Clarke as a feature film in 1979. Clarke had previously directed Peter Terson's *The Last Train Through the Harecastle Tunnel* (1969) and, for English Regions Drama, Ted Whitehead's *Thirty-Minute Theatre* play *Under the Age* (1972) and it was David Rose who suggested Clarke as a director for *Penda's Fen*. Rudkin was initially uncertain about Rose's suggestion and Clarke was equally uncertain about the 'intellectual' nature of the material. Rudkin, however, recognising that Rose 'wasn't given to perverse matchmaking', reassured Clarke about the subject matter of the play, suggesting that 'the important thing is the emotions' and noting that the basic story is not so dissimilar to that of other plays directed by Clarke:

I had not associated Alan Clarke with that type of what you might loosely call visionary, poetic material . . . He seemed to be identified with a naturalistic polemic and *Penda's Fen* doesn't seem to come under that rubric. But when the chips are down, *Penda's Fen* is just about somebody who has to kick things over, has to become free, and in the end it was the same story and the same issues which concerned Alan. (quoted in Kelly, 1998: 70)

Barry Hanson had previously worked with both Rudkin and Clarke – in fact Hanson had himself directed Rudkin's *Atrocity* (BBC2, 15 March 1973). Although he was not credited on *Penda's Fen*, Hanson was involved in helping to set up the production. He recognised just how remarkable and original the play was:

> If you're talking about writers who are distinctive, in a way there isn't anyone quite like Rudkin, and Alan appreciated that. And Alan himself had a mind that was rather bleak and elemental. *Penda's Fen* is a play of mystical Olde English, a boy beset by angels and devils, and a pagan king emerging through an earth that held various appalling nuclear secrets. It also had Mary Whitehouse thinly disguised in it, and all sorts of obsessions and fears that were abroad in that early part of the 1970s. You name it, they all cropped up, and Alan was perfectly at home in that environment. I remember a marvellous matte shot where the aisle of a church was rent asunder. You'd never get away with it on the BBC now. (quoted in Kelly, 1998: 68)

The playwright David Hare was also astonished by the originality and striking imagery of *Penda's Fen*. Hare was one of a number of writers and directors who gravitated towards BBC English Regions Drama in the 1970s, attracted by the creative environment David Rose was nurturing at Pebble Mill and conscious that plays were being produced there that were unlikely to get commissioned within the Drama Department in London:

> We were all working together on the same corridor at BBC Birmingham when Alan was making *Penda's Fen* – Stephen Frears and Mike Leigh, Alan Bleasdale and I, Willy Russell. And there was David Rose just being a wonderful impresario. When I saw *Penda's Fen*, I just couldn't believe it. And that is the whole BBC Birmingham culture right there, which was David Rose letting people do what they wanted and nobody in London knowing what was going on. You know: 'The Earth splits open? Oh yeah?' There's just no way a London producer and script editor would have been having that. But my God, that film went out at nine-thirty at night on a majority channel, it's incredible – an hour and a half long. And how bold to do it! (quoted in Kelly, 1998: 69)

It is significant that when *Penda's Fen* was repeated on Channel Four in 1990 it was shown as part of a series called *Film 4 Today*.[25]

Just as he had in 1974, Rudkin again referred to *Penda's Fen* as a 'film' rather than a play in his introduction to the Channel Four screening and the re-designation of this *Play for Today* as a *Film 4 Today* illustrates the categorical change which had taken place between the 1970s, when 'single play' was still a term in common currency, and the 1990s, when very few studio plays were being made and the single play had effectively been replaced by the television film. This development was largely as a result of Channel Four's investment in film-making in the 1980s, significantly under the leadership of David Rose who left Pebble Mill in 1981 to become Senior Commissioning Editor for Fiction at Channel Four.

In the 1970s, however, English Regions Drama, like most drama departments, was still producing a large amount of studio drama, partly to justify the investment in new studios at Pebble Mill, while taking every opportunity (especially within *Play for Today*) to make what were effectively television films. Shooting entirely on film increased production costs considerably and while a third of the dramas made for *Play for Today* from 1970 to 1984 were all-film dramas the majority were either studio recordings or a combination of studio and film. The drama 'hybrid' – where film is used for exterior scenes while interiors are recorded electronically in the studio – was very much in evidence in the 1970s, not only in plays but also in series and serials. The three English Regions Drama plays screened as part of the *Play for Today* series in January 1975 included two all-film plays and one 'hybrid', a mainly studio drama with filmed scenes at the beginning and end of the play.

The After Dinner Game (BBC1, 16 January 1975), written by Malcolm Bradbury and Christopher Bigsby, was the first *Play for Today* produced by English Regions Drama not to be shot entirely on film. Nevertheless, the sixty-five-minute play opens with an extended sequence on film, establishing the location as that of a new university and introducing the central characters as they return at the start of a new academic year. It is easy to see why film was used at the beginning – to establish the location – but film continues to be used in the opening scenes when the Vice-Chancellor delivers a speech in a large hall, inviting a new professor to make a statement about the need for an alliance between education and commerce in higher education (at which point several people leave the hall). Film continues to be used when staff are queuing in the canteen but as Mark Childers (Timothy West) sits down with colleagues there is a cut to video and a studio set, the quality of the image changing noticeably as the action scales down from the larger staging of the filmed opening scenes. Continuity is achieved (after a fashion) by the addition of canteen noises offscreen but the action remains with the smaller group of characters in a three-camera studio set-up. All subsequent scenes, until the end, are studio scenes and the play is dialogue-led as the central characters explore the central thesis of the drama: a discourse between the educational traditionalists and the modernists about the future of higher education, which takes place during and after a dinner party at the home of the Vice-Chancellor.

Unlike the previous English Regions Drama productions for *Play for Today*, *The After Dinner Game* was less intent on 'showing the region', other than in the establishing shots at the beginning, than it was in taking a satirical look at higher education. Befitting its subject, its narrative was far more discursive than that of the Terson, Plater and Collins plays and its 'regionality' less defined. This was an 'interior' drama, physically and intellectually, a play about new developments in academia and about opposing educational ideologies, which was more suited to the enclosed environment of the studio, where the claustrophobic 'after dinner game' could more easily be staged, than it was to the open spaces of the campus or the surrounding environment.

Malcolm Bradbury and Christopher Bigsby were writing very much from their own experience of higher education – both were lecturers at the new University of East Anglia (UEA) – and *The After Dinner Game* was an example of a different tradition of playwriting at Pebble Mill, what Michael Wearing refers to as the 'academic' tradition, as opposed to the popular, Northern working-class tradition represented by writers such as Terson and Plater:

> [T]here was a kind of populist route which was exemplified by people like Terson and in another way people like Alan Bleasdale and Willy Russell, you know, people who had a real sort of street grounding in life . . . and there was another aspect of it which was slightly more academic, which was people like Bradbury and in the end Ian McEwan, who of course had been at UEA doing Malcolm's Creative Writing course. So it was like a kind of weird alumni system, tentacles reaching out all over the place.[26]

Other 'routes', or traditions, within English Regions Drama included the poetic/*avant garde*/fantasy strand, represented initially by John Hopkins and David Rudkin and reinforced later on by writers such as Alan Garner (*The Red Shift*) and John Fletcher (*Stargazy on Zummerdown*). Another strand was the multicultural one represented by writers such as Tara Prem (*A Touch of Eastern Promise* and *The Olympian Way*), Barry Reckord (*Club Havana*) and Michael Abbensetts (*Black Christmas* and *Empire Road*).

The other all-film plays accompanying *The After Dinner Game* in the January 1975 *Play for Today* season included a further example of the Northern working-class tradition – Willy Russell's *The Death of a Young Young Man* (BBC1, 30 January 1975), a tragic story of Billy (Gary Brown), a young Liverpool lad who tries to escape the city estate where he lives to work on a farm, but finds he cannot escape the ridicule of his friends, whose goading of Benny, a farmhand with learning difficulties, leads to a tragic denouement in which Billy is killed. The contrast between the claustrophobia of the inner city scenes and the liberation of escaping to the countryside was well realised by director Viktors Ritelis and film cameraman Michael Williams, illustrating once again the advantage of shooting on film for achieving a 'sense of place'.

Meanwhile the filmed play that preceded *The After Dinner Game* on to the screen represented a completely new departure for English Regions Drama, and for *Play for Today*. Written by another Liverpool-born writer, Philip Martin, and set in Birmingham, with the author himself playing a villainous nightclub owner with a rich Birmingham accent, *Gangsters* (BBC1, 9 January 1975) confounded most people's expectations of what constituted a *Play for Today*. It was not only that the drama was an action-packed, fast-paced thriller, directed by Philip Saville in the style of a Hollywood B-movie, but that it featured the various ethnic communities living in the city in a story involving drug trafficking, heroin addiction, illegal immigration and sleazy nightclubs. For English Regions Drama this was a completely different concept of 'regionality' from that articulated in *The Fishing Party, Land of Green Ginger, The Lonely Man's Lover* and *Penda's Fen*. The iconography in *Gangsters* was resolutely urban and contemporary and the play was entirely lacking in any hint of melancholy or nostalgia for a disappearing way of life, ingredients that had characterised some of the department's previous dramas in the *Play for Today* series. The cast of *Gangsters* was multiracial (English, Irish, West Indian, Chinese, Indian, Pakistani) and the style of the drama was fast-paced and non-naturalistic. Generically this was a contemporary gangster film, with strong elements of *film noir*, evident in both the characterisation (a *femme fatale*, a heroic but flawed male protagonist) and the iconography. Many scenes were shot at night on neon-lit city streets, in nightclubs, in car parks and underpasses, with many typical features of the 1970s Birmingham cityscape: Spaghetti Junction, deserted canals, derelict industrial buildings. Furthermore, as might be expected of a play with a multi-racial cast, there was a wide array of voices and dialects, with the distinctive Birmingham accent of the nightclub owner Rawlinson (Philip Martin) prominent in the drama. Martin, who was returning to acting after a ten-year break during which he had concentrated on writing, felt that the rhythms of the Birmingham accent made it more distinctive than the 'thicker' Wolverhampton and Black Country accent, even though, geographically, these were neighbouring regions. Once again, dialect is one of the defining features of regionality in the play and Martin's distinction between the Birmingham and Black Country accents illustrates just how important accent can be in defining the regional specificity of a drama.[27]

According to producer Barry Hanson, the genesis of *Gangsters* lay in a trip David Rose made to London, to attend a meeting at the BBC, when he saw *The French Connection* (USA, 1971) at the cinema. On his return to Birmingham, Rose said to Hanson: 'Listen, it was a pretty good picture. Maybe we ought to do something like that here' (Hanson, 1983: 24). As David Rose explains, they decided to get Philip Martin to do some research to see if there was any mileage in the idea:

> Someone said to me, 'Look you've got some money in your budget you're not using, script editor money', so the suggestion was that Phillip should come to Birmingham. We invited him to come and live for three months in Birmingham and we paid him a sort of script editor fee, at that level, and said that if at the end of three months you find you've got something you'd like to write about by all means do it, if not, you know, goodbye and good luck. And he said he'd got this idea for *Gangsters*, which I think was not only regional, Birmingham very much based, but it was delving into our ethnic situation that television really hadn't touched a great deal.[28]

It is a sign of the autonomy enjoyed by English Regions Drama that the department was willing and able to finance Philip Martin for three months to research a project with no guarantee that anything would come of it. It is another example of what David Hare describes as the enlightened 'BBC Birmingham culture', with David Rose acting as 'a wonderful impresario'. That such a different kind of regional drama could be produced in Birmingham is also a sign of David Rose's willingness to consider all kinds of ideas for drama, especially if they departed from the dominant tradition of social realism. The highly contrasting examples of *The Fishing Party*, *Land of Green Ginger*, *Penda's Fen* and *Gangsters* provide ample evidence of this liberal and enlightened commissioning policy.

Philip Martin's research showed there was the potential for a contemporary thriller set in Birmingham about drug trafficking and the exploitation of illegal immigrants. He also wanted to explore the conditions that led to the rise of the National Front in the 1970s, and racism was an undercurrent throughout the play, but crucially he wanted to explore these issues through the genre of the gangster film/ *film noir*, rather than through a more 'realist' approach (such as that taken in David Edgar's 1978 *Play for Today* about the National Front, *Destiny*).

Gangsters was dismissed by most of the critics, who were clearly offended by this attempt to deal with serious issues in the style of a Hollywood B-movie, rather than through the more traditional *Play for Today* genre of social realism. One writer, however, was much more positive about the play. Writing in *New Society*, Albert Hunt recognised 'just how radical *Gangsters* was' and welcomed its attempt to engage with contemporary social reality using the values and tropes of popular culture:

> The play established from the beginning that we're not in the world of 'documentary reality'. The colour related to the garish colours of American horror comics, harsh purples, pinks and greens. Here, says the colour, is all the vulgarity of the comics plonked in the world of Spaghetti Junction.
>
> Again, the pace was that of the fast, hard-hitting Hollywood gangster movie, and also that of the quick-fire *Comedians* show, with its machine-gun patter of jokes. *Gangsters* opens and closes with a Brummy comedian telling the same joke: 'There was this Pakistani died of eating a Chinese curry . . .' The comedian becomes an image who's referred back to at various points throughout the play. He's part of the counterpoint in a tightly woven story involving protection rackets for illegal immigrants, the use of blacks as a hard squad, the murder of a black stripper, and the forced repatriation of an Indian who refuses to pay his protection dues . . .
>
> By applying the conventions of US movies to British reality, *Gangsters* made us see that reality in a new alarming way. Above all, it did so while

creating an entertainment that didn't have the mass audience reaching
for the switch to see if there was something more exciting on the other
side. (Hunt, 1975)

Indeed, *Gangsters* attracted an audience of eight million, exceeding
the audience tuned in to ITV and BBC2 at the same time, and in the
BBC Audience Research Report the play had a Reaction Index of 73,
'well above the average for the series, which is 58'. The report continued: 'The action of this "tough", "violent", "sordid" story about
the Birmingham underworld . . . made an excellent play, providing
both exciting and compelling viewing, it was mostly agreed' and one
viewer was quoted as saying 'This really was one of the best plays I've
seen for years. It had everything. I sat on the edge of my seat almost
the whole time. Fantastic production. When's the next one by this
team? When's the repeat? MORE PLEASE.'[29]

Philip Saville, who had previously directed one of the two *Second
City Firsts* to be filmed on location using a lightweight mobile OB
unit, wanted *Gangsters* to be fast-moving and entertaining and knew
it had to be made on film (it was shot in seven weeks on 16mm film
at an 'above-the-line' cost of £92,000).[30] Saville was also conscious
of the contemporary resonances in the play and its potential for
controversy:

> Barry said to me 'What do you think about this?' and I said 'I abso-
> lutely love it, but we have to be bold about it. It's not just social
> realism, it's heightened and we have to use the metaphor of the defini-
> tive gangster images, things like that, and integrate it and make it
> entertaining' . . .
>   That was really so ahead of its time on a purely political level, it
> was equivalent today to something that was very political, because
> there was a lot of interesting things done . . . the day it went out
> there was a complete uproar from the Birmingham Council . . . who
> denied any of these things were going on and they thought it was
> outrageous.[31]

As the minutes from the BBC's Television Weekly Review Committee
meeting show, BBC management also had some concerns about a
production 'which had given the service some anxieties, so that cuts
had had to be made in it before transmission and a warning included
in the opening announcement'.[32] The concerns were mainly to do
with the violence in the play and a cut was demanded in a torture
scene near the end, although the production team thought this

change actually heightened the effect because it involved a cutaway, leaving the viewer to imagine the incident rather than actually see it, making it potentially far more disturbing.[33]

In the event, the topicality of *Gangsters* was heightened by the coincidence of a boatload of illegal Asian immigrants being apprehended in the English channel in the same week *Gangsters* was screened. This event gave the play extra publicity and stimulated the debate about the appropriateness of using a popular form of entertainment, such as the gangster film, for the portrayal of serious contemporary issues. *Gangsters* undoubtedly made a considerable impact, more than any previous English Regions Drama production, and its popular success led to the development of two six-part serials by the department. Not only did the original play help to redefine what had previously been thought of as acceptable *Play for Today* material, suggesting that 'serious drama' did not necessarily have to take the form of social realism, it provided a new perspective in the mid-1970s on what a 'regional' television drama might be.

The next group of four English Regions Drama plays in the *Play for Today* series went out in January 1976 and included another significant production: the first play to be set in the South of the country, as opposed to the Midlands or the North. Mike Leigh's *Nuts in May* (BBC1, 13 January 1976) was his second production for English Regions Drama, following *The Permissive Society*, the *Second City First* he made the previous year. In the same year that he made his first *Play for Today*, the Tony Garnett-produced *Hard Labour* (1973), Leigh worked with Alison Steadman and Roger Sloman on a stage play called *Wholesome Glory* in which Steadman and Sloman developed the characters of Candice-Marie and Keith Pratt, who later became the central characters in *Nuts in May*. As Michael Coveney relates in his biography of Leigh, it was while working on *Wholesome Glory* that Leigh, Steadman and Sloman talked about

> how interesting it would be to see these characters enjoying the countryside, on location. The play as it stood was confined to bedsit-land, and when Leigh raised the subject with David Rose, Rose suggested making a film entirely on location around Corfe Castle in Dorset, for the simple reason that he came from Purbeck and no one ever made a film about it! (Coveney, 1997: 100).

Apart from wanting to see his home county on the screen Rose's penchant for filmed drama was evident from his suggestion to Leigh that the play should be shot entirely out of doors (*The Permissive Society* had been one of Leigh's rare studio plays):

> I told him about the quarries in the district and asked him to film every-thing out of doors, under the skies; he reneged only slightly on this condition – there is one sequence of about one minute twenty seconds, in the Greyhound pub near Corfe Castle, and one short scene in a toilet. Apart from that, the only interiors are those of some very small tents. (quoted in Coveney, 1997: 100)

Whereas the Garnett-produced *Hard Labour* had veered more towards social realism in style, *Nuts in May* was a comedy of manners which made excellent use of its Dorset locations, succeeding in 'showing the region' just as well as *The Fishing Party* and *Land of Green Ginger* had done in North Yorkshire and Humberside respec-tively. Although the play owed much to the performances of Alison Steadman and Roger Sloman, it brought Leigh to the attention of a wider public and has since become a cult classic to rival *Abigail's Party* (1977). It is also one of the first films where Leigh was accused of producing caricatures for comic effect, an accusation he vehemently denies, arguing that *Nuts in May* deals with issues of class and society just as seriously as, if not more so than, the more overtly 'social realist' *Hard Labour*:

> Whether in fact it's correct to analyse the likes of *Nuts in May* as caricature remains to be seen. Certainly the mode of the storytelling is more strip cartoon-like ... I would suggest that the nun in *Hard Labour* is much more a caricature in the pejorative sense than any characters, which are actually quite detailed and three dimensional, in *Nuts in May* ... In fact, *Nuts in May* was very consciously liberated from the notion that the only way to say anything about society was to talk about working-class people and say obvious things about them. I mean there are other ways of saying things, indeed that's what *Nuts in May* does. I don't think it has any less to say about class and society than *Hard Labour* and actually I suspect it has more to say in a more coherent and meaningful way than *Hard Labour*. I think *Hard Labour*'s a little bit kind of tautological really, which I don't think *Nuts in May* is. I also think *Nuts in May* has the distinction of being funnier, more entertaining than *Hard Labour*, which is important too. And also I did in *Nuts in May* what I've been doing ever since ... in one form or another, I was deliberately subverting the assumptions of the form. In other words, here was a *Play For Today* but I thought, well why should I make another play that looks like a *Play For Today*, let's get out and

do something fresh, and something that came very naturally to me, so I think that's important.[34]

Nuts in May was certainly very successful in terms of ratings, achieving an audience of nine and a half million, whereas the studio-based play which followed it in the *Play for Today* season, Eric Coltart's *Doran's Box* (BBC1, 20 January 1976), had an audience of just three and a half million (and a very low Reaction Index of 24, compared to the RI of 59 for *Nuts in May*).[35] That the filmed *Play for Today* preceding *Nuts in May*, Watson Gould's *The Other Woman* (BBC1, 6 January 1976), had an even larger audience of ten and a half million may suggest a growing audience preference for filmed plays over studio drama. The number of filmed plays made for *Play for Today* increased steadily during the 1970s, from just six in the 1970–71 season to fifteen in the 1979–80 season. In the 1975–76 season in which *Nuts in May* was shown, ten of the twenty-four plays were made on film, with English Regions Drama contributing three of them.

Like many directors working in television in the 1970s Mike Leigh went on to work in the film industry, making feature films with larger budgets and considerably more production time than was available for making a *Play for Today*. Yet, apart from some minor aesthetic considerations, Leigh felt there was no significant difference between making films for television and making feature films, even though most of the production team working on the films produced by English Regions Drama probably spent more time each year working on *Farming Today* than they did working on dramas for *Play for Today*:

So far as the so-called distinction between film and television, there isn't one really, as far as I'm concerned, because although, apart from the pieces I did in the studio, which just felt like sub-films really, at the end of the day a film is a film is a film and I'm not the only person to say that . . . I don't really think that any of the films that I made for television would have been necessarily especially different things, apart from the actual detailed difference of how you make a feature film from a television film, had I made them for the cinema. Obviously when we were working on *Play for Today* films there would be discussions where you would set up a long shot and then we'd say 'Well on an ordinary domestic receiver' – and in those days screens were smaller than they now are – 'that's going to be very tiny and so maybe we should go a bit closer', but that's about as far as we ever got in conscious terms in the direction of making a distinction.

Of course when you compare the way we made those films, and some were more sophisticated than others, for example the guys, who were perfectly good, who came out to shoot *Nuts in May* and *The Kiss of Death* from Pebble Mill, they were working on *Farming Today* for most of the year until the previous Friday and they just spent the whole year shooting nodding heads talking about the price of hay and whatever and out they'd come to shoot a *Play for Today* film and they'd gradually get more artistic as the days went by, but it was pointing a camera at things, throwing light at it and shooting.[36]

In the mid-1970s Leigh alternated between studio and filmed plays, with another *Second City First*, *Knock for Knock* (BBC2, 21 November 1976), suffering the fate of many taped plays when it was wiped after transmission. His next *Play for Today* for English Regions Drama, *The Kiss of Death* (BBC1, 11 January 1977), was a gloomy tale about an undertaker's assistant called Trevor (David Threlfall), whose lack of social skills stem from learning difficulties that none of his friends seems to recognise, resulting in a series of uncomfortable social situations which form the basis of the drama. Set in Lancashire, *The Kiss of Death* was another filmed *Play for Today*, followed later the same year by a studio recording of Leigh's successful stage play *Abigail's Party* (BBC1, 1 November 1977) which, ironically, has become his most famous television play.[37] After *Abigail's Party* all of Leigh's subsequent television work was made on film, up to the late 1980s when he concentrated on making feature films.

There was a diversification in English Regions Drama's single play production in 1977–78, with more plays being produced for BBC2, rather than *Play for Today* on BBC1. At the very beginning of the year, a week before the transmission of *The Kiss of Death*, there was an adaptation of Harold Brighouse's *The Game* (BBC2, 3 January 1977), a romance set in 1913 involving a footballer and the daughter of the Chairman of the football team he plays for, Blackton Rovers. Like some other English Regions Drama productions (*The Witches of Pendle, Our Day Out, The Blackstuff*) some production work on *The Game* was done in the BBC studios in Manchester (hence the 'BBC Manchester' credit in the *Radio* Times) but the play was produced by David Rose and adapted by the Northern playwright Henry Livings, who had written a *Thirty-Minute Theatre* play for English Regions Drama in 1972.

In July 1977 another Northern play was produced by English Regions Drama. *The Fosdyke Saga* (BBC2, 20 July 1977) was a television version of Bill Tidy's newspaper cartoon strip, which had been adapted for the theatre as a musical by Alan Plater. Tidy's newspaper strip was a satire on John Galsworthy's *The Forsyte Saga*, itself adapted for television in 1967, so it was appropriate that *The Fosdyke Saga* should also be produced for television by English Regions Drama as a satirical Northern, working-class 'response' to a classic BBC costume drama. This may explain why the English Regions Drama production was a recording of the stage play, performed in front of an audience, rather than a studio dramatisation which might have lost some of the raucous atmosphere of the stage show. Replying to a member of the BBC Weekly Programme Review Committee who 'wondered whether it might not have been better to have adapted the show for television rather than to televise it being played before an audience', the Head of BBC Drama, Shaun Sutton, insisted that 'Adaptation would have removed the real quality (described by Jimmy Gilbert [Head of Light Entertainment] as gutsy and theatrical) of the show. It was important to remember that television programmes were made for real people rather than for members of Programme Review Board.'[38] A tacit acknowledgement, perhaps, that the London-based BBC hierarchy did not necessarily have their fingers on the pulse of the popular (regional) working-class audience.

At the end of the year Michael Abbensetts's *Black Christmas* (BBC2, 20 December 1977) provided a multicultural perspective on the festive season, with a fifty-minute play about a black family in Birmingham getting together for Christmas. With excellent performances from Norman Beaton as the father and Carmen Munroe as the mother, a witty script from Guyanese writer Abbensetts and direction (on film) by Stephen Frears, this was a significant addition to the repertoire of English Regions Drama, paving the way for Abbensetts's *Empire Road* series in 1978–79.

Also in December 1977 English Regions Drama made its first contribution to the new BBC2 anthology series, *Play of the Week*. Willy Russell's *Our Day Out* (BBC2, 28 December 1977) was a location-based filmed drama, directed by Pedr James, with David Rose producing and Michael Wearing as script editor. Following his 1973 *Second City First, King of the Castle*, and a fifty-minute *Play for Today, The Death of a Young Young Man*, *Our Day Out* was Russell's first feature-length screenplay. It was about a day trip to North Wales for a group of Liverpool schoolchildren with reading and writing difficulties, whose strong Liverpool accents were one of the distinctive features of the play. As the school coach journeys from a rundown area of Liverpool to the North Wales coast, the play provides another illustration of the advantages of shooting on location, the change in environment having a liberating effect on the children while their authoritarian teacher, Mr Briggs (Alun Armstrong), does his best to keep them under strict control, complaining to the more liberal Mrs Kay (Jean Heywood): 'They're just like town dogs let off the leash in the country.' In a scene containing the ideological message of the play, Mrs Kay tells Briggs that the kids are just 'fodder for factory assembly lines'. She doesn't want to 'educate' them, as Briggs does, but to let them enjoy themselves.

Six days later another play by a Liverpool writer was screened as part of the 1977–78 *Play for Today* season. *Scully's New Year's Eve* (BBC1, 3 January 1978) was Alan Bleasdale's first full-length play for television, following his 1975 *Second City Firsts* debut, *Early to Bed*. Unlike *Early to Bed*, however, *Scully's New Year's Eve* was a studio drama, based on a teenage character about whom Bleasdale had written a series of stories which he adapted for various media: radio, theatre and a novel. Bleasdale's radio and theatre work in the 1970s was crucial to the development of his own personal style. As Millington and Nelson point out, reading his own stories on the radio enabled Bleasdale 'to develop an ear for dialogue and a sense of comic timing' (1986: 27), while seeing his plays performed in various Liverpool venues enabled him to appreciate which material worked with an audience and which did not. *Scully's New Year's Eve*, however, was not entirely successful, failing to sustain narrative interest over seventy minutes. One member of the BBC Weekly Programme Review Committee found the play 'too much of an imitation of *Abigail's Party*' while another felt it had been 'compassionate at moments, but then lost it again', to which Shaun Sutton responded 'the author Alan Bleasdale was rather that kind of writer'.[39] Nevertheless, *Scully's New Year's Eve* was a ratings success with 'eleven dropping to ten and a half million', considered to be 'a very good figure' by the Programme Review Committee.[40]

Bleasdale's next piece for television was a short drama called *Dangerous Ambition* (BBC1, 5 May 1978), about a priest who is led to question his vocation, made for a BBC North West series called *Sense of Place* and filmed on location in Liverpool.[41] Also in 1978 Bleasdale wrote the play that established his reputation as a writer and led to what became a seminal 'state of the nation' series. *The Blackstuff* (BBC2, 2 January 1980) was about a group of tarmac workers from

Liverpool who get a contract for a job in Middlesbrough, work being in short supply in Liverpool. While they are there four of the gang take on an extra job, only to be conned out of payment for it by the two Irish tinkers who have arranged it and sacked by their regular boss when he discovers they have been 'doing a foreigner', leaving them unemployed (and thus setting up the scenario for what would become *Boys from the Blackstuff*).

The Blackstuff was written by Bleasdale after *Scully's New Year's Eve* and filmed in September–October 1978, but it was not transmitted until January 1980. As a play for television it was more successful than *Scully's New Year's Eve*, for several reasons. Firstly, the acting was superior, especially among the central characters who formed the tarmac gang: Michael Angelis, Tom Georgeson, Bernard Hill, Alan Igbon and Peter Kerrigan, all of whom featured in the subsequent series. Secondly, unlike *Scully*, *The Blackstuff* was filmed on location, in Liverpool, Cheshire and Middlesbrough. Not only did the location filming open out the play (including some helicopter shots), it placed the characters in their environment, enabling the drama to develop more naturalistically than in *Scully's New Year's Eve*, which suffered from being confined to the studio. As a filmed drama *The Blackstuff* also benefited from the direction of Jim Goddard, whose previous credits included episodes of two Euston Films series: *The Sweeney* (1975–78) and Trevor Preston's crime serial, *Out* (1978). Bleasdale recognised the importance of Goddard's contribution, noting on the audio commentary accompanying the DVD release of *The Blackstuff* how Goddard's direction had enhanced the authenticity and pathos of the drama.[42]

Another significant factor in the success of *The Blackstuff* was that Bleasdale's writing was maturing. The characters and situations that featured in the play were close to his own experience – his family had an asphalt business and the focus on an all-male group enabled him to write authentic working-class dialogue, including a fair amount of Scouse humour, for characters with whom he was very familiar. Bleasdale admitted, however, that he was undergoing a learning process as a writer at the time:

> I actually did the classic five-year apprenticeship. I was an apprentice at this job from 1975 to 1980. From 1980 onwards my work was transformed because I quietly and slowly built up the application of my craft out of the talent that I had. From 1980 onwards slowly I found a way of doing things I'd always wanted to do, but didn't know how to. (quoted in Millington and Nelson, 1986: 28)

The Blackstuff was a seminal production for English Regions Drama. Not only did it consolidate the growing body of work coming out of Liverpool (especially in view of Granada's historical neglect of the city within its franchise region) but the play introduced all of the characters who were to become central to the series which followed. However it was over a year before a slot was found for *The Blackstuff* in the schedules, which was surprising given that it seemed to be classic *Play for Today* material. It was eventually screened at the beginning of 1980, outside of an anthology play series, on BBC2, just before the three plays that English Regions Drama contributed to the 1979–80 *Play for Today* season.

Bleasdale's next play, *The Muscle Market* (BBC1, 13 January 1981), was commissioned as a *Play for Today* and featured in the 1980–81 season. By this time Bleasdale had started work on the *Boys from the Blackstuff* series, but the delay in transmitting *The Blackstuff* meant there was a delay in getting the series into production. Michael Wearing, who worked closely with Bleasdale as script editor on *Scully's New Year's Eve* and *The Blackstuff*, was trying to get the series into production but, as Millington and Nelson record, was worried about the effect of the delays on Bleasdale, who had already delivered the first two scripts:

> Partly to reassure Bleasdale of his continuing commitment, Michael Wearing began to consider the possibility of using one of the available scripts for another single film of 'the Boys'. At this point of time, although there were not the funds for a series, the resources for a *Play for Today* on film *were* immediately available . . .
>
> To lift a single play out of a scheme in this way obviously threatened to weaken the viability of the rest of the series. However, it was important as far as the producer was concerned to demonstrate the strength of the Bleasdale scripts that were available for production. This was particularly important when contemporary, regional material was not seen by management as an attractive proposition for a series, and a projected series to follow up Bleasdale's successful *Scully's New Year's Eve*, taken to BBC-1 at editorials in 1979, had already been turned down. (Millington and Nelson, 1986: 43) [43]

Wearing's solution, therefore, was to turn one of Bleasdale's scripts into a *Play for Today*, partly to prevent Bleasdale getting disaffected because of the delays in getting approval for the series and partly in order to prove to BBC management that Bleasdale was capable of delivering a 'quality drama' based on 'contemporary, regional material'. In the event, the script that Bleasdale originally intended as the third episode of the series proved suitable for a stand-alone *Play for Today*, because it focused on the asphalt boss who had appeared in *The Blackstuff*, rather than 'the boys', and was therefore 'rather detached from the main thrust of the rest of the series: the problems of ordinary unemployed working men' (Millington and Nelson, 1986: 43). *The Muscle Market* was well received, Jennifer Reeks writing in *The Stage and Television Today*:

> Alan Bleasdale could almost be described as a writer of tragedies were it not for the fact that he writes comedies. His latest 'Play for Today', *The Muscle Market* . . . was the work of deep Liverpudlian melancholy with the built-in inexorability of Macbeth.
>
> But, most of all, it was a comedy in which the laughs flowed like substandard concrete, as Mr. Bleasdale raised his sights from the fiddling asphalters he immortalised in *The Blackstuff* to the bent bosses of the building trade who operate two steps behind the Mafia and one step ahead of the law. (Reeks, 1981)

The Muscle Market was Bleasdale's last single play for television, after which he concentrated on writing series and serials including *Boys from the Blackstuff* (1982), *Scully* (1984), *The Monocled Mutineer* (1986), *GBH* (1991) and *Jake's Progress* (1995).

The eclecticism in English Regions Drama's single play production is evident in the variety of plays produced for *Play for Today* from 1978 to 1982. The plays that followed *Scully's New Year's Eve* on to the screen in January 1978, for example, were David Hare's *Licking Hitler* (BBC1, 10 January 1978), about two people working for a British propaganda unit based in an English country house during the Second World War, and Alan Garner's *Red Shift* (BBC1, 17 January 1978), a complex historical drama, set in Cheshire, that moved freely between three periods: the present, the English Civil War and the Roman period. In the 1978–79 *Play for Today* season Ron Hutchinson's social realist drama about a building firm, *The Out of Town Boys* (BBC1, 2 January 1979), was followed by Dixie Williams's *Vampires* (BBC1, 9 January 1979), about two Liverpool schoolboys obsessed with the idea of vampires, and John Elliot's *The Chief Mourner* (BBC1, 16 January 1979). Other plays produced by English Regions Drama for *Play for Today* in 1979–82 included David Hare's *Dreams of Leaving* (BBC1, 17 January 1980), H.O. Nazareth and Horace Ove's *The Garland* (BBC1, 10 March 1981), which featured a largely

Asian cast, Tony Bicat's murder-mystery *A Cotswold Death* (BBC1, 12 January 1982) and Janey Preger's 'feminist' play about sexual politics, *Under the Skin* (BBC1, 19 January 1982).

There was a similar eclecticism in the five plays produced for *Play of the Week* in 1977–78 (which included another Janey Preger play), and in the nineteen plays produced for BBC2's *Playhouse* from 1980 to 1982, including plays by Michael Abbensetts, Tony Bicat, Mike Bradwell, Eva Figes, Philip Martin, Janey Preger and Peter Tinniswood. Most of these plays were recorded in the studio, in contrast to the plays made for *Play for Today*. With *Second City Firsts* having ended in 1978 there was evidently scope for the production of more studio drama at Pebble Mill to replace the half-hour plays that English Regions Drama had produced regularly since its inception. This may account for the decision to develop a new anthology series of plays in 1979, under the title of *The Other Side*. The series title suggested an alternative perspective on social and political issues, a suggestion which the title sequence, depicting a revolving television set, reinforced. The five fifty-minute plays in the series were produced by W. Stephen Gilbert, who had previously written a *Play for Today* called *Circle Line* (1971), and worked as a script editor and as a television critic. *The Other Side* was Gilbert's first stint as a producer and it turned out to be a baptism of fire.

Five plays were produced for the series, including *Underdog* (BBC2, 4 May 1979) by Jack Shepherd (directed by Michael Wearing), *A Greenish Man* (BBC2, 11 May 1979) by Snoo Wilson, and *Only Connect* (BBC2, 18 May 1979) by Noel Greig and Drew Griffiths. *Only Connect* took its title from E.M. Forster, who appeared in the play (played by Christopher Banks) giving a radio talk in 1944 about Edward Carpenter, 'an early socialist and pioneer for Gay Rights in the north of England' (*Radio* Times, 12 May 1979). Thirty years later, a young academic, Graham Johnson (Sam Dale), is researching a thesis on Edward Carpenter and arranges to visit John Bury (Joseph O'Conor), a former bus driver who knew Carpenter in the 1920s and who, Johnson discovers, once slept with Carpenter. Johnson finds that Bury's personal life is more interesting than Carpenter's politics and, emulating the situation between Bury and Carpenter, he stays the night with him. 'The personal is political' seemed to be the message of the play, in accordance with 1970s sexual politics.

Like all of *The Other Side* plays, *Only Connect* was recorded in the studio. But the series became notorious not for the plays that were made but for one that was not. *Solid Geometry* should also have been part of the series, but on the eve of its production it was banned by BBC management, who were concerned about a 'pickled penis' that featured in Ian McEwan's script, which he adapted from a story in his 1975 *First Love, Last Rites* collection. When Gilbert blew the whistle on the BBC's censorship of the play, releasing a press statement explaining 'the process by which the play had been stopped as we understood it' (Gilbert, 1980: 15), he was suspended on full pay.

In an article published in *Broadcast* a year after the event, Gilbert speculated about the reasons for the censorship of *Solid Geometry*, having never accepted the official reason given in a BBC Press Release that the play was 'too sexually explicit to be transmitted even at a late hour' (Gilbert, 1980: 14). In the wake of the BBC's banning of Dennis Potter's *Brimstone and Treacle* in 1976 and Roy Minton's *Scum* in 1977, BBC management was wary of any plays that might transgress its own codes of taste and decency, especially in the representation of sex and violence. The original single play of *Gangsters* preceded the controversies surrounding *Brimstone and Treacle* and *Scum* and had been subject to only one cut for 'violence', but in the more censorious climate of the late 1970s Gilbert speculated that BBC management may have wanted to send a message to departments such as English Regions Drama that had hitherto enjoyed considerable autonomy: '[The] theory was that any area of the BBC which enjoyed relative autonomy was being frightened into line and that David Rose's Drama Unit, like the Current Affairs Department, was seen as too independent; thus I provided a perfect opportunity for David to be given a fright' (Gilbert, 1980: 16). Gilbert, who had originally been hired by David Rose, suspected he had therefore become the 'sacrificial lamb' on behalf of English Regions Drama, although in the light of his decision to go public over the banning of *Solid Geometry* he had knowingly put himself in a difficult situation, leaving BBC management little choice but to suspend him.

The debacle of *Solid Geometry* may explain why *The Other Side* was a short-lived series. Subsequently, studio productions from English Regions Drama were divided between series such as *Empire Road* and single plays produced for *Playhouse* (fifteen of the nineteen plays produced for *Playhouse* from 1980 to 1982 were studio productions). Perhaps the most extraordinary of all the single plays produced by English Regions Drama was *Artemis 81* (BBC1, 29 December 1981), written by David Rudkin and directed by Alastair Reid. This three-hour filmed drama was David Rose's last production before leaving Birmingham to take up a position at the new Channel Four (in fact *Artemis 81* was transmitted eight months after he left) and it was both a swansong and perhaps a crowning achievement for Rose after ten years as Head of English Regions Drama. To describe *Artemis 81* as a 'single play' is really a misnomer. Such a description betrays the inadequacy of the term to describe a drama that was, in subject matter and style, much closer to the modernism of European art cinema than it was to the traditional television play.

Typically opaque, as one might expect of an epic narrative drama from David Rudkin which references Hitchcock as well as figures from classical mythology, *Artemis 81*, as David Ian Rabey observes,

> represents Rudkin's confluence of classical mythic forces with the artful tensions of modern film narrative to create a filmic poem of even more daring inventive range than that of *Penda's Fen*. Its startling effects, strata of meanings and moral vision remain rare in television film [. . .]
>
> One of Rudkin's most eclectic and original works, accessible yet challenging in its urgency, *Artemis 81* calls to be remade for cinema with greater resources of money, time and precision, as befits its design as *hommage* to Hitchcock. It is Rudkin's most vital and acutely reverberative dramatic formulation of the intimation that 'we do right to dream: and, for our sanity, learn to fall', and a visionary myth which testifies to premises recognized by Rudkin in Hitchcock's work. (Rabey, 1997: 117–18)

Following its transmission *Artemis 81* was described more simply as 'a futuristic fantasy' by Robert Ottaway in the *Radio Times*. In addition to noting the film's Hitchcockian elements and its eclectic cast (which included Hywel Bennett, the pop musician Sting and the horror film star Ingrid Pitt as a 'Hitchcock blonde'), Ottaway admired the film's 'searching sense of place – its locations ranging from Denmark, East Anglia and Liverpool, from the Midlands to North Wales [which] gives the narrative a wider scope, deliberate on Rudkin's part' (Ottaway, 1981–82). With its locations including Denmark and North Wales in addition to the English regions previously seen in the department's productions, *Artemis 81* is a testament to the increasing ambition of English Regions Drama, an ambition which could not, ultimately, be maintained within the remit and resources of the department, which may explain David Rose's departure to Channel Four where film budgets would be larger and the opportunities for location filming greater.

If a 'sense of place' is the primary feature distinguishing nearly all of the plays/films produced by English Regions Drama, the scope and ambition of *Artemis 81* was a fitting testimonial to the creative environment that David Rose nurtured in Birmingham during his ten years in charge of the department. The eclectic mix of esoteric Englishness, classical mythology and Hitchcockian mystery in Rudkin's epic narrative was a product of the enterprising commissioning policy operated by English Regions Drama, which enabled writers such as Rudkin, Peter Terson, Alan Plater, Malcolm Bradbury, Philip Martin, Michael Abbensetts, Janey Preger, Willy Russell and Alan Bleasdale to see their different interpretations of English regional culture and identity produced for a mass audience.

Series and serials: extending the range of regional drama

In its fourth year English Regions Drama was able to extend the range of its productions beyond the single play to series and serials. Alan Plater's *Trinity Tales* (BBC2, November–December 1975) was the first of these, a six-part serial inspired by Chaucer's *Canterbury Tales*, featuring a group of rugby supporters travelling from Wakefield to Wembley where their team, Wakefield Trinity, is due to play the next day in the Rugby League Cup Final. *Trinity Tales* might be better described as an 'episodic series' rather than a serial as each episode featured a discrete (but not discreet!) 'tale' told by one of the travellers during the course of the journey, hence the episode titles: 'The Driver's Tale', 'The Fryer's Tale', 'The Judy's Tale', 'The Joiner's Tale', 'The Wife of Batley's Tale', and 'The Man of Law's Tale'. As Albert Hunt explains:

> In the first episode, Nick the Driver finds himself forced to explain why he's going from Wakefield to London via Lincoln and King's Lynn. He tells the story of adventures which have led to his running away from both a crook, Big George, and the police. Everybody enjoys the story: they all agree that each of them should tell a story on the way to Wembley and that the teller of the best story will be given a free fish-and-chip supper by one of the party, Stan the Fryer, who owns a fish-and-chip shop. (Hunt, 1981: 148)

Each episode, therefore, has a dual narrative structure: the journey the group is making to London and the tale being told by one of them, with the same actors appearing as different characters in each narrative. This made the series quite complex, which was initially not to the liking of some viewers who, according to the BBC Audience Research Report on the first episode, 'disliked the constant switching from the journey to the "tale", finding the programme disjointed, muddled and altogether too "itsy-bitsy" – perhaps they would enjoy it better when they were more used to the style, one or two went on to remark'.[44] The Audience Research Report on the second episode, however, suggests the audience did warm to the series as they became used to its idiosyncratic style for it received a Reaction Index of 63, compared to 57 for the first episode, and the report noted how 'most of the reporting audience' were 'clearly entertained' and 'appreciated the "bawdy" humour ("in true Chaucer vein") of this very tall story'.[45]

The series was also stylistically complex as a result of the use of studio recording for interior scenes while both film and mobile video were used for recording exterior scenes. In this respect the series was a typical 1970s television drama hybrid of film and studio, but with the added dimension of mobile video for some exteriors providing an intermediary aesthetic between studio and film. Alan Plater explains how the series came to include this mixture of different technologies:

> *Trinity Tales* was an interesting hybrid, it was part studio, part film and part mobile VT. They'd just taken delivery of the first handheld, lightweight video camera at Pebble Mill and David said to me 'Do you think we could use this? Do you fancy using this?' All the scenes inside the minibus we shot using this camera, just to see what would happen, and it was that kind of adventurous 'Let's give it a go' spirit. So that's why there are moments when *Trinity Tales* looks as if it's been shot three different ways; it's because it has.
>
> I think if we were doing *Trinity Tales* again we would do it all on film, obviously, because film cameras ... everything is much lighter and easier to handle now but film was still ... conventional film cameras were still quite cumbersome and heavy, as were studio television cameras, I mean they were huge things, like tram-cars.[46]

This technological and stylistic mix did not seem to affect the audience's enjoyment of the series, the Audience Research Report on episode one noting that 'the location shots were particularly liked',[47] while for episode two the 'True-to-life settings from the motorway café to Dorothy's "lovely house" contributed to the main appreciation of a most satisfactory production',[48] both comments suggesting that the location filming, whether on film or video, gave the series greater verisimilitude.

As Albert Hunt has pointed out: 'The device of having stories within a story leaves Plater free to demolish the normal conventions of TV drama and to revel in the freedom to draw on a variety of styles' (Hunt, 1981: 148). So there are parodies of Dylan Thomas and Raymond Chandler, for example, as well as a self-conscious use of Hollywood stylistic clichés, such as waves lapping on a seashore to symbolise sexual passion, commented on self-reflexively by Judy, playing the wife in the tale: 'Hey up, here come the waves again.' The stylistic and structural innovations in *Trinity Tales* indicate the willingness of English Regions Drama to depart from the norms of television drama series and to give artistic licence to writers, such as Plater, who had already proved themselves capable of writing original regional drama for the department. Consequently, with *Trinity Tales*, Plater was given the opportunity to experiment and to enrich his artistic palette over five hours of screen time (each episode lasting fifty minutes) in a series featuring Northern, working-class characters on a meandering journey from Yorkshire to London which afforded plenty of opportunities for comedy and popular storytelling.

Following the success of the original *Play for Today*, the decision to commission *Gangsters* (BBC1, September–October 1976) as a six-part series provides further evidence of the enterprising nature of English Regions Drama's attitude towards series and serials. Whereas *Trinity Tales* was screened on BBC2, both series of *Gangsters* (a second series followed in 1978) were screened on BBC1, with the result that the audience for the first series was four times that for *Trinity Tales*, although the figures were less impressive for the second series, which took greater liberties in parodying genres and breaking the conventions of mainstream television drama.

The first series of *Gangsters* was just as innovative in style and content as the original play had been, even though director Alastair Reid was working with a much lower budget: £27,000 per hour, compared to twice that for the single play. Consequently the series was produced more quickly, each episode being completed in two weeks, with four days filming and two days for recording in the studio. Unlike the single play, the series was a hybrid of studio and film, but more film than usual was allocated for the shooting of the series, no doubt because, as with the original play, filming on location enabled a 'sense of place' to be conveyed – the urban environment of contemporary Birmingham being as important to the series as it was to the single play. Even in the studio scenes Alastair Reid tried to give the drama a 'filmic feeling' by shooting with a handheld camera, instead of the more cumbersome studio cameras, an unprecedented innovation in studio drama at the time.[49]

As with the single play, the series incorporated a number of stylistic innovations, including some 'Brechtian' elements, such as the moment in the first studio scene in 'Incident 1' (the episodes in the first series were numbered 'Incident 1', 'Incident 2', etc.) when the camera pulls back to reveal the whole studio set in a widescreen, 'letterbox' format, reminiscent of the way in which Jean-Luc Godard interrupted the narrative to reveal the artifice of the studio set in his Brechtian-influenced 1972 film *Tout va bien*. The technique is a classic example of Brecht's *verfremdungseffekt* (alienation effect) when the audience is literally distanced from the action, causing an interruption in the narrative flow. Similar moments of self-reflexivity occur throughout the serial, becoming increasingly evident in the second series (which may be one reason why the ratings dropped in series two).

The lack of budget and production time is sometimes evident during the series, with some uncertainty in the acting and direction resulting from limited rehearsal and filming time. The narrative was also confusing, partly because of the complexity of the plot – Philip Martin taking advantage of the extra screen time (the two series ran to a total of ten hours) to produce a multi-layered narrative – which tended to be a little too fragmented. Although the series was, as David Rose explained to the BBC Television Programme Review Committee, 'highly stylised' it was, nevertheless, 'rooted in deep reality', that of Birmingham's ethnic communities and the activities of the criminal underworld. In response to comments and criticisms made of the series by members of the Programme Review Committee, the minutes to the meeting on 20 October 1976, following transmission of 'Incident 5', record Rose as saying of the series that

> he considered it very accessible to the audience. He could vouch for the fact that it was rooted in deep reality; on the other hand the production was a highly stylised one. He had some reservations about Philip Martin's script, especially some lack of narrative clarity early on in the serial. On the other hand Mr. Rose was delighted that the BBC had here stuck its neck out a little.[50]

The final sentence highlights the fact that the initiative taken by English Regions Drama in commissioning a radical, multiracial serial such as *Gangsters* was ultimately dependent on the BBC having some faith in what the department was doing. While English Regions Drama enjoyed a certain degree of autonomy, there was no guarantee that everything it commissioned would be transmitted (as the *Solid Geometry* debacle was to prove) and it was to the credit of the BBC that such an unusual, and potentially controversial, series as *Gangsters* was scheduled in prime time on BBC1.

There were, however, some complaints from the audience about the 'language' in the second series, as recorded by the BBC Programme Review Committee minutes following transmission of episode two, 'The Red Executioner' (BBC1, 13 January 1978):

> M.D.Tel [Managing Director, Television] said the log reflected a large number of complaints about language. He was bound to record that he was put off by this and noted two occasions when he felt it had been gratuitous. Shaun Sutton [Head of Drama] said that cuts had in fact been made in the episode before transmission, but maybe not enough had been cut.[51]

Despite the fact that David Rose thought 'the story-lines were stronger perhaps than those of the first series, as was the element of hokum',[52] there were some concerns expressed by the Programme Review Committee, and by reviewers, about the abrupt changes in tone in the second series, when moments of tragedy would be juxtaposed with moments of comedy, parody with social realism. While the serial was intentionally parodic, using the conventions of Saturday morning cinema serials, complete with cliffhanger endings for each episode, as well as referring to (and sending up) 'Yellow Peril' and 'Fu Manchu' movies of the 1920s and 1930s and the recent wave of 'Kung Fu' films, reviewers (and some of the audience, judging by the declining viewing figures) found the mixture of parody and social realism difficult to handle. Contemporary social issues, such as immigration, racism and drug-taking, continued to feature in the second series alongside the more comic and parodic elements, creating a discomfiting mix of realism and comedy. Writing in the *Daily Telegraph*, Richard Last complained that *Gangsters* was like a

> compound of leavings from *The Avengers*, *Monty Python*, early *Laurel and Hardy*, late Ken Russell, *Who Do You Do?* and *Batman* . . . with a touch of *The Prisoner* thrown in . . . You can't get too many laughs from a W.C. Fields impersonation when it is liable to be followed by painful death and wild realistic grief, or relax with jokes like a tombstone inscribed Sacred To The Memory of Bryan Cowgill when a few frames further on

an elderly Asian will be beaten up by white hooligans. Mr Martin was trying to play tennis without benefit of net or marker lines and it can't be done. Without rules of any kind credibility perishes. (quoted in Kerr, 1981: 75)

The mixture of parody, social commentary and generic hybridity in *Gangsters* suggests an early manifestation of postmodernism in television drama, several years before the term was used in relation to television. In this respect, as well as the way in which the serial featured a multiracial cast within a popular generic format, the serial was ahead of its time. That it was also a regional drama, set in the urban environment of contemporary Birmingham, suggests that English Regions Drama was breaking new ground with *Gangsters* in more ways than one.

Another Birmingham serial that was ahead of its time was *Empire Road* (BBC2, 1978–79), a black soap opera written by Michael Abbensetts and produced by Peter Ansorge. While *Gangsters* had no pretensions to be 'politically correct' in its portrayal of black and Asian characters, as a result of its deliberate transgression of acceptable conventions, it did not escape the accusation that it was reproducing stereotypes of blacks and Asians as criminals, with Chinese, Indian, Pakistani and West Indian characters involved in various illegal activities, from drug-smuggling to illegal immigration. *Empire Road*, in contrast, set out to challenge the stereotyping of black and Asian characters in the media by focusing on the everyday lives of ordinary families living in Birmingham.

Empire Road was written by the Guyanese writer Michael Abbensetts, whose play about a West Indian family, *Black Christmas*, was produced by English Regions Drama in 1977. Abbensetts says that the idea for *Empire Road* came from a visit to Birmingham for the filming of *Black Christmas*:

> I went to stay with a friend in Handsworth, and it struck me that the atmosphere was very different from London. It was more relaxed. Everybody seemed to have more time, and it was easy to see what people's problems were. It was very mixed: Blacks, Whites and Asians living next door to each other. And you could hear all of them talking in the same Brummie accent. All that happens in London, but in Birmingham I could see it with greater clarity. (quoted in Phillips, 1978: 21)

Abbensetts was commissioned to write a five-part series, which was transmitted in October–November 1978. The series was based around the character of Everton Bennett (Norman Beaton), a West Indian 'godfather' who owns several houses and a shop in a multi-racial street ('Empire Road') in a Birmingham suburb. While some of the action was played for comedy, such as the relationship between Everton Bennett and his brother-in-law Walter (Joe Marcell), social 'issues' were also dealt with, such as that of the 'mixed-race' relationship between Everton's son Marcus (Wayne Laryea) and his girlfriend Ranjanaa (Nalina Moonasar). Yet, although the series was welcomed in some quarters as 'a down to-earth appraisal of the struggles of West Indians and Asians in Britain' (Khan, 1979: 64), the pre-publicity was concerned to stress that the series would not be issue-led: 'It might be black, but it wouldn't be "political" or "heavy". Its intention was to "amuse and entertain"' (Khan, 1979: 64).

For Peter Ansorge, who joined English Regions Drama as a script editor in 1975, having previously been editor of the theatre magazine *Plays and Players*, *Empire Road* was his first job as a producer. One of the first plays Ansorge had worked on at Pebble Mill as a script editor was Barry Reckord's *Club Havana* (BBC2, 25 October 1975), a *Second City First* about a West Indian family living in Birmingham and the first black drama to be produced by English Regions Drama. Ansorge was also script editor on Michael Abbensetts's *Black Christmas* and he explains how *Empire Road* evolved out of the play, suggesting there was pressure in the late 1970s to be producing series rather than single plays as the BBC became more conscious of the need to compete with ITV. In the light of criticisms of the lack of black and Asian characters in other programmes on British television, including *Coronation Street*, a black soap opera offered the prospect of attracting new viewers while, at the same time, fulfilling the BBC's public service commitment:

> We'd done a film called *Black Christmas* which I script edited . . . I'd known from my *Plays and Players* days a writer called Michael Abbensetts, who's Guyanese . . . and he just simply said 'I want to write a piece about a black Christmas' . . . and it was the first time a black family really had been treated in a purely domestic way . . . they were a normal family and I did think this was quite interesting . . .
>
> There was a certain pressure to find more series ideas. David I'm sure will deny this, but there was . . . that was already starting, that you could somehow get a bigger profile for something that was not just a one off . . . so that's how it came about . . . We changed the name of the family, we changed the role [of the Norman Beaton character], he

wasn't a postman any more, but it came out of that and then David said
well you should produce this . . .

After the first week it went out these letters arrived and the first lot of
letters that arrived were from black kids, a school teacher had got them
talking about it in the classroom and he suggested they write a letter to
the characters. He sent me these twenty-five letters. I showed them to
David Rose and he said, 'Well that alone was worth it' . . . Of course it
was not just watched by black people, otherwise it would have got no
audiences at all . . . We were getting about two, two and half million on
BBC2, which is not bad.[53]

Whereas *Gangsters* was transmitted on BBC1, the transmission of
Empire Road on BBC2, in an early-evening slot from 6.50 to 7.20
pm, suggested some uncertainty on behalf of the BBC about how
popular the series might be. Initially audiences were small, with only
half a million for the first episode, but by the end of the first series the
audience had grown to four and a half million.[54]

Subsequently a second series of ten episodes was commissioned
and transmitted on BBC2 from August to October 1979, in peak
time, from 8.00 to 8.30 pm. While Michael Abbensetts wrote all the
episodes for both series, different directors were involved, including
the West Indian director Horace Ove, whom Peter Ansorge brought
in to direct three episodes in the second series. Ove had previously
made low-budget independent films about the black community and
black culture, such as *Pressure* (1975), and his work on *Empire Road*
was his first experience of working in a television studio, which he did
not much enjoy. Consequently he tried to shoot as much as possible
outside, using an OB unit. Norman Beaton recalls how Ove's involve-
ment had an interesting effect on the programme, not just in terms
of how it was recorded but because he brought a different cultural
perspective to it:

When Horace Ove came in to direct some episodes in the second series,
that immediately introduced a different voice. I don't think Horace was
terribly interested in the scripts, he was more interested in the people.
And so all the structures of English acting that we had been using went
out the window and, suddenly, we were doing big arm movements and
using West Indian language in the way that we do back home. That
was a wonderful experience. So when Horace came in to direct the
episodes, we had a black soap written by a black man, directed by a
black man, with a black cast. It was wonderful! (quoted in Pines, 1992:
116–17)

Ove himself gives an interesting account of the difficulty of trying to do something different in television (see Pines, 1992: 124–6), but he felt that the series was ground breaking in its representation of black and Asian characters:

> I think *Empire Road* was well received within the black community, and also within the white community, because people hadn't seen anything like it on television before. They had seen other things but not a black family owning a shop, their problems, and the problems of the Asians, and the interaction between blacks and whites in dramatic situations. I think we got pretty close to accurately reflecting those realities. (quoted in Pines, 1992: 126)

Michael Abbensetts, though, is sceptical about whether black audiences had actually watched the series in large numbers, believing that black audiences were much less likely to watch BBC2. He sees this as a significant factor in the failure of the programme to go to a third series because the ratings for it on BBC2 simply were not high enough, whereas if the BBC had scheduled it on BBC1 it might well have attracted a much bigger audience:

> I think we had problems getting a third series because the ratings for the second series, although better than for the first, were not good enough or as large as everyone had hoped they would be. But if you examine it, I think you will find that black audiences were more likely to watch ITV or BBC1, especially in those days. A lot of the black viewers just didn't watch BBC2. So many of them probably would not have watched *Empire Road*. (quoted in Pines, 1992: 134–5)

With its other commitments it is doubtful whether English Regions Drama would have had the resources to sustain a long-running serial and the BBC evidently saw no potential in *Empire Road* as a mainstream alternative to the existing soaps on ITV. After fifteen episodes the series was terminated. It remains the only example of a black soap opera produced on British television.

The series and serials produced by English Regions Drama from 1975 to 1982 replicate the diversity to be found in the single plays produced by the department. Not only were *Trinity Tales*, *Gangsters* and *Empire Road* each very different, so too were the other ten series and serials produced by the department in that period. The diversity can partly be explained by the 'policy' of not conforming to established traditions, of encouraging originality and difference and by generally avoiding social realism in order to have, as David Rose put it, 'bright lights shining through as well'.

Between the two series of *Gangsters* there was a three-part adaptation, by Thomas Ellice, of a novel by Emma Smith called *Maidens' Trip* (BBC2, 13–27 June 1977), about women working on canal boats during the Second World War. *Maidens' Trip* was a female counterpart to Peter Terson's *Shakespeare – or Bust*, in which his three male heroes travelled to Stratford-upon-Avon by canal boat, and it was perhaps an acknowledgement that the department's drama output had been very male-orientated up to that time. In *Maidens' Trip* each forty-five-minute episode featured one of the three women in the series (Tina Heath, Liz Bagley and Tricia George) who were working as boaters on the Grand Union Canal. Not only was the series based on a novel by a woman, with three women as the leading actors, it was also produced and directed by women: Anthea Browne-Wilkinson and Moira Armstrong respectively.

At the same time as *Maidens' Trip* was showing on BBC2, a second series by Alan Plater was screening on BBC1. *The Middlemen* (June–July 1977) was a six-part series featuring Frank Windsor and Francis Matthews in a slightly surreal comedy drama, as Alan Plater recollects:

> I got this idea of doing something for my two favourite actors, Francis Matthews and Frank Windsor, because I'd worked with both of them and liked them both very much and I thought they would make an interesting combination, and it was a fantasy about a world where there were no jobs and it was about these two guys shambling through life looking for alternatives to work, because there was no work, and it was on the edge of science fiction and I think it's fair to say it was pretty well blasted out of the water by the press, except for Joan Bakewell, I remember Joan absolutely raved about it . . . It was consciously, self-consciously, surrealistic.[55]

The episode titles in themselves give a flavour of the idiosyncratic nature of the series: 'Rich Is Best', 'A Little Bit of Heaven', 'A Young Lady From Gloucester', 'A Bag of Mixed Nuts', 'Read Any Good Books Lately?' and 'Fresh Fields and Slightly Used Pastures', all typical of Alan Plater's quirky approach in a series more admired within the BBC – Shaun Sutton commenting that it was 'well worth watching for the writing alone' – than it was by critics and audiences who, Sutton thought after the second episode, 'were finding the programme unusual because it was different', not least because it was a comedy programme without audience laughter so 'viewers did not really know if they were meant to laugh'.[56]

Another unusual comedy series followed in 1978 with Mike Stott's five-part *Pickersgill People* (BBC2, April–May 1978), featuring Richard Wilson and Anthony Sher, while Janey Preger's *Two Up and Two Down* (BBC1, May–June 1979) was a six-part half-hour comedy series on BBC1 which saw one of English Regions Drama's few women writers moving into the mainstream after a *Second City First* and a *Play of the Week. Two Up and Two Down* overlapped with a very different serial from English Regions Drama on BBC1. *The Deep Concern* (BBC1, June–July 1979) was a six-part thriller written by Elwyn Jones, an established writer and well-known BBC figure whom David Rose had worked with in the Drama-Documentary Unit in the late 1950s and early 1960s.

Jones was the exception among the writers producing series and serials for English Regions Drama. All of the other writers, with the exception of Philip Martin, who subsequently wrote a single play for the department, and Thomas Ellice, whose adaptation of *Maidens' Tale* was his only work for English Regions Drama, had previously written either a half-hour or full-length play for the department. In the case of Alan Bleasdale, Ron Hutchinson, Alan Plater, Janey Preger and Mike Stott the pattern was a half-hour play followed by a full-length play and then a series or serial.

Ron Hutchinson, having written a *Second City First* and a *Play for Today*, wrote two serials for the department in the early 1980s, both produced by Michael Wearing. The six-part *Bull Week* (BBC1, May–June 1980) explored the tensions between three brothers working in a Birmingham factory, one in management, one on the factory floor and one who was a union shop steward. Shot partly on location, on film, and partly in the studio, *Bull Week* explored the politics of the workplace in a gritty, realist style, with Birmingham accents in plentiful evidence among the factory workers. The serial, which was set in the week before the annual fortnight holiday, when the factory employees 'work like bulls' to earn some extra money, was a precursor both of *Boys from the Blackstuff* – but set at a time before the policies of the new Thatcher government had really had an impact and people still had jobs – and of the later *Clocking Off* (BBC1, 2000–3), another regional, factory-based drama, set in Manchester, where the social realist conventions employed in *Bull Week* are given a postmodern makeover (see Cooke, 2005b). Hutchinson followed *Bull Week* with a four-part thriller, *Bird of Prey* (BBC1, April–May 1982), which was followed by a sequel in 1984.

Between *Bull Week* and *Bird of Prey* Michael Wearing also produced *The History Man* (BBC2, 4–25 January 1981), a four-part adaptation by Christopher Hampton of the novel by Malcolm Bradbury, featuring Anthony Sher as a sociology lecturer at a fictional campus university. In contrast to the other serials produced by English Regions Drama, *The History Man* was clearly in the 'academic' tradition of Bradbury's earlier *Play for Today, The After Dinner Game*. Later the same year, Tara Prem's *The Olympian Way* (BBC1, July–August 1981), a six-part serial set in a health club, saw her return to writing for the first time since *A Touch of Eastern Promise* in 1973, after seven years working as script editor, director and producer for English Regions Drama. Prem's decision to take a break from producing opened up the opportunity for Michael Wearing to step up from script editing to producing, with Stephen Davis's *Playhouse* drama, *Trouble With Gregory* (BBC2, 23 February 1980) and Ron Hutchinson's *Bull Week* his first tasks as a producer. Like Peter Ansorge, who developed a specialism in 'multicultural' drama, working with black and Asian writers, Wearing's interests saw an increase in the production of realist, social–concerned drama at Pebble Mill with *Bull Week, The History Man, Bird of Prey* and *Boys from the Blackstuff*.

Michael Wearing began working with Alan Bleasdale on *Boys from the Blackstuff* (BBC2, October–November 1982) well before Bleasdale's single play, *The Blackstuff*, was transmitted. According to Millington and Nelson: 'Ideas for *Boys from the Blackstuff* first surfaced in conversation during the shooting of *The Black Stuff* in the autumn of 1978 . . . Alan Bleasdale had the idea of writing a play about unemployment, using the same group of characters as they returned from Middlesbrough to the Liverpool dole queue' (Millington and Nelson, 1986: 32).

In November 1978 Bleasdale wrote to David Rose and Michael Wearing outlining a proposal for 'at least five fifty-minute plays' which would develop some of the themes in the original play. In his letter Bleasdale emphasised the social concerns that lay behind the proposal:

> I think it is very important right now to write about the Dole as seen from the point of view of those who are on it, and to side with them against the

people and papers who would like us to believe, despite the million and a half out of work and mass redundancies at every opportunity, that the majority of the unemployed are malingerers and rogues. It is my belief that at least ninety per cent of those who are out of work, want to work. (Millington and Nelson, 1986: 179)

Bleasdale's letter led to a commission, in May 1979, for six forty-five-minute plays which was subsequently changed to a commission for a seven-part series when Bleasdale submitted outlines for seven stories, in August 1979. The process of development of *Boys from the Blackstuff* was protracted, partly because of the delay in transmitting *The Blackstuff* and because of concerns about the potential cost of the series at a time when BBC production budgets were being cut (see Millington and Nelson, 1986, chapter 4). As we have already seen, one of Bleasdale's scripts, 'McKenna's Story', which was originally to be episode three of the series, was produced separately as a *Play for Today* called *The Muscle Market* (BBC1, 13 January 1981) in order for Michael Wearing 'to reassure Bleasdale of his continuing commitment' to the series (Millington and Nelson, 1986: 43). *The Muscle Market* was transmitted a year after the (delayed) transmission of *The Blackstuff* and nearly two years before the series for which it was originally intended.

Boys from the Blackstuff was eventually approved, at a budget of £860,000. In order to produce five fifty-minute plays on that budget it was decided to shoot four episodes on video, using Outside Broadcast cameras, at a cost of £147,500 per episode, while one episode would be shot on film, at a cost of £266,000, the difference illustrating the extra cost of shooting on film. Bleasdale's main concern in writing the series was to highlight the impact mass unemployment was having on working-class people and, in order to show the reality of social deprivation in Liverpool, where the drama is set, it was essential to be able to 'show the city' by filming on location. As a regional drama, however, it was not only through the visual signifiers that the impact of industrial deprivation was communicated but also through Bleasdale's deployment of a typically Liverpudlian black humour, conveyed through the mocking intonation and rhythms of the Scouse dialect. Through a combination of the visual, the linguistic and the affective performances of the actors *Boys from the Blackstuff* presented a sustained evocation of the impact of Thatcherite policies on one of the regional heartlands of industrial Britain. By the time the series was completed unemployment in Britain had risen to over three million, for the first time since the 1930s, and *Boys from the Blackstuff* consequently became a television 'event', tapping in to the increasing public outcry about the social impact of Thatcherite policies on traditional, industrial working-class communities. Repeated on BBC1 within weeks of its initial screening, the series increased its audience by fifty per cent, with the final episode attracting eight million viewers.

Character-based, rather than plot-driven, *Boys from the Blackstuff* used its characters as a means to explore the condition of the working class, especially the Liverpudlian working class, in contemporary Britain. The seminal figure of Yosser Hughes (Bernard Hill) became an iconic character in the series whose repeated refrain, 'Gizza job, I can do that', became a national catchphrase. Taken up and sung by thousands on the terraces of Liverpool Football Club, the phrase entered into popular currency, a defiant cry capturing the desperation and disenfranchisement of a whole class.

It was in the final episode, however, that the most profound statements were made about Britain's industrial decline and the 'death of socialism', represented by the death of George Malone (Peter Kerrigan), the trade unionist whose politics had been shaped in the Depression of the 1930s. Filmed in the derelict, abandoned Liverpool docks, there was extreme pathos in George's dying words, 'I can't believe there's no hope . . . I can't', as the camera zoomed out to reveal the deserted dockyard, a symbol of Liverpool's industrial decline. Like the final image of the series, of Chrissie (Michael Angelis), Loggo (Alan Igbon) and Yosser walking forlornly past the Tate and Lyle factory as it is demolished, the image of the deserted Liverpool docks seemed to undermine the optimism of George's final lament, suggesting little hope for the future.

Yet the bleakness of these images is counter-balanced by the expressions of optimism uttered by characters such as George, not to mention the anger shown by two of the female characters in this male-dominated drama, the dramatically significant outburst of George's wife (Jean Heywood) when reacting against the defeatism shown by her sons and the exasperation shown by Angie (Julie Walters) in trying to get Chrissie to fight back against the system that has emasculated him. Unlike George, the younger men have been ground down, lacking his resolution and experience of fighting mass unemployment in the 1930s, and it is left to the women to try to rekindle some of that fighting spirit in their demoralised menfolk.

Nevertheless, the images of industrial decay all around them certainly provide grounds for the boys' pessimism, the all too visible destruction of Liverpool's industrial heritage standing as a metaphor for the systematic destruction of industrial Britain by the Conservative government. As Pawling and Perkins point out, the realistic style of the series enabled the actual industrial destruction that was taking place in Liverpool at the time to be conveyed in almost documentary fashion:

> The 'subject' of the drama was not simply the 'Boys', but Liverpool itself as a city under intense pressure. So the location shots of the derelict docks or the demolition of the Tate and Lyle refinery in 'George's Last Ride', were not just signifiers of a generalised backcloth of dereliction, but acted as *specific* records of the concrete destruction of people's working lives at that particular moment in time. This, then, was no dramatic recreation for visual effect, but actuality footage of Liverpool's devastation as it occurred, brick by brick. (Pawling and Perkins, 1992: 54)

The use of video cameras may have contributed to this look of 'actuality', video connoting 'immediacy' and 'the present' where film more often connotes 'the past', but the series was not a 'documentary' drama in the tradition of Loach and Garnett. Bleasdale has said he does not see himself as a 'political' writer, in the Jim Allen mould – 'I have no tendencies to be Marxist' (quoted in Millington, 1984: 11) – and *Boys from the Blackstuff* deliberately took a different approach from the more strident one adopted by Allen in plays such as *The Lump* and *The Big Flame*.

While the 'realism' of the series was a major factor in its success, drawing audiences into recognition with situations and circumstances that were a part of their everyday lives, the comedy that Bleasdale injected into the series was also important in alleviating the grimness of the 'stories' that were being told, as well as enhancing the verisimilitude of the series, as one Liverpudlian viewer noted:

> There's a lot of humour in the series, a lot of tragedy. Someone once said, your life in Liverpool was a tragedy played as if it were a comedy. Well, the trouble with that is that we tend to put a brave face on things if we can manage it, so we don't talk to each other about the problems we, as unemployed people, have. But since the series has been on, people have

been saying, yes, we've been through that, I've thought like that, and it isn't just a question of individual characters. All of us have been, at some time or another, as desperate as Yosser, or feeling stripped of dignity as Chrissie. At times, maybe, we felt as optimistic as George, but it's like all the characters were facets of us put together; the kind of life all of us have, and that's a great achievement to make. He's given us words to communicate with each other about our own experiences. (Archer, 1984: 49)

It was the blend of realism and humour, especially the use of black comedy as a 'stylistic device used to defuse the emotional intensity of a scene' (Millington, 1984: 18), that made *Boys from the Blackstuff* unique, not only contributing to the powerful and lasting effect the series had on its audience but marking a new development in British social realist drama. In its searing indictment of the effect that government policies were having on working-class communities, the series demonstrated that it was possible, through television drama, to give a voice to the millions of people who were suffering as a consequence of Thatcherite policies in the early 1980s.

In a way *Boys from the Blackstuff* represented the end of an era at English Regions Drama. That it had been produced at all was a consequence of the department's commitment towards producing contemporary regional drama by regional writers, especially writers new to television such as Alan Bleasdale, whose relationship with English Regions Drama was nurtured from his very first play, *Early to Bed*, through *Scully's New Year's Eve*, *The Blackstuff* and *The Muscle Market*. The creative environment David Rose established at Pebble Mill not only gave opportunities to many new regional writers such as Bleasdale, it also enabled other important television careers to develop, not least those of the department's script editors-turned-producers: Barry Hanson, Tara Prem, Peter Ansorge and Michael Wearing. It was Wearing's productive relationship with Alan Bleasdale, established as a script editor on *Scully's New Year's Eve* and *The Blackstuff*, which saw *Boys from the Blackstuff* through to completion after the vicissitudes of a protracted production process.

By the time *Boys from the Blackstuff* was completed, however, David Rose had left the department to take up a position as Senior Commissioning Editor for Fiction at the new Channel Four. Not long after, Peter Ansorge joined him there and many of the writers and directors who had been working for English Regions Drama followed

Rose and Ansorge to Channel Four. Michael Wearing also left, going to the Drama Department in London to produce the final season of *Play for Today* in 1983–84 and Troy Kennedy Martin's *Edge of Darkness* (1985). Although Wearing, and later Barry Hanson, subsequently returned to Birmingham to take up the position of Head of Drama at Pebble Mill the regional ethos that David Rose established in the 1970s dissipated following his departure, as Peter Ansorge testifies: 'I think it did decline and then they tried to bring back Barry and Michael . . . and it's not that no good work was done after that, but the breadth of the work that was done and the sort of excitement and discoveries and in a sense that collegiate atmosphere that we had, I don't believe they ever regained that.'[57]

Rather than appoint Ansorge or Wearing as Head of English Regions Drama following Rose's departure, which might have made possible some continuity in the regional ethos that had been established through contacts with regional writers, a new Head of Department was appointed and 'the whole BBC Birmingham culture', as David Hare once described it, began to change, as Michael Wearing explains:

> Well what happened was it sort of broke up a bit because Peter went off with David to Channel Four and by that time he and I were the key producers, I suppose; neither of us reaped the inheritance, and they brought Robin Midgley in and Robin had all sorts of retro ideas about live drama in the studio and all that and I sort of stuck it through that because I wanted to do *Boys from the Blackstuff*, obviously, and Robin, to be fair, was a huge, huge supporter of that.[58]

While some of the spirit of the department lived on in plays such as Peter Terson's *Atlantis* (1983) and Farrukh Dhondy's five-part series *Come to Mecca* (1983), Robin Midgley brought a different approach, developing, among other things, what Wearing clearly considered to be 'retro' drama – a series of 'live' plays produced in the Pebble Mill studios, by writers such as Keith Dewhurst, Bernard Kops and Fay Weldon. There was even a play directed by the veteran Granada director Silvio Narizzano: John Wain's *Young Shoulders* (BBC1, 14 February 1984), a studio drama produced for the final season of *Play for Today*. The great regional drama initiative which began in 1971, when English Regions Drama was established at Pebble Mill, had come to an end and many of its key players migrated to an exciting new venture in British television: Channel Four.

Notes

1　David Rose, interviewed by the author, 26 February 2003.
2　BBC Written Archives Centre (WAC), 'An Audience Research Report: *That Quiet Earth*', 22 March 1972.
3　David Rose, interviewed by the author, 26 February 2003.
4　See *In Two Minds* (BBC1, 1 March 1967), directed by Ken Loach.
5　Peter Ansorge, interviewed by the author, 2 June 2005.
6　Ibid. Ansorge is referring here to the camera rehearsal and recording all being done on one day in the studio. Prior to going into the studio the director would spend five days rehearsing with the actors.
7　Willy Russell, email to the author, 19 November 2010.
8　BBC WAC, Television Weekly Programme Review Minutes, 27 February 1974, p. 12.
9　In fact, *The Actual Woman* was not in 'the last series' of *Second City Firsts* to be shown (which would have been series four) but the second series. Three plays from the first two series were repeated between series four and five, in May and October 1975: *Girl* and *The Actual Woman* from series two, and *Mrs Pool's Preserves* (also directed by Philip Saville) from the first series.
10　Neville Smith had previously co-written a *Wednesday Play*, directed by Ken Loach, called *The Golden Vision* (BBC1, 17 April 1968), a drama-documentary about Everton FC in which Smith played an Everton supporter, which he was. Smith had also written screenplays for a London Weekend Television film directed by Ken Loach, *After a Lifetime* (1971), and for a feature film, Stephen Frears's *Gumshoe* (1971).
11　For more on the work of Mike Leigh see Carney and Quart (2000), Coveney (1997), Raphael (2008), Watson (2004) and Whitehead (2007).
12　See Cooke (2005b: 196) for an example of how writing for *Coronation Street* for ten years had a debilitating effect on Paul Abbott: 'it took me two years to get over it'.
13　See *BFI TV 100: A Selection of the Favourite British Television Programmes of the 20th Century* (London: BFI, 2000) in which *Abigail's Party* was third in the Single Drama category and *Boys from the Blackstuff* number one in the Drama Series and Serials category. For critical assessments of canonicity in television see Bignell (2006), Creeber (2004) and Ellis (2005 and 2007).
14　For contractual reasons Jack Gold was required to shoot ten per cent of *The Lump* in the studio, as producer Tony Garnett explained in an interview with the author on 29 February 2000 (see Cooke, 2003: 73).
15　Dialogue transcribed from a video recording of the play.
16　David Rose, interviewed by the author, 13 November 2003.

17 BBC WAC, 'An Audience Research Report: *Shakespeare – or Bust*', 5 March 1973.

18 Peter Terson later reworked the formula in a fourth *Play for Today* for English Regions Drama: *Atlantis* (BBC1, 29 March 1983) featured three similarly comic characters, played by different actors this time, and a similarly light-hearted and poignant narrative in which they try to realise a dream by restoring an old canal boat.

19 For a more detailed analysis of *Land of Green Ginger* see Rolinson (2007).

20 BBC WAC, '*The Roses of Eyam*', Television Weekly Programme Review (Minutes), 13 June 1973, p.13. C.P.S.Tel. = Controller Programme Services (Television); H.D.G.Tel. = Head of Drama Group (Television); H.E.R.D. = Head of English Regions Drama; C.BBC-2 = Controller BBC2.

21 BBC WAC, 'An Audience Research Report: *The Roses of Eyam*', 29 June 1973.

22 Michael Wearing, interviewed by the author, 2 June 2005.

23 Tragically, shortly after his appearance in *Diary of a Madman*, Henry had a serious accident which left him in a coma, from which he never recovered.

24 Transcribed from David Rudkin's introduction to the screening of *Penda's Fen* on Channel Four, 22 July 1990.

25 *Film 4 Today* (C4, July–August 1990) was a short season of six BBC English Regions Drama plays: *Licking Hitler*, *Nuts In May*, *Penda's Fen*, *Our Day Out*, *The Muscle Market* and *The Fishing Party*, all of which had been shot on film.

26 Michael Wearing, interviewed by the author, 2 June 2005.

27 Comments by Philip Martin on the Birmingham accent can be found on the audio commentary accompanying the DVD release of *Gangsters* (BBC Worldwide, 2006).

28 David Rose, interviewed by the author, 26 February 2003.

29 BBC WAC, 'An Audience Research Report: *Gangsters*', 27 January 1975.

30 Information on the play's budget obtained from the audio commentary accompanying the DVD release of *Gangsters*. The 'above-the-line' costs did not include such 'hidden' costs as the facilities available within the BBC or the salaries of BBC production staff, all of which were calculated as 'below-the-line' costs. On the DVD audio commentary to the first episode of the series, which he directed, Alastair Reid says he was told by the Production Manager that the budget for the single play was £117,000, which may have been the total cost.

31 Philip Saville, interviewed by the author, 11 June 2004.

32 BBC WAC, '*Play for Today: Gangsters*', Television Weekly Programme Review (Minutes), 15 January 1975, p. 11.

33 Audio commentary accompanying the DVD release of *Gangsters*.

34 Mike Leigh, interviewed by the author, 14 July 2000.

35 BBC WAC, Television Weekly Programme Review (Minutes), 28 January 1976 and 4 February 1976.

36 Mike Leigh, interviewed by the author, 14 July 2000.

37 *Abigail's Party* was not an English Regions Drama production.

38 BBC WAC, Television Weekly Programme Review (Minutes), 27 July 1977, p. 8.

39 BBC WAC, Television Weekly Programme Review (Minutes), 4 January 1978, p. 19.

40 BBC WAC, Television Weekly Programme Review (Minutes), 18 January 1978.

41 *Sense of Place* was a rare example of a regional BBC drama series not made by English Regions Drama. There were two series, in 1978–79, of half-hour dramas by writers from the North West, including Alan Bleasdale, Shelagh Delaney, Alan Garner, Henry Livings and Janey Preger (who also wrote several plays and a series for English Regions Drama).

42 On several occasions during the DVD audio commentary on *The Blackstuff*, which was included as part of the DVD release of *Boys from the Blackstuff* (BBC Worldwide, 2003), Bleasdale draws attention to the effectiveness of particular shots, endorsing the contribution made to the drama by Jim Goddard and the camera team.

43 The *Scully* series was eventually produced by Granada and transmitted on Channel Four in May–June 1984.

44 BBC WAC, 'An Audience Research Report: *Trinity Tales: The Driver's Tale*', 22 December 1975.

45 BBC WAC, 'An Audience Research Report: *Trinity Tales: The Fryer's Tale*', 29 December 1975.

46 Alan Plater, interviewed by the author, 11 June 2004.

47 *The Driver's Tale*, ibid.

48 *The Fryer's Tale*, ibid.

49 Information obtained from the audio commentary accompanying the DVD release of *Gangsters*.

50 BBC WAC, Television Weekly Programme Review (Minutes), 20 October 1976, p. 8.

51 BBC WAC, Television Weekly Programme Review (Minutes), 18 January 1978, p. 11.

52 BBC WAC, Television Weekly Programme Review (Minutes), 11 January 1978, p. 17.

53 Peter Ansorge, interviewed by the author, 2 June 2005.

54 Figures from the BBC Television Weekly Programme Review minutes for 15 November 1978 and 13 December 1978. Peter Ansorge's estimated audience of 'two, two and half million' suggests an average audience.

55 Alan Plater, interviewed by the author, 11 June 2004.
56 BBC WAC, Television Weekly Programme Review (Minutes), 22 June 1977 and 29 June 1977.
57 Peter Ansorge, interviewed by the author, 2 June 2005.
58 Michael Wearing, interviewed by the author, 2 June 2005.

Conclusion

Granada Television and BBC English Regions Drama provide contrasting models of regional television drama production in the 'second age' of British television, from 1955 to 1982. A comparison of the two – one a major company producing a range of programming for the ITV network, the other a small department within the BBC established specifically to produce regional drama for the BBC network – illustrates the range of regional television drama produced in a duopolistic era when only three channels (and only two before 1964) were available to the television audience.

Coming on air a year after ITV began broadcasting in the London region, Granada Television produced a wide range of regionally based drama, mostly written by Northern writers, portraying regional culture and regional identities for both a 'local' audience – inhabiting an area of the North of England which Sidney Bernstein famously dubbed 'Granadaland' – and a national audience, as nearly all of its drama production was networked. This is not to say that all of the drama produced by Granada in this period portrayed the regional culture and identity of the North West of England, but it is to argue that indigenous drama production helped to forge Granada's reputation as a regional broadcaster.

BBC English Regions Drama, on the other hand, although regionally based in Birmingham, produced a diversity of regional representations as a result of its remit to commission regionally based writers from all over England, with a view to these dramas being screened for a national audience on BBC1 and BBC2. English Regions Drama productions were set in Birmingham, Hull, Liverpool, Newcastle, Derbyshire, Lancashire, Worcestershire, Yorkshire, and many other parts of England, including Dorset (Mike Leigh's *Nuts in May*) in a rare foray down south.

Both Granada and BBC English Regions Drama valued and cultivated regional writers: Granada initially drawing on an earlier tradition of Lancashire drama with its adaptations of 'Manchester School'
plays, before developing its own school of Northern writers, including
Cyril Abraham, Harry Driver, Peter Eckersley, John Finch, Harry
Kershaw and Jack Rosenthal, many of whom began their writing
careers on *Coronation Street*; meanwhile BBC English Regions Drama
commissioned writers such as Alan Bleasdale, Henry Livings, Alan
Plater, Janey Preger, David Rudkin, Willy Russell and Peter Terson
from a variety of different English regions, not just the North, in an
attempt to promote a diversity of regional voices and counter the
metropolitan hegemony of London.

Both Granada and BBC English Regions Drama produced a mixture
of studio-based drama and location-based drama. Granada pioneered
drama production on location using Outside Broadcast units, initially,
before moving into filmed drama in the late 1960s. For BBC English
Regions Drama, producing its first drama in 1972, film was important
from the beginning, with John Hopkins's *That Quiet Earth* the first of
many filmed dramas to be produced by the department. While English
Regions Drama experimented with new lightweight video equipment
in 1973–74 a film aesthetic was preferred for its ability to convey
a 'sense of place' with greater verisimilitude, complementing and
enhancing the regionality of the writing.

By no means all of Granada's drama was set in its own region.
The Fellows (1967), for example, was a thirteen-part detective serial
set in Cambridge, while the gangster serial *Big Breadwinner Hog* was
set in London, and the long-running series *Adam Smith* was about a
vicar in a Scottish village. There were also historical/costume dramas
such as *The Caesars*, about the Roman emperors, *Judge Dee*, a six-
part costume/detective drama set in seventh-century China, and the
lavish *Brideshead Revisited* with its glamorous locations ranging from
Oxford to Venice. BBC English Regions Drama, on the other hand,
rarely ventured abroad, or into the past, but produced a variety of
mainly contemporary drama set in a wide range of English locations,
all outside London.

As one of the 'big five' ITV companies, Granada had the resources to
commit to long-running serials like *Coronation Street* as well as major
productions like the fifty-two episodes of *A Family at War* and the
thirty-nine episodes of *Sam*. As a regional department within the BBC,
English Regions Drama was more limited in terms of staff and funding

and its drama serials only once extended beyond six episodes, to the fifteen episodes of *Empire Road*, although its ratio of filmed drama to studio drama was probably higher than that of Granada, the BBC investing more in filmed drama during the 1970s than did Granada.[1]

Both Granada and BBC English Regions Drama were part of larger organisations, Granada Television being part of the Granada Group, as well as part of the Independent Television network. But Granada TV established a reputation early on in its history for being fiercely independent within ITV, and this was an important factor in Granada developing a reputation for original, innovative programming. While the company produced its fair share of low-cost popular drama for the network, especially in the early days of ITV, it gradually developed a reputation for distinctive 'quality' drama, both in its single plays produced for networked series such as *Television Playhouse* and *Play of the Week* and in its innovative anthology series, such as *City '68*, *Country Matters* and *Red Letter Day*, as well as with its original drama series and serials, from *Coronation Street* to the spy series *The XYY Man* and the Northern police drama *Strangers* (1978–82).

Although BBC English Regions Drama was a small department based at BBC Birmingham, itself a regional outpost (albeit one of the main regional production centres) within the BBC, the influence and achievements of the department far exceeded its size. From its establishment at the new Pebble Mill studios in 1971, David Rose was intent on maintaining a creative as well as physical distance from the metropolitan centre of the BBC, declining the invitation from the Head of Plays to attend regular meetings in London, as noted in Chapter 4. The advantage of this creative autonomy is evident in the body of work produced at Pebble Mill from 1972 to 1982 (see Appendix 2), a sustained period of original, innovative and culturally diverse drama which has no parallel in the history of British television.

It was because English Regions Drama was based in the regions, rather than London, closer to the flourishing regional repertory theatre movement of the 1970s, from which the department drew many of its writers and other personnel, that it was able to produce such an original and innovative body of work, the writers benefiting from the freedom they were given, feeding off the creative atmosphere nurtured by David Rose, in a way that might not have been possible had their work been commissioned in London. Only Granada, with its greater resources, has managed to produce a comparable body of regional television drama, over a longer period of time, and arguably without the diversity that is to be found in the portfolio of drama produced at Pebble Mill in the 1970s and early 1980s.

The carefully cultivated autonomy of English Regions Drama at Pebble Mill was mainly due to the beneficent, protective leadership of David Rose during his ten years as head of the department. W. Stephen Gilbert was just one of many people given an opportunity by Rose to produce original, sometimes controversial, drama at Pebble Mill. Despite the chastening experience of the banned *Solid Geometry*, Gilbert acknowledged the important role played by Rose and English Regions Drama in giving progressive writers, directors and producers the creative space in which to work without pressure or interference, even if such freedom sometimes incurred the disapproval of the BBC hierarchy:

> Rose and his Birmingham-based team 'got away with' things that no-one would dare try in London – not in the sense of affronting the audience, but in their approach to working methods, in their willingness to go for broke with a difficult subject, an untried director, a new writer. The result was the most consistently adventurous and constructive drama output anywhere in television. (Gilbert, 1980: 12)

Being based in Birmingham undoubtedly enabled David Rose, Barry Hanson, Tara Prem, Peter Ansorge, Michael Wearing and the other producers at Pebble Mill to 'get away with' things they might not have got away with in London. According to Peter Ansorge the autonomy enjoyed by English Regions Drama was entirely due to Rose's leadership and the fact that Rose had been at the BBC a long time and enjoyed a good working relationship with Head of Drama Shaun Sutton was also important:

> Shaun Sutton, who was Head of Drama, had been very, very close with David, they worked on *Z Cars* together and was David's kind of protector if there were any controversial problems and would quietly say to David 'Well I think they'd like a bit of this, you know what I mean?', very close. We didn't really know because David had always protected us.[2]

When David Rose left to take up the position of Senior Commissioning Editor for Fiction at Channel Four Ansorge felt that the BBC 'didn't quite know what to do with us, because we were such a separate entity and we'd come up with brilliant results, we'd come up with the most bizarre things, they couldn't identify [with] it'.[3] Michael Wearing stayed on to produce *Boys from the Blackstuff* but left shortly afterwards. Peter Ansorge stayed for a while longer, producing Farrukh Dhondy's *Come to Mecca* series at Birmingham in 1983, before joining David Rose at Channel Four as Commissioning Editor for Series and Serials. With the departure of these key personnel the creative momentum that had been built up at Pebble Mill dissipated and the autonomous regional initiative that Rose had established in Birmingham went into decline, as writer Philip Martin observed:

> When David and Peter left, the power of that position in the Midlands, of the English Regions, was downgraded, and it was never the same again. The people that followed didn't have the power to manage their own budgets, to make their own choices, to develop their own talent and it was like a Golden Age that came to an end then.[4]

Industrial circumstances were beginning to change in the early 1980s, in television as in other industries, as Thatcherite economic policies began to take effect. As Philip Martin highlights, subsequent Heads of Department at English Regions Drama 'didn't have the power to manage their own budgets, to make their own choices, to develop their own talent' and the creative autonomy enjoyed by David Rose, Barry Hanson and others at Pebble Mill began to be reined in as steps were taken to make television production more cost-effective. This eventually impacted on the freedom that 'progressive' producers, writers and directors had previously enjoyed at the BBC which, since the early 1960s, had been relatively free from political interference and market pressure.

While Granada also had a commitment to innovation and to its regional writers, directors and producers – who were extremely loyal to the company, recognising that Granada was special among the ITV companies – there were nevertheless commercial pressures on Granada from its establishment in the mid-1950s to produce popular programmes for the ITV network. The different circumstances within which the company operated make its achievements, as far as the production of regional television drama is concerned, of a different order to those of BBC English Regions Drama.

There is no doubt that series and serials such as *Coronation Street, The Younger Generation, The Villains, City '68, A Family at War, Sam, The Stars Look Down* and *Hard Times*, plus individual plays such as *Roll On Four O'Clock, The Mosedale Horseshoe* and *Another Sunday and Sweet F.A.*, were regionally distinctive, original works of drama, mostly from Northern writers, directors and producers who had a commitment not only to the company but to the region they were portraying. These plays, series and serials were also popular with audiences, a consideration which may have been important to BBC English Regions Drama but which was not the imperative that it was for a commercial company.

There was also a vast body of original work produced by writers, producers and directors at Granada, such as Robin Chapman, Richard Everitt, Julia Jones, Hugh Leonard, Philip Mackie, Peter Wildeblood, Derek Bennett, June Howson, Claude Whatham, Herbert Wise and Michael Cox, which was not necessarily 'regional', in the sense of portraying the region, but which made an original contribution to the portfolio of drama produced by the company in the 1960s and 1970s, very often raising the standards of drama on the ITV network and providing a distinct challenge to the often more celebrated plays and drama serials on the BBC.

Yet despite its many achievements it is debatable as to whether Granada was able to match the diverse range of innovative regional drama produced by BBC English Regions Drama in the 1970s and early 1980s. Granada's drama portfolio was of a different nature, often more realist in form and eschewing the stylistic innovations evident in such BBC English Regions Drama productions as *That Quiet Earth, Penda's Fen, Gangsters, The Red Shift, Rotten* and *Artemis 81*. This is not to deny the extent of Granada's contribution to regional television drama in the period but to acknowledge that the company was subject to other, more commercial, considerations – namely the need to attract audiences to the ITV network – which may have tempered the artistic ambitions of its writers and directors and limited the opportunities for experiment and innovation.

While some of the drama series with which Philip Mackie was involved (e.g. *Saki, The Victorians, The Liars*) were original, often formally adventurous, 'quality' dramas, they were also studious (and studio-bound) literary dramas. Neither Mackie nor any of his Granada colleagues went as far as writers such as John Hopkins, David Rudkin or Philip Martin at BBC English Regions Drama in stretching the boundaries of television drama. Furthermore, Granada's drama was rarely as 'political', or as socially conscious, as some of the drama produced at Pebble Mill by writers such as Tony Bicat, Alan Bleasdale, David Hare, Ron Hutchinson and Janey Preger.

It is significant that the landmark dramas produced by Granada and BBC English Regions Drama at the end of the period under consideration were, respectively, *Brideshead Revisited* and *Boys from the Blackstuff*. The contrast between these two British television 'classics' perhaps encapsulates a major difference between Granada and the BBC at a time when British television was moving into a more competitive era. This moment, 1981–82, is a significant one in British television culture, marking the beginnings of a shift towards a global broadcasting culture. From this moment Granada's drama was increasingly made with an overseas market in mind, hence the shift in production towards such 'heritage' dramas as *Brideshead Revisited*, *The Jewel in the Crown* and *The Adventures of Sherlock Holmes*.

It is worth noting that Granada's overseas sales company, Granada International, was established at this time. At a Granada seminar in February 1981, held to consider the prospects for the next decade following the successful renewal of its franchise, chairman Denis Forman, after outlining how television was changing, asserted that Granada was in a good position 'to take advantage of these new opportunities'. He explained that the company had plans 'to expand our production capacity in Manchester substantially' and that it would also apply for a transponder on the British satellite 'to provide a satellite service in the UK and Northern France'. With its rental business it was 'well suited to hire out the equipment required in the home for all of these new forms of video' and furthermore 'for international production and marketing of software we have Granada International. We also have money. All in all, the Group is poised to jump' (Granada, 1981a: 7–8). From that moment the role of Granada International became increasingly important, not only to the Granada Group but to ITV as a whole.[5]

At the end of the 1980s Margaret Thatcher's Conservative government proposed far-reaching changes in broadcasting in a White Paper entitled 'Broadcasting in the 1990s: Competition, Choice and Quality'. Among the initiatives, which subsequently became law in the 1990 Broadcasting Act, was the controversial proposal to put the ITV franchises up for auction when the contracts expired in 1991. This paved the way for a series of mergers and takeovers among the ITV companies leading to the eventual establishment of one consolidated 'national' company in February 2004 (although Scottish Television, Grampian, Ulster and Channel TV remained separate). The economic rationale for consolidation was that it would enable ITV plc to compete more effectively in a global marketplace. One consequence of consolidation, however, was that the previous commitment to regional broadcasting was downgraded in favour of the production of more 'quality' dramas designed for an international market, e.g. *Agatha Christie's Poirot* (1989 to present), *Doctor Zhivago* (2002), *The Forsyte Saga* (2002) and *Downton Abbey* (2010 to present). While regionally based ITV production centres still produce 'regional' drama these now tend to take the form of tried and tested long-running serials, such as *Coronation Street* and *Emmerdale*, which are not only popular in Britain but also marketable abroad.

In the new era of 'Competition, Choice and Quality' there has been a decline in the range and variety of indigenous regional television drama that existed prior to the emergence of a global market. Consolidation has also brought an increasing centralisation within ITV, with regional production centres being closed or scaled down. As Steve Barnett noted when reporting in *The Observer* on the closure of Granada's historic Manchester studios in November 2003:

> This is the logical outcome of modernising a system meant for a different era and a different marketplace. The whole point of a system that divided the UK into 14 somewhat arbitrary regional entities was that each successful licensee would have roots firmly in its own region. Not just the board directors, but senior executives, programme makers, scriptwriters and reporters would reflect and enhance local identity because they were part of it. That philosophy was undermined by the 1990 Broadcasting Act and has been unravelling ever since. (Barnett, 2003)

However, another clause in the 1990 Broadcasting Act – the requirement that both the BBC and ITV take 25 per cent of their programming from independent production companies – introduced a potential counterweight to the centralising and globalising tendencies encouraged in other parts of the Act. The establishment of Channel Four in the early 1980s as a publisher, rather than producer, of programmes led to the emergence of dozens of small independent production companies competing to provide programmes for the new channel. While many of these companies fell by the wayside and a process of mergers led to the emergence of several 'super-indies', with ambitions to compete in an international marketplace, the establishment of a 25 per cent quota of independent production (admittedly not always achieved by the BBC and ITV) enabled some enterprising independents, such as Company Pictures (*The Lakes, Shameless, Skins*), Red Production Company (*Queer as Folk, Clocking Off, Linda Green*), Tiger Aspect (*Playing the Field, Teachers, Fat Friends*) and

World Productions *(Ballykissangel, The Cops, No Angels)*, to produce regional television drama for a national audience, screened on the main terrestrial channels.

That only one of the twelve dramas listed was commissioned by ITV *(Fat Friends)* is indicative of the crisis in ITV as the company tried to reposition itself as an international broadcaster, choosing to stick with its established drama series and long-running serials rather than risk commissioning new regional drama from independent production companies.[6] This seems to confirm a prediction made by Geraint Talfan Davies in 1999 that 'the regional character of the ITV system will weaken and that, almost as a mirror image of this trend, the BBC's national provision for Scotland, Wales and Northern Ireland and its local provision in England will grow in scale and importance' (Kidd and Taylor, 2002: 88).

While ITV has been closing regional studios and reducing its regional television production, the BBC has been investing in new regional studios in Birmingham, Cardiff, Glasgow and Manchester. Following the closure of the BBC's Pebble Mill studios in 2004, BBC drama relocated to a new Drama Village based at the University of Birmingham's Selly Oak campus, where there is a purpose-built set for the daytime serial *Doctors* (2000 to present) and where other daytime drama series such as *The Afternoon Play* (2003–7), *Moving On* (2009–11) and *Land Girls* (2009–11) have been produced. A similar Drama Village opened in Cardiff in 2011 to produce networked drama from BBC Wales, including the revived *Doctor Who* (2005 to present), its spin-offs *Torchwood* (2006 to present) and *The Sarah Jane Adventures* (2007 to present), and series such as *Casualty* (1986 to present), which was previously produced in Bristol, and the Welsh-language soap opera *Pobol y Cwm* (1974 to present). New BBC Scotland studios opened in Glasgow in 2007, and a major new development at Salford Quays, formerly the site of the Manchester docks became the home of BBC North in 2011, subsuming BBC North West, which had studios in central Manchester.

While the 'drama villages' in Birmingham and Cardiff represent significant investments in drama production at the BBC, it is arguable as to whether the programmes being produced at these production facilities reflect regional culture and regional identities in the way that dramas from Granada and BBC English Regions Drama previously did. In an article highlighting the BBC's investment in new regional studios, director general Mark Thompson unwittingly acknowledged that a series like *Torchwood*, while it may be produced by a regional BBC studio, is unequivocally global in terms of its ambition and target audience:

> Last week I stood on the steps of City Hall in Los Angeles watching an episode of Torchwood being shot. A large American crew, substantial American investment, a programme filmed on location in the United States and in Wales and seen by audiences around the world including licence payers in the UK – but a core creative team which is Welsh to its fingertips. (Thompson, 2011)

In the twenty-first-century global marketplace, regionally produced television drama has to appeal beyond its locality and target as wide an audience as possible. In the case of *Torchwood* this means acquiring American investment and filming in international locations.

Not all recent regionally produced BBC drama operates on this scale. The budgets and production schedules for BBC Birmingham's daytime dramas are more limited and some of these series have been filmed in regional locations in Birmingham, Liverpool and Manchester. Yet because of their daytime scheduling these dramas do not have the profile of such landmark regional dramas as *Boys from the Blackstuff*, *Empire Road*, *Gangsters*, *Land of Green Ginger* and *Penda's Fen*, produced by BBC English Regions Drama at Pebble Mill in the 1970s to 1980s.

Nevertheless, the creation of new 'drama villages' by the BBC in recent years, together with the commissioning of dramas from independent production companies, suggests that the future of regional television drama is being taken more seriously by the BBC than it is by ITV, despite ITV's historic role in this area. The lack of initiative shown by ITV in commissioning from independent production companies has enabled the BBC and Channel Four to benefit from the 'new wave' of regional drama produced by these companies since the mid to late 1990s (see Cooke, 2005a). Because of their smaller size and regional contacts, independent production companies such as Company Pictures, Red Production Company, Tiger Aspect and World Productions are often better positioned to produce regional drama than the increasingly centralised and globally oriented national broadcasters.

In this respect independent production companies are maintaining the regional traditions established by Granada and BBC English Regions Drama: nurturing regional writers and regional actors, filming in regional locations, portraying regional culture and regional identities for both regional and national audiences.[7] The 'national' audiences, in this case, are principally those of England, Scotland, Wales and Ireland (although some of these dramas have been sold abroad), whereas the 'regional' audiences are those communities in the English regions that form the English national audience in all its social, cultural and ethnic diversity.

In the rapidly changing ecology of British broadcasting, independent production companies now provide a progressive counter balance to the more conservative regional drama produced by the national broadcasters, the popularity of which was confirmed in a report from the media regulator Ofcom in April 2006 which revealed that regional audiences often have a preference for programmes made in their own region, as *The Guardian* reported at the time:

> Viewers show strong loyalty to their regional identity. The Cornwall drama *Doc Martin* is the fourth favourite show in the region, while *Emmerdale* and *Heartbeat* are second and fourth in their home county of Yorkshire. Among the top shows in the HTV West region are *Holby City* and *Midsomer Murders*, both set in the west of England. (Tryhorn, 2006: 25)

In contrast to these highly popular, long-running series there are other regional dramas being produced by independent production companies that are less conservative in their representations and often more stylistically innovative (e.g. *Queer as Folk*, *The Cops*, *Shameless* and *Skins*). These 'alternative' regional dramas, from independent production companies, are the ones maintaining the innovative traditions of Granada and, especially, BBC English Regions Drama, to which, in terms of size, creative personnel and independence, they bear some resemblance.

If these two kinds of regional television drama – from national broadcasters and from independent production companies – represent two models of regional drama production today there is the possibility of a third model with the development of local television available on new digital media platforms. While national broadcasters tend to develop 'rural heritage'-style regional drama, with a view to selling such programmes abroad, and independent production companies deliver contemporary urban representations of the 'new regionalism' evident in provincial English cities at the beginning of the twenty-first century, developments in new technology are making possible new forms of low-cost regional drama for distribution via the internet.

One example of this is The Rural Media Company, based in the West Midlands, which, since 1992, has been working 'To empower people in rural communities, particularly those most disadvantaged, to develop understanding, skills and a "voice" through creative media'.[8] While the short films and videos produced by Rural Media embrace all forms, including drama, they provide a genuinely 'local' example of regional media production which emerges from the interests and needs of the local community. This new form of regional media production represents a move towards democratising the media at a time when media production has become increasingly concentrated in the hands of fewer and fewer large organisations with global ambitions:

> As we witness the globalisation and commercialisation of the media, the growth of community media is providing an essential counterbalance, often challenging the mainstream. Almost every month digital technologies are providing new opportunities for individuals and groups to produce and distribute their own content.
>
> Our community projects encourage diversity, participation and creativity and enable people to articulate the important issues in their lives, giving them the confidence to address them. We are exploring many different approaches: local TV, digital stories, the large-scale community film, personal testimony, citizen journalism and online publishing.
>
> Rural Media is working in partnership at a national and international level to advocate for access to new communications technology and media skills to be recognised as an essential part of democratic culture.[9]

With younger television viewers in the sixteen to twenty-four age range now spending more time surfing the internet than watching television it may well be that this kind of low-cost digital drama will become an increasingly important force in the next few years. Such drama may lack the production values of the other two models of regional drama, guaranteeing their continued existence, but it could provide an important alternative to mainstream drama production, producing forms of regional representation not found on the national television channels and nurturing a seedbed of regional talent to feed the independent production companies and the mainstream broadcasters.

Of the three types of regional broadcasting referred to by Mike Kidd and Bill Taylor in their introduction to the ITC report on *Television in the Nations and Regions* – the production of regional programmes outside of London, the broadcasting of regional programmes in specific regions, and the broadcasting of regional programmes on national networks – the authors conclude: 'It is apparent that all three components will continue to be essential if the important social and cultural benefits which regional programming can promote – binding the UK together, plurality, diversity, the promotion of the democratic process – are to continue' (Kidd and Taylor, 2002: 90). These three components are complemented by the three models of regional television production outlined above. In the 'third age' of British television such a tripartite structure might ensure that the 'golden age' of regional British television drama, from 1956 to 1982, did not completely disappear with the demise of BBC English Regions Drama and Granada Television. In these different ways, regional culture, regional identity and the notion of a 'sense of place' persist in British television drama.

Notes

1 Thames Television was the only ITV company to invest heavily in filmed drama in the 1970s when it set up Euston Films.
2 Peter Ansorge, interviewed by the author, 2 June 2005.
3 Ibid.
4 From the DVD audio commentary to *Gangsters: Incident 1* (BBC Worldwide, 2006)
5 Since the consolidation of the regional ITV companies into one company, Granada International has been subsumed within ITV Studios Global Entertainment.
6 For more on ITV's endeavours in the international marketplace see Steemers (2004 and 2005).
7 In collaboration with Channel Four, Red Production Company set up a scriptwriting competition called Northern Soul in 1999, which unearthed a number of new writers.
8 www.ruralmedia.co.uk/about-us (accessed 6 April 2011).
9 www.ruralmedia.co.uk/community-media (accessed 6 April 2011).

Appendix 1

Granada TV Drama: 1956–82

Date of first transmission	Chronological list of productions (in order of transmission): series and serials, including Granada's anthology series, in bold (selected credits and notes in parentheses)
1956	
31/10/56	Play of the Week: Shooting Star
28/11/56	Play of the Week: Look Back in Anger (John Osborne)
6/12/56	Television Playhouse: The Lion's Share
1957	
16/1/57	Play of the Week: Another Part of the Forest
31/1/57	Television Playhouse: Guest in the House
20/2/57	Play of the Week: Home of the Brave
28/2/57	Television Playhouse: The Sand Castle
19/3/57–21/3/57	**Whispering Smith Hits London** (3 episodes)
20/3/57	Play of the Week: An Enemy of the People (Ibsen, adapted by Arthur Miller)
15/5/57	Play of the Week: Accolade
23/5/57	Television Playhouse: Saloon Bar
12/6/57	Play of the Week: Boy Meets Girl
28/6/57–28/8/57	**Workshop** (5 plays – not networked)
10/7/57	Play of the Week: The Glass Cage (J.B. Priestley)
18/7/57	Television Playhouse: The Confidence Man
15/8/57	Television Playhouse: My Heart's in the Highlands
4/9/57	Play of the Week: The Wooden Dish
16/9/57–24/6/59	**Shadow Squad** (2 series/detective drama)
2/10/57	Play of the Week: Rope (Patrick Hamilton, ad. Kenneth Hoare, dir. Henry Kaplan)
11/10/57	Television Playhouse: Thunder on Sycamore Street
30/10/57	Play of the Week: The Guinea Pig
8/11/57	Television Playhouse: The Staring Match
27/11/57	Play of the Week: Death of a Salesman (Arthur Miller)

6/12/57	Television Playhouse: Pick-up Girl
1958	
22/1/58	Play of the Week: Johnny Belinda
31/1/58	Television Playhouse: Cry Silence
19/2/58	Play of the Week: Montserrat
10/3/58	Doomsday for Dyson (J.B. Priestley)
19/3/58	Play of the Week: The Iron Harp
16/4/58	Play of the Week: The Myth Makers
25/4/58	Television Playhouse: Now Barabbas …
14/5/58	Play of the Week: All My Sons (Arthur Miller)
23/5/58	Television Playhouse: The Pony Man
11/6/58	Play of the Week: The Troublemakers
20/6/58	Television Playhouse: The Browning Version
1/7/58–15/3/63	**The Verdict Is Yours** (initially unscripted, later scripted, TV courtroom drama)
9/7/58	Play of the Week: The Kidders
18/7/58	Television Playhouse: Cornelius (J.B. Priestley)
6/8/58	Play of the Week: The Curious Savage
15/8/58	Television Playhouse: High Tension
23/8/58	Television Playhouse: Don't Listen Ladies
3/9/58	Play of the Week: Mary Broome (Allan Monkhouse)
12/9/58	Television Playhouse: Rest in Violence
1/10/58	Play of the Week: The Liberty Man
10/10/58	Television Playhouse: The Voyagers
29/10/58	Play of the Week: The Strong Are Lonely
7/11/58	Television Playhouse: Breakdown
26/11/58	Play of the Week: Playboy of the Western World
5/12/58	Television Playhouse: A Sense of Justice
1959	
2/1/59	Television Playhouse: A Village Wooing
25/1/59	Play of the Week: The Education of Mr. Surrage (Allan Monkhouse)
30/1/59	Television Playhouse: No Fixed Abode (Clive Exton)
17/2/59	Play of the Week: Garden of Loneliness
27/2/59	Television Playhouse: A Memory of Two Mondays (Arthur Miller)
17/3/59	Play of the Week: The Skin of Our Teeth (Thornton Wilder)
14/4/59	Play of the Week: Ebb Tide (Donald Pleasance)
24/4/59	Television Playhouse: A Bit of Happiness (Alexander Baron)
29/4/59–24/6/59	**In Court Today** (unscripted courtroom drama, 9 episodes)

12/5/59	Play of the Week: Sheppey (Somerset Maugham)
22/5/59	Television Playhouse: Promenade (Peter Nichols)
9/6/59	Play of the Week: Sugar in the Morning
2/7/59–10/2/60	**Skyport** (*Shadow Squad* spin-off)
7/7/59	Play of the Week: For Services Rendered (Somerset Maugham)
17/7/59	Television Playhouse: Longitude 49
4/8/59	Play of the Week: Shadow of a Pale Horse
14/8/59	The Queen's Corporal (single play)
1/9/59	Play of the Week: The Younger Generation (Stanley Houghton)
11/9/59	Television Playhouse: The Silk Purse (Clive Exton)
9/10/59	Television Playhouse: The Blood Fight (Alexander Baron)
13/10/59– 29/12/59	**Knight Errant '59** (12-episode modern-day crusader adventure series/created by Philip Mackie)
3/11/59	Play of the Week: The Crucible (Arthur Miller)
6/11/59	Television Playhouse: Ticket for Tomorrow
24/11/59	Play of the Week: South
4/12/59	Television Playhouse: Shadow and Substance
1960	
1/1/60	Television Playhouse: The Small Servant
5/1/60–1/7/60	**Knight Errant '60** (25-episode second series of Knight Errant '59)
19/1/60	Play of the Week: In Search of Happiness
29/1/60	Television Playhouse: The Bush and the Tree
16/2/60	Play of the Week: A Member of the Wedding
26/2/60	Television Playhouse: Fiddler's Four (Harold Brighouse)
25/3/60	Television Playhouse: Act of Terror
29/3/60	Play of the Week: Double Indemnity (James M. Cain)
1/4/60–12/10/60	**Biggles** (children's drama series)
22/4/60	Television Playhouse: Think of the Day (Keith Dewhurst, dir. Herbert Wise)
10/5/60	Play of the Week: Beyond the Horizon (Eugene O'Neill)
20/5/60	Television Playhouse: Private and Confidential
7/6/60	Play of the Week: The Upstart (Harold Brighouse)
17/6/60	Television Playhouse: A Place of My Own
28/6/60	Play of the Week: The Shrike
8/7/60–9/9/60	**On Trial** (10 re-enactments of famous trials, produced by Peter Wildeblood)
14/7/60	Television Playhouse: Country Cousins
2/8/60	Play of the Week: Ladies of the Corridor

11/8/60	Television Playhouse: The Queen's Palace
30/8/60	Play of the Week: Vitriol (Harold Brighouse, dir. Herbert Wise)
8/9/60	Television Playhouse: The Harsh World
15/9/60–22/6/61	**Knight Errant Limited** (38-episode third series of Knight Errant)
27/9/60	Play of the Week: The Protest
6/10/60	Television Playhouse: Penelope
14/10/60–2/12/60	**Kipps** (8-part serial)
25/10/60	Play of the Week: Tiger at the Gates
3/11/60	Television Playhouse: Independent Means (Stanley Houghton)
22/11/60	Play of the Week: The Silver Whistle
1/12/60	Television Playhouse: The Honeymooners
9/12/60 to present	**Coronation Street**
20/12/60	Play of the Week: The Girl in the Window (Allan Monkhouse)
29/12/60	Television Playhouse: A Boy Next Door
1961	
12/1/61	Television Playhouse: The Zoo Story
17/1/61	Play of the Week: The Ring of Truth
14/2/61	Play of the Week: The Plough and the Stars
23/2/61	Television Playhouse: Ben Spray (Peter Nichols)
14/3/61	Play of the Week: The Girl on the Via Flaminia
23/3/61	Television Playhouse: The Widowing of Mrs Holroyd
11/4/61	Play of the Week: The Midnight Sun
20/4/61	Television Playhouse: Marking Time
9/5/61	Play of the Week: Soldier in the Snow
18/5/61	Television Playhouse: The Reception (Peter Nichols)
6/6/61	Play of the Week: Fairy Tales of New York
15/6/61	Television Playhouse: A Walk on the Water
28/6/61–7/12/61	**Family Solicitor** (24 episodes)
30/6/61–8/9/61	**The Younger Generation** (11-play anthology series)
4/7/61	Play of the Week: Life With Father
13/7/61	Television Playhouse: Paris Round the Corner
1/8/61	Play of the Week: Ivanov
10/8/61	Television Playhouse: The Dumb Waiter (Harold Pinter)
29/8/61	Play of the Week: Over the Bridge
7/9/61	Television Playhouse: The Square
26/9/61	Play of the Week: Barchester Towers
5/10/61	Television Playhouse: The Room (Harold Pinter)

24/10/61	Play of the Week: Sergeant Musgrave's Dance (John Arden)
2/11/61	Television Playhouse: The Gold Hunter
14/11/61	Play of the Week: Joker's Justice
30/11/61	Television Playhouse: A Resounding Tinkle
19/12/61	Play of the Week: The Visitors
28/12/61	Television Playhouse: Winner Takes the Lady (Harold Brighouse)

1962

11/5/62–13/9/63	**The Odd Man** (3 series/24 episodes, police series)
5/6/62	Play of the Week: You in Your Small Corner (Barry Reckord)
3/7/62	Play of the Week: My Three Angels
6/7/62–24/8/62	**Saki** (8 episodes; dramatisation of stories by H.H. Munro)
28/8/62	Play of the Week: The Lark (Jean Anouilh)
25/9/62	Play of the Week: Hobson's Choice (Harold Brighouse)
5/10/62	Television Playhouse: A Choice of Weapons
23/10/62	Play of the Week: Major Barbara (Bernard Shaw, dir. Stuart Burge)
30/10/62	Play of the Week: Misalliance
6/11/62	Play of the Week: Don Juan in Hell
13/11/62	Play of the Week: The Apple Cart
30/11/62	Television Playhouse: When Silver Drinks
28/12/62	Television Playhouse: The Interview

1963

11/1/63	Television Playhouse: The Cage
29/1/63	Play of the Week: Time and the Conways (J.B. Priestley)
8/2/63	Television Playhouse: There's No Room for You Here for a Start
22/2/63	Television Playhouse: The Wedding Dress (Edna O'Brien, dir. John McGrath)
5/3/63	Play of the Week: Eden End
19/3/63	Play of the Week: Dangerous Corner (J.B. Priestley)
22/3/63	Television Playhouse: Ben Again (Peter Nichols)
26/3/63	War and Peace (single play)
23/4/63	Play of the Week: Ever Since Paradise (J.B. Priestley)
21/5/63	Play of the Week: The Rainmaker
31/5/63–19/7/63	**The Victorians** (8 plays produced by Philip Mackie)
20/6/63–25/10/63	**Maupassant** (2 series; dramatisations of short stories by Guy de Maupassant)
6/8/63	Play of the Week: For King and Country – Out There

13/8/63	Play of the Week: For King and Country – The Barricade
20/8/63	Play of the Week: For King and Country – Tunnel Trench
27/8/63	Play of the Week: For King and Country – The Enemy
27/8/63	Leap in the Dark (single play)
8/10/63	Play of the Week: The Fixers
1/11/63–13/12/63	**Friday Night** (7-play anthology series)
25/12/63	Mr. Pickwick (single play)

1964

3/1/64–23/4/65	**It's Dark Outside** (Police/detective drama: 2 x 8-episode series)
13/1/64	Play of the Week: The Rose Tattoo (Tennessee Williams)
20/1/64	Play of the Week: The Glass Menagerie (Tennessee Williams)
27/1/64	Play of the Week: Camino Real (Tennessee Williams)
28/2/64–19/2/65	**The Villains** (3 series/27 episodes)
27/4/64–18/5/64	**A Question of Happiness** (4 episodes)
17/7/64–28/8/64	**Triangle** (7 episodes – each comprising three short plays by Robin Chapman, Michael Hastings and Hugh Leonard)
10/8/64–31/8/64	**A Choice of Coward** (4 Noel Coward plays)
4/9/64–25/9/64	**It's a Woman's World** (4-part series featuring women, but written by men)
7/9/64	The Other Man (single play)
2/10/64–6/11/64	**Paris 1900** (6 plays)
13/11/64–4/12/64	**Victoria Regina** (4 plays by Laurence Housman, ad. and prod. Peter Wildeblood)

1965

4/1/65	**Blood and Thunder**: The Changeling (Thomas Middleton, ad. Philip Mackie, dir. Derek Bennett)
11/1/65	**Blood and Thunder**: Women Beware Women (Thomas Middleton, ad. Philip Mackie, dir. Gordon Flemyng)
30/4/65–4/6/65	**Six Shades of Black** (intriguing-sounding series of six plays, all written by Peter Wildeblood)
3/5/65–24/5/65	**The Edwardians** (4 plays)
11/6/65–1/7/66	**The Man In Room 17** (detective drama: 2 series)
28/6/65	The Death of Bessie Smith (single play)
5/7/65	The American Dream (single play)
16/8/65	Play of the Week: The Way of the Flesh
6/9/65	Strife (single play)

1966

3/1/66–30/10/67	**The Stories of D.H. Lawrence** (14 plays shown in 3 series)
7/1/66–30/3/66	**The Liars** (11 dramatisations of short stories, produced by Philip Mackie, adapted by Mackie and Hugh Leonard)
4/7/66	Plays of Action 1: The Cretan (Arden Winch)
7/7/66–18/8/66	**You Can't Win** (7 episodes)
18/7/66	Plays of Action 2: Blue As His Eyes, The Tin Helmet He Wore
1/8/66	Play of the Week: An Experience of Evil
26/8/66–16/9/66	**The Corridor People** (stylish 4-part adventure series)
5/9/66–27/9/66	**Plays of Married Life** (4 plays)
1/11/66	Dear Liar (single play)

1967

19/1/67	Play of the Week: Love on the Dole (Walter Greenwood, adapted by John Finch, produced by Derek Bennett)
17/2/67–5/12/68	**Mr. Rose** (3 series; detective drama)
9/3/67	The Investigation (single play)
19/5/67–11/8/67	**The Fellows** (13-part detective drama set in Cambridge)
25/5/67	The Division (single play)
1/6/67	The Trial and Error of Colonel Winchip (single play)
18/8/67–22/9/67	**Escape** (6 episodes – 2 directed by Michael Apted)
21/8/67	Summer Playhouse: One Fat Englishman
11/9/67	Summer Playhouse: Travelling Light
27/9/67–12/12/67	**The Flower of Gloster** (children's drama series)
29/9/67–1/12/67	**Inheritance** (10 episodes)
8/12/67–1/3/68	**City '68** (13-part anthology series devised by John Finch)
11/12/67	Playhouse: Top of the Ladder

1968

5/2/68–14/6/69	**Rogues' Gallery** (2 series/10 episodes)
6/2/68	Sarah (single play)
19/4/68–24/5/68	**Spindoe** (6 episodes)
17/6/68–25/10/69	**Murder** (2 series / 11 plays)
1/7/68	Playhouse: In Killer's Odds (dir. Michael Cox)
12/7/68–26/7/68	**The War of Darkie Pilbeam** (trilogy written by Tony Warren about a black marketeer)
30/7/68–24/9/68	**The System** (6 plays – including *Them Down There* – first all-film play)

21/9/68–2/11/68	**The Caesars** (6 plays written and produced by Philip Mackie)
30/9/68	Playhouse: There's a Hole in Your Dustbin, Delilah (Jack Rosenthal, dir. Michael Apted; film)
7/10/68	Playhouse: Number Ten (ad. John Finch, dir. Michael Apted)
9/12/68	Playhouse: Your Name's Not God, It's Edgar (dir. Michael Apted)
16/12/68	Playhouse: If Only the Trains Came

1969

8/4/69–13/5/69	**Judge Dee** (6-part costume/detective drama set in seventh-century China)
11/4/69–30/5/69	**Big Breadwinner Hog** (8-part crime drama starring Peter Egan, set in London)
30/6/69	Playhouse: The Beast in the Jungle (Henry James)
4/8/69	Playhouse: The John Hilarian Salt Exhibition and Numerous Illustrated Slides (Roy Clarke)
11/8/69–24/7/70	**The Stables Theatre Company** (7 plays, shown in the Playhouse series)
5/9/69–26/9/69	**The Contenders** (John Wain – 4 parts)
30/9/69–31/8/70	**The Dustbinmen** (2 series/20 episodes, comedy-drama, devised by Jack Rosenthal)
11/10/69	Saturday Night Theatre: In Another Country (dir. Derek Bennett)
18/10/69	Saturday Night Theatre: Murder – The Colonel and the Naturalist
25/10/69	Saturday Night Theatre: Murder – The Blood Relation (dir. Mike Newell)
1/11/69	Saturday Night Theatre: It's Called the Sugar Plum
21/12/69–8/2/70	**The Owl Service** (Alan Garner; children's drama serial)

1970

19/1/70	Playhouse: The Pueblo Affair (drama-documentary)
24/1/70	Saturday Night Theatre: Mrs. Mouse, Are You Within? (Frank Marcus, ad. Geoffrey Lancashire, dir. Mike Newell)
26/1/70	Playhouse: The People's Jack (Stables Theatre Company)
14/4/70–16/7/72	**A Family at War** (1939–45 wartime drama about middle-class family in Liverpool – 3 series)
4/5/70	Playhouse: Don't Touch Him, He Might Resent It (Henry Livings, dir. Michael Apted)

11/5/70	Playhouse: Arthur Wants You for a Sunbeam (dir. Mike Newell)
18/5/70	Playhouse: Thursday's Child
3/7/70–11/9/70	**Confession** (11-part anthology series; 1 shot on film)
4/7/70	Saturday Night Theatre: The Gingham Dog
29/7/70–12/8/70	**Husbands and Lovers** (3-part series)
1/8/70	Saturday Night Theatre: Dear Janet Rosenberg . . . Dear Mr. Kooning
19/8/70–13/9/71	**The Sinners** (2 series/12 episodes; 2.5 shot on film)
24/8/70	Playhouse: The Style of the Countess (Gavin Lambert, sc. Simon Gray, dir. Michael Apted)
15/12/70	Playhouse: The Day They Buried Cleaver (dir. Mike Apted)
20/12/70	Roll On Four O'Clock (Colin Welland; prod. Ken Trodd; film)

1971

3/1/71	The Dead (James Joyce)
21/2/71	Sunday Night Theatre: Big Soft Nellie (dir. Michael Apted)
21/3/71	Sunday Night Theatre: Pandora
23/3/71	Playhouse: The Mosedale Horseshoe (Arthur Hopcraft; film)
18/4/71–16/5/71	**Persuasion** (5 episodes)
23/5/71	Sunday Night Theatre: The Silver Collection
13/6/71	Sunday Night Theatre: Paper Roses (Dennis Potter; prod. Ken Trodd; film)
14/6/71–19/7/71	**Seasons of the Year** (6 episodes)
27/6/71	Sunday Night Theatre: Square (prod. Ken Trodd)
15/8/71	Sunday Night Theatre: The Chaps
22/8/71	Sunday Night Theatre: Giants and Ogres (dir. Christopher Morahan)
29/8/71	Sunday Night Theatre: Green Julia
9/11/71	Playhouse: The Panel (Arthur Hopcraft; dir. Leslie Woodhouse; film)
16/11/71	Playhouse: Funny
5/12/71	Sunday Night Theatre: The Birthday Run (Arthur Hopcraft; dir. Richard Everitt; film)
8/12/71	The Last Journey (single play)
12/12/71	Sunday Night Theatre: Some Distant Shadow (dir. Christopher Morahan)

1972

2/1/72–20/2/72	**The Intruder** (children's drama series)

9/1/72–3/12/72   Sunday Night Theatre (Granada contributed 10 plays to this ITV anthology series, including Jack Rosenthal's *Another Sunday and Sweet F.A.*, 9/1/72; film)

23/1/72–25/3/73   **Adam Smith** (2-series / 39-episode drama about a clergyman in a Scottish village)

14/2/72–20/3/72   **Home and Away** (7-part series written by Julia Jones, prod. Ken Trodd)

29/5/72   Playhouse: A Splinter of Ice (Fay Weldon)

27/6/72   Playhouse: The Substitute

20/8/72–11/3/73   **Country Matters** (2 series / 13 episodes – 8 shot on film; based on stories by H.E. Bates and A.E. Coppard)

1/9/72–6/10/72   **Holly** (6 episodes)

18/10/72–29/3/84   **Crown Court** (long-running daytime courtroom drama, with 3-episode storylines)

18/12/72   Playhouse: Buggins' Ermine (Arthur Hopcraft; film)

1973

20/2/73   A Point In Time (single play)

27/2/73   Playhouse: Putting on the Agony

6/3/73   Playhouse: Operation Magic Carpet

28/3/73   Late Night Theatre: The Death of Captain Doughty

4/4/73   Late Night Theatre: The Eagle Has Landed

15/4/73–16/12/73   Sunday Night Theatre (Granada contributed 5 plays to this ITV anthology series)

24/4/73   Playhouse: Vinegar Trip (Kenneth Cope)

12/6/73–25/8/75   **Sam** (3 series / 39 episodes)

20/6/73   Late Night Theatre: 1939

11/7/73–22/8/73   **Shabby Tiger** (7-episode adaptation of Howard Spring novel)

18/7/73   Late Night Theatre: Yesterday's Girl

12/8/73–9/9/73   **Once Upon A Time** (anthology series of 5 plays, prod. Jonathan Powell)

28/10/73   Sunday Night Theatre: Katapult (Arthur Hopcraft; film)

3/12/73   Life and Soul (single play)

16/12/73   Sunday Night Theatre: In the Heel of the Hunt (Jim Allen; film)

18/12/73   Late Night Theatre: Little Fears

1974

7/1/74–18/2/74   **A Raging Calm** (7-part adaptation by Stan Barstow from his own novel)

5/2/74   Playhouse: Lucky (Alun Owen; film)

31/3/74–26/5/74   Sunday Night Theatre (Granada contributed 4 plays to this ITV anthology series, which ended 26/5/74)

21/4/74–26/5/74	**Childhood** (6-part anthology series; 5 shot on film)
21/4/74	Childhood: Baa Baa Black Sheep (Arthur Hopcraft / Rudyard Kipling; film)
7/5/74	Playhouse: Dear Love
19/6/74	Playhouse: The Finest Family in the Land
8/7/74	Late Night Drama: I Know What I Meant (White House tapes and public statements, edited by David Edgar, dir. Jack Gold, prod. Michael Cox)
16/7/74–6/7/75	**Village Hall** (anthology series; 2 series / 14 plays)
4/8/74	The Nearly Man (ITV Playhouse/Arthur Hopcraft)
25/8/74	A Private Matter (single play)
1/9/74	Occupations (Trevor Griffiths; single play)
8/9/74	Ceremony of Innocence (single play)
9/9/74	Late Night Drama: Starmaker (Ray Davies)
15/9/74–10/11/74	**Soldier and Me** (children's drama series)
15/10/74	Playhouse: Norma (Alun Owen; film)
23/12/74	Haunted: The Ferryman (Kingsley Amis / Julian Bond; film)
30/12/74	Haunted: Poor Girl (Elizabeth Taylor / Robin Chapman; film)
1974	Passengers (Susan Pleat)
1975	
14/1/75–25/2/75	**Nightingale's Boys** (7 episodes)
2/2/75	Lost yer Tongue? (Peter Terson, dir. Mike Newell; film)
27/4/75	Parole (single play)
4/5/75	The Place of Peace (single play)
4/9/75–27/11/75	**The Stars Look Down** (13-episode adaptation of A.J. Cronin novel)
4/11/75–16/12/75	**The Nearly Man** (7 episodes)
9/11/75	The Greenhill Pals (film)
1976	
11/1/76	**Red Letter Day**: Ready When You Are, Mr. McGill (Jack Rosenthal, dir. Mike Newell; film)
18/1/76	**Red Letter Day**: The Five Pound Orange
25/1/76	**Red Letter Day**: Well Thank You, Thursday
1/2/76	**Red Letter Day**: Amazing Stories (Howard Schuman)
8/2/76	**Red Letter Day**: Matchfit (film)
15/2/76	**Red Letter Day**: For Services to Myself (film)
8/2/76	**Red Letter Day**: Bag of Yeast (Neville Smith; dir. Mike Grigsby; film)
21/3/76	A Land of Ice Cream (film)
25/4/76–30/1/77	**The Ghosts of Motley Hall** (children's drama series – 12 episodes)

23/5/76	Benny Lynch (single play)
3/7/76–29/8/77	**The XYY Man** (2 series spy drama: 3-parter in 1976 followed by 10 episodes in 1977)
11/7/76	Buns For Elephants (single play)
3/9/76–15/10/76	**Victorian Scandals** (7 plays)
10/11/76	Heyday's Hotel (Philip Purser)
17/11/76	Our Young Mr. Wignall (film)
24/11/76	The Launderette
5/12/76–15/1/78	**Laurence Olivier Presents** (6 adaptations of stage plays)

1977

25/1/77–19/4/77	**This Year Next Year** (13-part series about Harry Shaw who moves from Yorkshire Dales to London; by John Finch)
26/4/77	ITV Playhouse: Blind Love (film)
31/5/77	ITV Playhouse: Philby, Burgess and Maclean (Ian Curteis, dir. Gordon Flemyng; film)
17/7/77	The Sunday Drama: A Good Human Story
25/10/77–15/11/77	**Hard Times** (4-part Dickens adaptation written by Arthur Hopcraft)
13/11/77	The Caledonian (single play)
18/12/77	The Sunday Drama: Charm (Brian Thompson, dir. Mike Newell; film)

1978

19/1/78	ITV Playhouse: Some Enchanted Evening
15/2/78	Mirage (film)
1/3/78–12/4/78	**Send in the Girls** (7 episodes)
5/6/78–20/10/82	**Strangers** (5 series/32 episodes; Manchester-based police drama)
9/7/78–16/7/78	**Clouds of Glory** (2 films about Wordsworth and Coleridge; sc. Melvyn Bragg, dir. Ken Russell; film)
20/8/78	The Sunday Drama: End of Season (John Finch; film)
27/8/78	The Sunday Drama: You Are My Heart's Delight
10/9/78	The Sunday Drama: Wings of Song
14/11/78–20/12/79	**Fallen Hero** (2 x 6-episode series)
25/10/1978	Power Struggle (drama-documentary; film)

1979

20/2/79	Collision Course (drama-documentary, dir. Leslie Woodhead; film)
23/2/79–6/4/79	**The House of Caradus** (7-part series)
10/3/79	Father's Day (film)

26/5/79	Print Out (film)
10/6/79–3/7/80	**The Mallens** (2 series/13 episodes; derived from 3 novels by Catherine Cookson)
29/7/79	Screenplay: Gossip From The Forest (film)
5/8/79	Screenplay: Talent (Victoria Wood's first TV play)
11/11/79	Screenplay: The Sound of the Guns
23/12/79	Screenplay: Waxwork
1980	
27/1/80–18/8/81	**The Spoils of War** (3 series / 20 episodes; Second World War family drama by John Finch)
27/2/80	Secret Orchards (single play)
13/4/80–10/5/81	**Cribb** (2 series/13-episode Victorian police drama)
21/6/80	Screenplay: Lives of Our Own
19/7/80	Closing Ranks (film)
20/7/80–21/8/81	**Ladykillers** (2 series / 14-episode anthology of real-life murder cases)
10/8/80–21/9/80	**Watch All Night** (7 episodes)
19/8/80	Invasion (David Boulton, dir. Leslie Woodhead; drama-documentary; film)
21/9/80	Screenplay: The Zoo
28/12/80	Staying On (adapted by Julian Mitchell from the novel by Paul Scott, dir. Silvio Narizzano; film)
2/12/1980	Life for Christine (Fay Weldon; film)
1981	
1/1/81	Christmas Spirits (single play)
6/3/81–17/4/81	**My Father's House** (7 episodes)
15/4/81	The Good Soldier (film)
9/6/81	Madge (single play)
23/6/81	Screenplay: Paradise Is Closing Down
26/7/81	Noddy (single play)
9/8/81	Screenplay: Happy Since I Met You
24/8/81–26/8/81	**The Member for Chelsea** (3 episodes)
12/10/81–22/12/81	**Brideshead Revisited** (11-episodes)
28/11/81–12/12/81	**Knife Edge** (3 episodes)
16/12/81	Strike (drama-documentary; film)
11/2/1981	L.S. Lowry – A Private View (drama-documentary; film)
1982	
4/4/82–6/6/82	**A Kind of Loving** (10-part adaptation by Stan Barstow from his own novel)
8/5/82	Visiting Day (single drama)

25/7/82–29/8/82	**All For Love** (anthology series; 6 episodes, 5 on film; second series of 6 followed in 1983)
25/10/82– 29/11/82	**Foxy Lady** (6 episodes, second series of 7 episodes followed in 1984, both series written by Geoffrey Lancashire)
31/10/82– 19/12/82	**Young Sherlock – The Mystery of the Manor House** (9 episodes)

Appendix 2

BBC English Regions Drama: 1972–82

Channel/date of first transmission	Chronological list of productions (in order of transmission): series and serials in bold (writer's name in parentheses)
1972	
BBC2, 21/2/72	Thirty-Minute Theatre: An Arrow for Little Audrey (Brian Finch)
BBC2, 28/2/72	Thirty-Minute Theatre: That Quiet Earth (John Hopkins)
BBC2, 6/3/72	Thirty-Minute Theatre: Said the Preacher (Arthur Hopcraft)
BBC2, 13/3/72	Thirty-Minute Theatre: That Time of Life (David Cregan)
BBC2, 20/3/72	Thirty-Minute Theatre: Under the Age (Ted Whitehead)
BBC2, 27/3/72	Thirty-Minute Theatre: Bypass (David Rudkin)
BBC2, 3/4/72	Thirty-Minute Theatre: And for My Next Trick (Jack Rosenthal)
BBC2, 10/4/72	Thirty-Minute Theatre: The Sit In (Keith Dewhurst)
BBC1, 1/6/72	Play for Today: The Fishing Party (Peter Terson)
BBC2, 12/10/72	Thirty-Minute Theatre: Scarborough (Donald Howarth)
BBC2, 19/10/72	Thirty-Minute Theatre: Tonight We Meet Arthur Pendlebury (Alan Plater)
BBC2, 26/10/72	Thirty-Minute Theatre: Ronnie's So Long at the Fair (Jay Humber)
BBC2, 2/11/72	Thirty-Minute Theatre: Ten Torrey Canyons (Brian Clark)
BBC2, 9/11/72	Thirty-Minute Theatre: I Wouldn't Tell On You, Miss (Susan Pleat)
BBC2, 16/11/72	Thirty-Minute Theatre: You're Free (Henry Livings)

1973

BBC1, 8/1/73	Play for Today: Shakespeare or Bust (Peter Terson)
BBC1, 15/1/73	Play for Today: Land of Green Ginger (Alan Plater)
BBC2, 8/2/73	A Touch of Eastern Promise (Tara Prem)
BBC2, 15/2/73	And All Who Sail in Her (Andy Ashton)
BBC2, 22/2/73	You and Me and Him (David Mercer)
BBC2, 1/3/73	The Great Acrobile (Roy Minton)
BBC2, 8/3/73	I Want To Marry Your Son (David Cregan)
BBC2, 15/3/73	Atrocity (David Rudkin)
BBC1, 14/5/73	Play for Today: Steps Back (David Halliwell)
BBC2, 11/6/73	This Story Is True (Don Taylor) – documentary about *The Roses of Eyam*
BBC2, 12/6/73	The Roses of Eyam (Don Taylor)
BBC2, 23/8/73	The Diary of a Madman (dramatised by Michael Wearing and Victor Henry)
BBC2, 15/10/73	Second City Firsts: The Medium (Denise Robertson)
BBC2, 22/10/73	Second City Firsts: Mrs Pool's Preserves (Michael Sadler)
BBC2, 29/10/73	Second City Firsts: If a Man Answers (Brian Glover)
BBC2, 5/11/73	Second City Firsts: The Movers (Ian Taylor)
BBC2, 12/11/73	Second City Firsts: King of the Castle (Willy Russell)
BBC2, 19/11/73	Second City Firsts: Patrons (Eric Berger)
BBC2, 26/11/73	Second City Firsts: That Time of Life (David Cregan) – originally transmitted as a Thirty-Minute Theatre play, 13/3/72

1974

BBC1, 17/1/74	Play for Today: The Lonely Man's Lover (Barry Collins)
BBC2, 18/2/74	Second City Firsts: Humbug, Finger or Thumb? (Arthur Hopcraft)
BBC2, 25/2/74	Second City Firsts: Girl (James Robson)
BBC2, 4/3/74	Second City Firsts: Bold Face – Condensed (Peter Rawsley)
BBC2, 11/3/74	Second City Firsts: The Actual Woman (Jack Shepherd)
BBC2, 18/3/74	Second City Firsts: Match of the Day (Neville Smith)
BBC1, 21/3/74	Play for Today: Penda's Fen (David Rudkin)
BBC2, 25/3/74	Second City Firsts: Lunch Duty (Rony Robinson)
BBC1, 28/3/74	Play for Today: Pidgeon – Hawk or Dove? (Michael Sadler)
BBC1, 11/4/74	Play for Today: Three for the Fancy (Peter Terson)
BBC2, 28/10/74	Second City Firsts: Pig Bin (Brian Glover)

BBC2, 4/11/74	Second City Firsts: Sunday Tea (Edwin Pearce)
BBC2, 11/11/74	Second City Firsts: Silence (John Fletcher)
BBC2, 18/11/74	Second City Firsts: Fight for Shelton Bar (adapted by Peter Cheeseman)
BBC2, 25/11/74	Second City Firsts: Squire (Tom Pickard)
BBC2, 2/12/74	Second City Firsts: Too Hot To Handle (Jim Hawkins)
BBC2, 16/12/74	Second City Firsts: The Festive Poacher (Ian Taylor)
1975	
BBC1, 9/1/75	Play for Today: Gangsters (Philip Martin)
BBC1, 16/1/75	Play for Today: The After Dinner Game (Malcolm Bradbury and Christopher Bigsby)
BBC1, 30/1/75	Play for Today: The Death of a Young Young Man (Willy Russell)
BBC2, 20/3/75	Second City Firsts: Early to Bed (Alan Bleasdale)
BBC2, 27/3/75	Second City Firsts: Swallows (John McGahern)
BBC2, 3/4/75	Second City Firsts: Waiting at the Field Gate (James Robson)
BBC2, 10/4/75	Second City Firsts: The Permissive Society (Mike Leigh)
BBC2, 17/4/75	Second City Firsts: The Frank Crank Story (Alan Taylor)
BBC2, 24/4/75	Second City Firsts: Released (Stephen Wakelam)
BBC2, 25/10/75	Second City Firsts: Club Havana (Barry Reckord)
BBC2, 1/11/75	Second City Firsts: The Writing on the Wall (devised by Mike Bradwell and Hull Truck)
BBC2, 8/11/75	Second City Firsts: How It Is (Anita Bronson)
BBC2, 15/11/75	Second City Firsts: On the Good Ship Yakky Ikky Doola (Bob Mason)
BBC2, 21/11/75– 26/12/75	**Trinity Tales** (Alan Plater) – 6 episodes
BBC2, 22/11/75	Second City Firsts: Thwum (Mike Stott)
BBC2, 29/11/75	Second City Firsts: The Healing (Laura Lemson)
1976	
BBC1, 6/1/76	Play for Today: The Other Woman (Watson Gould)
BBC1, 13/1/76	Play for Today: Nuts in May (Mike Leigh)
BBC1, 20/1/76	Play for Today: Doran's Box (Eric Coltart)
BBC1, 27/1/76	Play for Today: Packman's Barn (Alick Rowe)
BBC2, 13/3/76	Second City Firsts: Trotsky Is Dead (Tony Bicat)
BBC2, 20/3/76	Second City Firsts: The Visitor (Denise Robertson)
BBC2, 3/4/76	Second City Firsts: Do You Dig It? (John Harding and John Burrows)
BBC2, 10/4/76	Second City Firsts: Jack Flea's Birthday Celebration (Ian McEwan)

BBC2, 17/4/76	Second City Firsts: Blackbird Shout (Paul Hyland)
BBC2, 24/4/76	Second City Firsts: Travelling Free (Sean McArthy)
BBC2, 19/6/76	The Witches of Pendle (Barry Collins)
BBC1, 9/9/76–21/10/76	**Gangsters** (Philip Martin) – 6 episodes
BBC2, 14/11/76	Second City Firsts: Summer Season (Brian Glover)
BBC2, 21/11/76	Second City Firsts: Knock for Knock (devised by Mike Leigh)
BBC2, 28/11/76	Second City Firsts: Glitter (Tony Bicat)
BBC2, 5/12/76	Second City Firsts: Dreamboat (Ian Taylor)
BBC2, 12/12/76	Second City Firsts: Percy and Kenneth (Mary J. O'Malley)

1977

BBC2, 3/1/77	The Game (Harold Brighouse – adapted by Henry Livings)
BBC1, 4/1/77	Play for Today: Love on a Gunboat (Malcolm Bradbury)
BBC1, 11/1/77	Play for Today: The Kiss of Death (devised by Mike Leigh)
BBC1, 18/1/77	Play for Today: Our Flesh and Blood (Mike Stott)
BBC2, 3/5/77	Second City Firsts: Twelve off the Belt (Ron Hutchinson)
BBC2, 10/5/77	Second City Firsts: Postcards from Southsea (J.C.W. Brooke)
BBC2, 17/5/77	Second City Firsts: Daft Mam Blues (David Halliwell)
BBC2, 24/5/77	Second City Firsts: In the Deadspell (James Robson)
BBC2, 31/5/77	Second City Firsts: Waifs and Strays (Chris Bailey)
BBC2, 6/6/77	Second City Firsts: Fattening Frogs for Snakes (Janey Preger)
BBC2, 13/6/77–27/6/77	**Maidens' Trip** (Thomas Ellice – based on the novel by Emma Smith) – 3 episodes
BBC1, 15/6/77–20/7/77	**Middlemen** (Alan Plater) – 6 episodes
BBC2, 20/7/77	The Fosdyke Saga (Bill Tidy and Alan Plater)
BBC2, 20/12/77	Black Christmas (Michael Abbensetts)
BBC2, 28/12/77	Play of the Week: Our Day Out (Willy Russell)

1978

BBC1, 3/1/78	Play for Today: Scully's New Year's Eve (Alan Bleasdale)
BBC1, 6/1/78–10/2/78	**Gangsters** (Philip Martin) – 6 episodes
BBC1, 10/1/78	Play for Today: Licking Hitler (David Hare)
BBC1, 17/1/78	Play for Today: The Red Shift (Alan Garner)

BBC2, 1/2/78	Play of the Week: The Dissolution of Marcus Pleischman (Stephen Davis)
BBC2, 8/2/78	Play of the Week: The O'Hooligan File (Janey Preger)
BBC2, 15/2/78	Play of the Week: The Turkey Who Lives on the Hill (Sean McCarthy)
BBC2, 15/3/78	Play of the Week: Stargazy on Zummerdown (John Fletcher)
BBC2, 8/4/78	Second City Firsts: The Back Page (Andrew Nickolds and Stan Hey)
BBC2, 15/4/78	Second City Firsts: Shall I See You Now? (Mary O'Malley)
BBC2, 17/4/78–15/5/78	**Pickersgill People** (Mike Stott) – 5 episodes
BBC2, 22/4/78	Second City Firsts: The Lady Irene (Tom Hadaway)
BBC2, 6/5/78	Second City Firsts: Mucking Out (Robert Holman)
BBC2, 13/5/78	Second City Firsts: Rotten (Alan Brown)
BBC2, 22/5/78	Curriculae Curricula (Alan Plater and Dave Greenslade)
BBC2, 31/10/78–28/11/78	**Empire Road** (Michael Abbensetts) – 5 episodes
1979	
BBC1, 2/1/79	Play for Today: The Out of Town Boys (Ron Hutchinson)
BBC1, 9/1/79	Play for Today: Vampires (Dixie Williams)
BBC1, 16/1/79	Play for Today: The Chief Mourner (John Elliot)
BBC2, 14/4/79	Penny Whistles of Robert Louis Stevenson (Mike Maran and David Sheppard)
BBC2, 27/4/79	The Other Side: Connie (Derrick Buttress)
BBC2, 4/5//79	The Other Side: Underdog (Jack Shepherd))
BBC2, 11/5/79	The Other Side: A Greenish Man (Snoo Wilson)
BBC2, 18/5/79	The Other Side: Only Connect (Drew Griffiths and Noel Greig)
BBC2, 25/5/79	The Other Side: Contacts (Stephen Davis)
BBC1, 11/5/79–15/6/79	**Two Up and Two Down** (Janey Preger) – 6 episodes
BBC1, 7/6/79–12/7/79	**The Deep Concern** (Elwyn Jones) – 6 episodes
BBC2, 23/8/79–25/10/79	**Empire Road** (Michael Abbensetts) – 10 episodes
1980	
BBC2, 2/1/80	The Blackstuff (Alan Bleasdale)
BBC1, 10/1/80	Play for Today: Keep Smiling (Paul Joyce)

BBC1, 17/1/80	Play for Today: Dreams of Leaving (David Hare)
BBC1, 24/1/80	Play for Today: Thicker Than Water (Brian Glover)
BBC2, 9/2/80	Playhouse: The Enigma (adapted by Malcolm Bradbury from a book by John Fowles)
BBC2, 16/2/80	Playhouse: Hester for Example (Michael Sullivan)
BBC2, 23/2/80	Playhouse: Trouble With Gregory (Stephen Davis)
BBC2, 18/4/80	Playhouse: The Dig (James Robson)
BBC2, 25/4/80	Playhouse: Happy (Derrick Buttress)
BBC1, 1/5/80–5/6/80	**Bull Week** (Ron Hutchinson) – 6 episodes
BBC2, 2/5/80	Playhouse: Mary's Wife (David Cook)
BBC2, 9/5/80	Playhouse: Games Without Frontiers (devised and directed by Mike Bradwell)
BBC2, 16/5/80	Playhouse: The Unborn (Philip Martin)
BBC2, 23/5/80	Playhouse: Electric in the City (Tony Bicat)
BBC1, 25/11/80	Play for Today: Number on End (Gordon Flemyng)
1981	
BBC2, 4/1/81–25/1/81	**The History Man** (adapted by Christopher Hampton from the novel by Malcolm Bradbury) – 4 episodes
BBC1, 13/1/81	Play for Today: The Muscle Market (Alan Bleasdale)
BBC1, 20/1/81	Play for Today: A Brush With Mr. Porter on the Road to Eldorado (Don Haworth)
BBC2, 13/2/81	Playhouse: Days at the Beach (Malcolm Mowbray)
BBC2, 20/2/81	Playhouse: Bobby Wants to Meet Me (Janey Preger)
BBC2, 27/2/81	Playhouse: Days (Eva Figes)
BBC2, 6/3/81	Playhouse: Clapperclaw (Jack Shepherd)
BBC1, 10/3/81	Play for Today: The Garland (H.O. Nazareth and Horace Ove)
BBC2, 13/3/81	Playhouse: The Potsdam Quartet (David Pinner)
BBC2, 15/5/81	Playhouse: The Day War Broke Out (Peter Tinniswood)
BBC1, 1/7/81–12/8/81	**The Olympian Way** (Tara Prem) – 6 episodes
BBC1, 21/12/81	If Winter Comes (Janos Nyiri)
BBC1, 29/12/81	Artemis 81 (David Rudkin)
1982	
BBC1, 12/1/82	Play for Today: A Cotswold Death (Tony Bicat)
BBC1, 19/1/82	Play for Today: Under the Skin (Janey Preger)
BBC1, 22/4/82–13/5/82	**Bird of Prey** (Ron Hutchinson) – 4 episodes
BBC2, 14/5/82	Playhouse: Jake's End (Desmond Lowden)
BBC2, 21/5/82	Playhouse: Housewarming (Stephen Bill)

BBC2, 28/5/82	Playhouse: Easy Money (Michael Abbensetts)
BBC2, 4/6/82	Playhouse: Potatohead Blues (Bill Morrison)
BBC2, 10/10/82–7/11/82	**Boys from the Blackstuff** (Alan Bleasdale) – 5 episodes
BBC1, 26/10/82	Play for Today: 3 Minute Heroes (Leslie Stewart)

Bibliography

ABC Television (1959), *The Armchair Theatre*, London: Weidenfeld and Nicolson.

Allen, John, Massey, Doreen and Cochrane, Allan (1998), *Rethinking the Region*, London: Routledge.

Anon.(1956), 'Independent TV Comes to the North: Sir Kenneth Offers Viewers More Drama', *Manchester Guardian*, 4 May.

Anon.(1961), 'Interesting Experiment in Television Play Production', *North-Western Evening Mail*, 24 June.

Anon.(1964a), 'Proper Villains!', *TV Times (Midland Edition)*, 12 June.

Anon.(1964b), 'Filming I.T.V. Thriller at Pott Shrigley', *Macclesfield County Express*, 18 June.

Anon.(1968), 'Viewpoint', *Oldham Evening Chronicle*, 25 September.

Anon.(1972), 'The English Regions', *BBC Handbook 1973*, London: British Broadcasting Corporation.

Ansorge, Peter (1983), 'Drama Production at BBC Birmingham' in Jayne Pilling and Kingsley Canham (eds), *The Screen on the Tube: Filmed TV Drama*, Norwich: Cinema City.

Ansorge, Peter (1997), *From Liverpool to Los Angeles: On Writing for Theatre, Film and Television*, London: Faber and Faber.

Archer, John (1984), 'The *Did You See . . .* Interviews' in Richard Paterson (ed.), *BFI Dossier 20: Boys from the Blackstuff*, London: British Film Institute.

Bainbridge, Beryl (1987), *Forever England: North and South*, London: BBC.

Baker, Alan and Billinge, Mark (eds) (2004), *Geographies of England: The North–South Divide, Material and Imagined*, Cambridge: Cambridge University Press.

Barnett, Steve (2003), 'ITV Faces a Little Local Difficulty', *The Observer*, 30 November.

BBC (1969), *Broadcasting in the Seventies*, London: British Broadcasting Corporation.

BBC (1971), *BBC Handbook 1971*, London: British Broadcasting Corporation.

BBC (1972), *BBC Handbook 1973*, London: British Broadcasting Corporation.

Bernstein, Sidney (1954), 'Commercial TV: My Plans', *The Star*, 11 November.

Bignell, Jonathan, Lacey, Stephen and Macmurraugh-Kavanagh, Madeleine (eds) (2000), *British Television Drama: Past, Present and Future*, Basingstoke: Palgrave.

Bignell, Jonathan (2006), 'Programmes and Canons', *Critical Studies in Television*, 1:1, Spring.

Black, Peter (1972), *The Mirror in the Corner: People's Television*, London: Hutchinson.

Blyth, Alan (1964), 'The Other Man', *TV Times (Midland Edition)*, 4 September.

Briggs, Asa (1995), *The History of Broadcasting in the United Kingdom, Volume 5: Competition*, Oxford: Oxford University Press.

Broadcast Debate, The (2003), 'Heading for a Regional Renaissance', *Broadcast*, 28 November.

Buscombe, Edward (ed.) (1981), *BFI Dossier Number 9 – Granada: The First 25 Years*, London: British Film Institute.

Buscombe, Ed (1993), 'Nationhood, Culture and Media Boundaries: Britain', *Quarterly Review of Film and Video*, 14: 3.

Campbell, Patrick (1972), 'The Quiet Revolution in BBC Drama', *The Stage and Television Today*, 10 February.

Carney, Ray and Quart, Leonard (2000), *The Films of Mike Leigh: Embracing the World*, Cambridge: Cambridge University Press.

Carter, Martin (1973), *Communications Media: Wayland Regional Studies – The Midlands*, London: Wayland.

Caughie, John (2000), *Television Drama: Realism, Modernism, and British Culture*, Oxford: Oxford University Press.

Childs, Peter (1997), 'Place and Environment: Nation and Region' in Mike Storry and Peter Childs (eds), *British Cultural Identities*, London: Routledge.

Clark, Colin (2003), 'What Was the Secret?' in John Finch (ed.), *Granada Television: The First Generation*, Manchester: Manchester University Press.

Cook, John R. (1995), *Dennis Potter: A Life on Screen*, Manchester: Manchester University Press.

Cooke, Lez (2003), *British Television Drama: A History*, London: British Film Institute.

Cooke, Lez (2005a), 'A "New Wave" in British Television Drama', *Media International Australia*, 115, May.

Cooke, Lez (2005b), 'The New Social Realism of *Clocking Off*' in Jonathan Bignell and Stephen Lacey (eds), *Popular Television Drama: Critical Perspectives*, Manchester: Manchester University Press.

Cooke, Lez (2005c), 'Regional British Television Drama in the 1960s and 1970s', *Journal of Media Practice*, 6:3.

Cooke, Lez (2007a), *Troy Kennedy Martin*, Manchester: Manchester University Press.

Cooke, Lez (2007b), 'BBC English Regions Drama: *Second City Firsts*' in Helen

Wheatley (ed.), *Re-viewing Television History: Critical Issues in Television Historiography*, London: I.B. Tauris.

Corner, John (ed.) (1991), *Popular Television in Britain: Studies in Cultural History*, London: British Film Institute.

Coveney, Michael (1997), *The World According to Mike Leigh*, London: Harper Collins.

Cox, Michael (2003), 'Primary Television' in John Finch (ed.), *Granada Television: The First Generation*, Manchester: Manchester University Press.

Creeber, Glen (ed.) (2004), *Fifty Key Television Programmes*, London: Arnold.

Crissell, Andrew (1997), *An Introductory History of British Broadcasting*, London: Routledge.

Crozier, Mary (1965), 'Television', *The Guardian*, 23 January.

Curran, Charles (1970), 'A Decade in Prospect', *BBC Handbook 1970*, London: British Broadcasting Corporation.

Darlow, Michael (2004), *Independents Struggle: The Programme Makers who Took on the TV Establishment*, London: Quartet.

Davies, Geraint Talfan (2002), 'Centralised Organisation – Centralised Mindset', in Mike Kidd and Bill Taylor (eds), *Television in the Nations and Regions*, London: Independent Television Commission.

Dyer, Richard, Geraghty, Christine, Jordan, Marion, Lovell, Terry, Paterson, Richard, Stewart, John (1981), *Coronation Street*, London: British Film Institute.

Ellis, John (2005), 'Importance, Significance, Cost and Value: Is an ITV Canon Possible? in Catherine Johnson and Rob Turnock (eds) (2005), *ITV Cultures: Independent Television over Fifty Years*, Maidenhead: Open University Press.

Ellis, John (2007), 'Is It Possible to Construct a Canon of Television Programmes? Immanent Reading versus Textual Historicism' in Helen Wheatley (ed.), *Re-viewing Television History: Critical Issues in Television Historiography*, London: I.B. Tauris.

Elton, Harry (2003), 'The Programme Committee and *Coronation Street*', in John Finch (ed.), *Granada Television: The First Generation*, Manchester: Manchester University Press.

Evans, Jeff (1995), *The Guinness Television Encyclopedia*, London: Guinness Publishing.

Eyles, Allen (1998), *The Granada Theatres*, London: Cinema Theatre Association / British Film Institute.

Finch, Brian (1964), 'Man of the Narrow Boats', *TV Times (Midland Edition)*, 3 April.

Finch, John (1967), 'A City Gives Up Its Secrets', *TV World*, 2–8 December.

Finch, John (2003), 'The Tools of the Trade' in John Finch (ed.), *Granada Television: The First Generation*, Manchester: Manchester University Press.

Finch, John, with Michael Cox and Marjorie Giles (eds) (2003), *Granada Television: The First Generation*, Manchester: Manchester University Press.

Finch, John (2004), 'From the North', *UK Writer*, Autumn.

Fitzwalter, Ray (2008), *The Dream That Died: The Rise and Fall of ITV*, Leicester: Matador.

Forman, Denis (1981), 'Television in 1959' in Edward Buscombe (ed.), *BFI Dossier Number 9 – Granada*, London: British Film Institute.

Forman, Denis (1997), *Persona Granada*, London: André Deutsch.

Gaunt, John (1955), 'Northern Scrapbook', *Oldham Evening Chronicle and Standard*, 24 February.

Gilbert, E.W. (1951), 'Geography and Regionalism' in G. Taylor (ed.), *Geography in the Twentieth Century*, London: Methuen.

Gilbert, E.W. (1960), 'The Idea of the Region', *Geography*, XLV.

Gilbert, W. Stephen (1980), 'An Angle on *Solid Geometry*', *Broadcast*, 17 March.

Granada TV Network (1962), *Granada's Manchester Plays: Television Adaptations of Six Plays Recalling the Horniman Period at the Gaiety Theatre*, Manchester: Manchester University Press.

Granada Television (1981a), *Granada Television: The Next Decade – A discussion*, Manchester: Granada.

Granada Television (1981b), *As Others See Us*, Manchester: Granada.

Hajkowski, Thomas (2010), *The BBC and National Identity in Britain, 1922–53*, Manchester: Manchester University Press.

Hallam, Julia (2003), 'Introduction: The Development of Commercial TV in Britain' in John Finch (ed.), *Granada Television: The First Generation*, Manchester: Manchester University Press.

Hanson, Barry (1983), 'Making *Gangsters*' in Pilling, Jayne and Kingsley Canham (eds), *The Screen on the Tube: Filmed TV Drama*, Norwich: Cinema City.

Hanson, Barry (2000), 'The 1970s: Regional Variations' in Jonathan Bignell, Stephen Lacey and Madeleine Macmurraugh-Kavanagh (eds), *British Television Drama: Past, Present and Future*, Basingstoke: Palgrave.

Harvey, Sylvia and Robins, Kevin (eds) (1993), *The Regions, the Nation and the BBC*, London: British Film Institute.

Herbertson, A.J. (1905), 'The Major Natural Regions', *Geographical Journal*, XXV.

Hetherington, Peter (2004), 'Northern Exposure', *Society Guardian*, 27 October.

Hill, John (2007), 'A "new drama for television"?: *Diary of a Young Man*' in Laura Mulvey and Jamie Sexton (eds), *Experimental British Television*, Manchester: Manchester University Press.

Hobson, Dorothy (2002), 'Creating and Representing Culture', in Mike Kidd and Bill Taylor (eds), *Television in the Nations and Regions*, London: Independent Television Commission.

Holmwood, Leigh (2003), 'Vive la Difference', *Broadcast*, 17 April.

Holmwood, Leigh (2004), 'BBC's Big Regional Idea', *Broadcast*, 3 December.

Holt, Hazel (1975), 'A Play of Many Virtues', *Television Today*, 16 October.

Hopcraft, Arthur (2003), 'I Can See What You're Trying to Do', in John Finch (ed.), *Granada Television: The First Generation*, Manchester: Manchester University Press.

Hunt, Albert (1975), 'Television's Real Life', *New Society*, 30 January 1975 (reprinted in Jayne Pilling and Kingsley Canham (eds), *The Screen on the Tube: Filmed TV Drama*, Norwich: Cinema City, 1983).

Hunt, Albert (1981), 'Alan Plater' in George Brandt (ed.), *British Television Drama*, Cambridge: Cambridge University Press.

Hynd, Steuart (1956), 'Adventure in Drama for Vance', *TV Times (Midland Edition)*, 6 July.

IBA (1979), *Drama on Independent Television: A report of an IBA Consultation Held at St. Andrews, July 1979*, November.

Jacobs, Jason (2000), *The Intimate Screen: Early British Television Drama*, Oxford: Oxford University Press.

Jewell, Derek (1964), 'Group Think: Portrait of the Television Writer as a Committee', *Sunday Times Magazine*, 28 June.

Jewell, Helen M. (1994), *The North–South Divide: The Origins of Northern Consciousness in England*, Manchester: Manchester University Press.

Johnson, Catherine and Turnock, Rob (eds) (2005), *ITV Cultures: Independent Television over Fifty Years*, Maidenhead: Open University Press.

Jordan, Marion (1981), 'Realism and Convention' in Richard Dyer et al., *Coronation Street*, London: British Film Institute.

Kelly, Richard (ed.) (1998), *Alan Clarke*, London: Faber and Faber.

Kennedy Martin, Troy (1964), 'Nats Go Home: First Statement of a New Drama for Television', *Encore*, 48, March–April.

Kerr, Paul (1981), '*Gangsters*: Conventions and Contraventions' in Tony Bennett et al (eds), *Popular Television and Film*, London: British Film Institute / Open University.

Kershaw, Harry V. (1967), '*City '68*', *TV Times*, 2 December.

Kershaw, H.V. (1981), *The Street Where I Live*, London: Book Club Associates.

Kershaw, John (1964), 'Synthetic Gossip', *Contrast*, 3:4, Summer.

Khan, Naseem (1979), 'Black Comedy', *Radio Times*, 18 August.

Kidd, Mike and Taylor, Bill (2002), *Television in the Nations and Regions: Television Broadcasting and Production outside London*, London: Independent Television Commission.

Lacey, Stephen (1995), *British Realist Theatre: The New Wave in Its Context 1956–1965*, London: Routledge.

Laing, Stuart (1986), *Representations of Working-class Life 1957–1964*, Basingstoke: Macmillan.

Lewis, Jim and Townsend, Alan (eds) (1989), *The North–South Divide: Regional Change in Britain in the 1980s*, London: Paul Chapman.

MacDonald, Barrie (1993), 'ITV Franchises and Programme Companies, 1955–1993' in James Ballantyne (ed.), *Researcher's Guide to British Film and Television Collections*, London: British Universities Film & Video Council.

Mackie, Philip (1964), 'Reaction: Replies to Troy Kennedy Martin's Attack on Naturalistic Television Drama', *Encore*, 49, May–June.

Macmurraugh-Kavanagh, Madeleine (1997), 'The BBC and the Birth of "The Wednesday Play", 1962–66: Institutional Containment versus "Agitational Contemporaneity"', *Historical Journal of Film, Radio and Television*, 17:3.

Maconie, Stuart (2007), *Pies and Prejudice – In Search of the North*, London: Ebury Press.

Marlow, Jane (2003), 'Out of the Regions', *Broadcast* (Indies 2003 Supplement), 28 March.

Marris, Paul (2001), 'Northern Realism: An Exhausted Tradition?', *Cineaste*, 26:4, Autumn.

McDougall, Gordon (2003), 'En Route to the Stables' in John Finch (ed.), *Granada Television: The First Generation*, Manchester: Manchester University Press.

McEwan, Ian (1981), *The Imitation Game: Three Plays For Television*, Jonathan Cape.

McGill, David (1971), 'No Room for Stars in the Cloth Cap Theatre of the Potteries', *TV Times (Midland Edition)*, 25 February.

Medhurst, Jamie (2010), *A History of Independent Television in Wales*, Cardiff: University of Wales Press.

Millington, Bob (1984), 'Making *Boys from the Blackstuff*: A Production Perspective' in Richard Paterson (ed.), *BFI Dossier 20: Boys from the Blackstuff*, London: British Film Institute.

Millington, Bob (1993), '*Boys from the Blackstuff* (Alan Bleasdale)' in George W. Brandt (ed.), *British Television Drama in the 1980s*, Cambridge: Cambridge University Press.

Millington, Bob and Nelson, Robin (1986), *Boys from the Blackstuff: The Making of TV Drama*, London: Comedia.

Ottaway, Robert (1981–82), 'A Tale with a Sting', *Radio Times*, 19 December–1 January.

Paget, Derek (1990), *True Stories? Documentary Drama on Radio, Screen and Stage*, Manchester: Manchester University Press.

Paget, Derek (1998), *No Other Way To Tell It: Dramadoc/docudrama on Television*, Manchester: Manchester University Press.

Paterson, Richard (1981), 'The Production Context of *Coronation Street*' in Richard Dyer et al., *Coronation Street*, London: British Film Institute.

Paterson, Richard (ed.) (1984), *BFI Dossier Number 20 – Boys from the Blackstuff*, London: British Film Institute.

Pawling, Chris and Perkins, Tessa (1992), 'Popular Drama and Realism: The Case of Television' in Adrian Page (ed.), *The Death of the Playwright*, London: Macmillan.

Pettinger, John W. (2007), *From Dawn Till Dusk: A History of Independent Television in the Midlands*, Studley: Brewin Books.

Phillips, John L. (1968), 'Came Across with Considerable Impact', *The Stage and Television Today*, 3 October.

Phillips, Mike (1978), 'Colour Television', *Radio Times*, 28 September 1978.

Pilling, Jayne and Canham, Kingsley (eds) (1983), *The Screen on the Tube: Filmed TV Drama*, Norwich: Cinema City.

Pines, Jim (ed.) (1992), *Black and White in Colour: Black People in British Television Since 1936*, London: British Film Institute.

Plater, Alan (1977), 'Twenty-Five Years Hard: A Playwright's Personal Retrospective', *Theatre Quarterly*, 25, Spring.

Purser, Philip (1961), 'Landscape of TV Drama', *Contrast*, 1:1, Autumn.

Purser, Philip (2003), 'Granada Drama from 1956' in John Finch (ed.), *Granada Television: The First Generation*, Manchester: Manchester University Press.

Rabey, David Ian (1997), *David Rudkin: Sacred Disobedience*, Amsterdam: Harvard Academic.

Raphael, Amy (ed.) (2008), *Mike Leigh on Mike Leigh*, London: Faber and Faber.

Read, Donald (1964), *The English Provinces c.1760–1960: A Study in Influence*, London: Edward Arnold.

Reeks, Jennifer (1981), untitled review of *The Muscle Market*, *The Stage and Television Today*, 22 January (reprinted in Jayne Pilling and Kingsley Canham (eds), *The Screen on the Tube: Filmed TV Drama*, Norwich: Cinema City, 1983).

Rolinson, Dave (2007), '"The Surprise of a Large Town": Regional Landscape in Alan Plater's *Land of Green Ginger*', *Journal of British Cinema and Television*, 4:2.

Rowell, George and Jackson, Anthony (1984), *The Repertory Movement: A History of Regional Theatre in Britain*, Cambridge: Cambridge University Press.

Rudkin, David (1974), 'I Wanted to Write Something that Grew Out of the Landscape', *Radio Times*, 14 March.

Sandford, Jeremy (1976), *Cathy Come Home*, London: Marion Boyars.

Scannell, Paddy (1993), 'The Origins of BBC Regional Policy', in Sylvia Harvey and Kevin Robins (eds), *The Regions, the Nation and the BBC*, London: British Film Institute.

Scrivens, Michael and Roberts, Emily (eds) (2003), *Group Identities on French and British Television*, New York and Oxford: Berghahn Books.

Sergeant, Jean-Claude (2003), 'Adjusting to Diversity: The Case of England and France' in Michael Scriven and Emily Roberts (eds), *Group Identities on French and British Television*, Oxford: Berghahn Books.

Sexton, Jamie (2003), '"Televerite" Hits Britain: Documentary, Drama and the Growth of 16mm Filmmaking in British Television', *Screen*, 44:4, Winter.

Shellard, Dominic (1999), *British Theatre Since the War*, New Haven and London: Yale University Press.

Smith, David (1989), *North and South: Britain's Economic, Social and Political Divide*, London: Penguin.

Steemers, Jeanette (2004), *Selling Television: British Television in the Global Marketplace*, London: British Film Institute.

Steemers, Jeanette (2005), 'No Longer "the Best in the World"': The Challenge of Exporting British Television Drama', *Media International Australia*, 115, May.

Taylor, Don (1990), *Days of Vision*, London: Methuen.

Taylor, John Russell (1962a), *Anatomy of a Television Play: An Inquiry into the Production of Two ABC Armchair Theatre Plays*, London: Weidenfeld & Nicolson.

Taylor, John Russell (1962b), *Anger and After: A Guide to the New British Drama*, London: Methuen, 1962.

Thompson, Mark (2011), 'There's a British in BBC', *The Guardian*, 12 February.

Trodd, Kenith (1983), 'The Trodd Index' in Jayne Pilling and Kingsley Canham (eds), *The Screen on the Tube: Filmed TV Drama*, Norwich: Cinema City.

Trodd, Kenith (2003), 'The Bear Hug' in John Finch (ed.), *Granada Television: The First Generation*, Manchester: Manchester University Press.

Tryhorn, Chris (2006), 'Local Shows for Local People', *The Guardian*, 27 April.

Tunstall, Jeremy (1983), *The Media In Britain*, London: Constable, ch. 4: 'Television' and ch. 15: 'The regions'.

Turpie, Jonnie (2004), 'Base the PSP in Brum', *Broadcast*, 3 December.

Vahimagi, Tise (1996), *British Television: An Illustrated Guide*, Oxford: Oxford University Press, 2nd edition.

Vice, Sue (2009), *Jack Rosenthal*, Manchester: Manchester University Press.

Watson, Garry (2004), *The Cinema of Mike Leigh: A Sense of the Real*, London: Wallflower.

Weatherby, W.J. (1962), 'Granada's Camino Real', *Contrast*, 1:4, Summer.

West Midlands Arts (1980), *Films and Plays from Pebble Mill: Ten Years of Regional Television Drama*, Stafford: West Midlands Arts.

Whatham, Claude (2003), 'The Younger Generation' in John Finch (ed.), *Granada Television: The First Generation*, Manchester: Manchester University Press.

White, Leonard (2003), *Armchair Theatre: The Lost Years*, Tiverton: Kelly Publications.

Whitehead, Tony (2007), *Mike Leigh*, Manchester: Manchester University Press.

Wilson, Anthony (2002), 'Granadaland, Please', in Mike Kidd and Bill Taylor, *Television in the Nations and Regions*, London: Independent Television Commission.

Wise, Herbert (2003), 'Once Were Giants' in John Finch (ed.), *Granada Television: The First Generation*, Manchester: Manchester University Press.

Wood, David (2004), 'Birmingham: Drama Central', *Broadcast*, 3 December.

Wyver, John (1981), 'An Outline Sketch' in Edward Buscombe (ed.), *BFI Dossier Number 9 – Granada*, London: British Film Institute.

Index

Note: page numbers in bold refer to main entries; 'n.' after a page reference indicates the number of a note on that page.